DOES POLITICS MATTER?

DOES POLITICS MATTER?

THE DETERMINANTS OF PUBLIC POLICY

L. J. SHARPE
AND
K. NEWTON

CLARENDON PRESS · OXFORD
1984

Oxford University Press, Walton Street, Oxford OX2 6DP

London Glasgow New York Toronto
Delhi Bombay Calcutta Madras Karachi
Kuala Lumpur Singapore Hong Kong Tokyo
Nairobi Dar es Salaam Cape Town
Melbourne Auckland

and associated companies in
Beirut Berlin Ibadan Mexico City Nicosia

Oxford is a trade mark of Oxford University Press

Published in the United States
by Oxford University Press, New York

British Library Cataloguing in Publication Data
Sharpe, L. J.
    Does politics matter?   The determinants
    of public policy
    1. Municipal service—England
    I. Title   II. Newton, K.
    363'.0942   HD4645
    ISBN 0-19-827461-0

Library of Congress Cataloging in Publication Data
Sharpe, L. J. (Laurence James)
    Does politics matter?
    Bibliography: p.
    Includes index.
    1. Municipal government—Great Britain.   2. Local
government—Great Britain.   3. Municipal services—
Political aspects—Great Britain.   4. Political parties
—Great Britain.   I. Newton, Kenneth, 1940-
II. Title.
JS3091.S52   1983   352'.0072'0942   83-13486
ISBN 0-19-827461-0

Typeset by Hope Services, Abingdon, Oxfordshire
and printed in Great Britain
at the University Press, Oxford

For
PAT
and
DEE

PREFACE

This book has been a long time in the making and this was partly due to that all too common academic vice of taking on new assignments before we were able to complete our writing up. But the main time-consuming factor has been the collection, cleaning, and analysis of our data. We have taken special care in all three tasks and in the Appendices we have tried to lay bare for the interested reader all the background information on our analytical procedures and the origins of the data base on which the book is built. We venture to suggest that our study is the most comprehensive output study undertaken in this country, not only in terms of its time span and the range and number of the variables employed, but also because it covers county boroughs and counties. This also made us anxious to provide as comprehensive a set of explanatory Appendices as possible.

In order to make the study as comprehensive as possible, it was imperative that we collected time series data; however, in the mid-1970s when the project was planned an entirely new system of local government had only just been established in England and Wales. This meant that in order to obtain an adequate time series we had perforce to confine our analyses to the old order. To those who therefore conclude that this makes our study history rather than political science, we would only say that all output studies, if they are to be of any value, must be historical. The process of translating an intention into action that changes the status quo is a monstrous consumer of time. This is true for politics no less than political science!

Moreover, the fact that the structure of British local government changed quite radically in the 1970s does not mean that the determinants of output performance of the sytem have changed equally radically. Furthermore, when the time comes to undertake an output study of the new system; that is to say, when sufficient time has elapsed to provide an adequate time series, our study will provide an irreplaceable basis for a comparative study, one of the primary objectives of which will be precisely to try to ascertain what difference structural change made on output performance.

Although this study is wholly confined to local government, we have deliberately attempted wherever possible to relate it to cross-national output studies. This is because it is our firm belief that the two genres have been too compartmentalized. We do not claim that the two levels of government are the same — obviously there are some fundamental differences — only that the basic similarities are such that continuing apartheid can only be to the ultimate detriment of both. It could be particularly unfortunate for cross-national research, the scope of which is necessarily, and perhaps irretrievably, limited by the absence of the necessary data.

We are aware that in making this link between sub-national and cross-national research we run the risk of upsetting both traditional local government specialists, who may be suspicious of the output approach in any case, and cross-national specialists, who, because of compartmentalization (and, dare we add, just a touch of academic snobbery), are only too likely to be blissfully unaware of the enormous body of research that has been done on sub-national outputs.

In addition to the conscious attempt to link our findings with national level research, we wish to emphasize that we have sought also and more importantly to bring out two broad themes. The first — the importance of the unitary model — is in one sense directly derived from national level research, for the model, with its emphasis on the role of the polity within an external system, is, in effect, the heart and soul of the study of international relations — the nation state. The results of our study suggest that the unitary model may not attain the status of the nation state in IR, but it will, we feel sure, have a vital place in all future local output research.

Our second overriding objective has been to restore in output research the status of the political party in all its measurable ramifications. By the mid-1970s it had received a severe battering at the hands of some output analysts. Although left for dead by the economic determinists and the end of the ideology ideologists, it is overwhelmingly clear from our results that there is still considerable life left in the party as a policy determinant. For those with even only a passing interest in the future of political sicence this can only be a happy outcome, for it remains as true today as it has for the past twenty years that the exploration of the party in every conceivable manifestation and role prior to the formation of public policy has been one of the central activities of that discipline. It is this lop-sided concentration which spurred on our interest in the fortunes of political parties, since if output studies had all but confined them to the academic dust-bin, such an untimely fate had been indirectly aided and abetted by the party specialists. For they had rarely asked whether the object of their lavish attentions made any difference to what governments did. It is our hope that this study will prompt such a question being posed more often, if only because we have given it a title that is likely to catch the eye of at least some of the party specialists.

This book is very much a joint effort, so that there is something of both authors in every chapter, save that Ken Newton has been the prime mover for the data analysis. There has also been a fairly clear division of labour to the extent that it is possible to attribute each chapter as having been the main responsibility of one author. The division has been: Chapters 1, 2, 4, 9, and 10 — L.J.S; Chapters 3, 5, 6, 7, 8, and the Appendices — K.N.

Some of the material covered in one or two chapters has appeared elsewhere.

The relevant chapters and earlier form are:

Chapter 1: *Policy and Politics*, 5 (1977),

Chapters 6 and 9: in K. Newton (ed.), *Urban Political Economy* (London, Frances Pinter, 1981).

The rest of the study is entirely original and we take the usual responsibility for it, fully absolving all those mentioned below from any responsibility for what follows.

ACKNOWLEDGEMENTS

This book began life with a grant from the Centre for Environmental Studies and both authors acknowledge a considerable debt of gratitude to the Centre and its then Director, David Donnison, for backing our project. We would also like to express our profound regret at the precipitate and some would say ideologically prejudiced closing of the Centre by the government in 1980.

We must also express our thanks to the Warden and Fellows of Nuffield College, Oxford where the great bulk of the work on the book was undertaken. The authors are particularly grateful for the facilities which the College provided, including those for data processing. We wish to express our thanks for the assistance of various members of the College, in particular thanks are due to Sir Norman Chester, Philip Williams (who kindly supplied some important election data), and to Ann Collinson, Keith Hope, Terence Karran, and Clive Payne for their advice and help in processing our data and statistical analysis. Mrs Moira Bell of the University of Dundee must also be thanked for her assistance in data processing at a later stage in the project.

At the beginning of the study in 1975 the authors arranged a small inter-disciplinary conference at Nuffield College on output analysis and the authors wish to record their thanks to all who attended, whose advice they fully appreciated though did not always take, and to the Politics and International Relations Committee of the SSRC who generously funded the conference.

A further very special debt of gratitude is owed to the Research Assistant to the project, Jo Garcia, without whom the massive and complex task of collecting, processing, and cleaning the data would have been impossible. Throughout the time she worked on the project she showed exemplary patience and skill in amassing a large quantity of accurate data, and in drawing up a seventy-page code book which is a masterpiece of detailed precision in its own right.

Thanks are also due to Conservative Central Office who very kindly gave us access to their collection of local election results.

Many others have advised and helped the authors in various ways, far too many for each to be mentioned individually here, but there were some whose help went beyond the normal line of academic duty. They include Michael Aiken, Douglas Ashford, Terry Clark, Patrick Dunleavy, George Jones, Paul Knox, and Tore Hansen.

Finally, this book would never have reached the printers without the patience and fortitude of a number of secretaries, among whom the authors would like to single out for special mention Doris Tindal, for her immaculate typing and secretarial skills, and Lynne Summersbee and Trude Hickey, who similarly brought order and clarity to some very rough drafts.

October 1982   L. J. S. and K. N.

CONTENTS

LIST OF TABLES

LIST OF FIGURES

1. WHY DO PUBLIC POLICIES DIFFER?

1 The Output Approach

Introduction

If politics is the art of the possible, then so is research into politics. Of all the possible approaches open to the political scientist in pursuit of the answers to some of the more intractable questions of the discipline, the study of the fiscal and budgetary policies of government is one of the most vital. This is because these policies reflect such fundamental aspects of government as the setting of priorities, the allocation of resources, and the scope of the public sector itself. The budget is, in effect, financial short-hand for the government's policy commitments. Wildavsky has even suggested: 'Perhaps the "study of budgetting" is just another expression for the "study of politics".'[1] The fiscal approach also provides one way of answering the primordial question that arises in any comparative government exercise, why is there such an extraordinary variation in the policies that governments pursue despite an apparent similarity of aims and of conditions?

Until a couple of decades or so ago it is fair to say that most political scientists assumed that the primary determinants of such policy variation were political, if we define political in its broadest sense. That is to say, they confined their attention to the political process, especially to the pre-legislative process — elections, voting behaviour, parties, pressure groups, and political attitudes; and to the legislative process — parliament and legislative behaviour. For various reasons a change has taken place and attention has shifted to post-legislative politics; to, as it were, the object of the political exercise, to services, policy, and outputs.

One of the consequences of this shift to the study of policy has been a corresponding shift in assumptions about the origin of policy variation. Instead of assuming that all can be explained by the political process, there has also been a much greater willingness to open up the causal nexus and to see how far the underlying, non-political structures of the polity — its economic or its social characteristics — have a bearing on the policy-making process. To some extent this movement may have gone too far (we shall come to that problem in a moment) and there is no doubt that some of the early studies which attempted to assess the relative impact of the non-political aspects of the polity on policy were somewhat crude and lacking in theoretical refinement.

One of the problems immediately facing the new approach was the difficulty of comparing policy variation in national states, and of amassing sufficient comparable data to make the exercise a satisfactory one. So, although there have

been some cross-national studies, as we shall see, most studies of this kind —
what we shall call output studies — have been undertaken in relation to a local
government system within a single nation state, or in the case of federal states,
especially the United States (where, as usual, most work has been done), to the
constitutent states of the federation. In this way the number of constants can be
maximized since the sub-national government system of each country usually
operates within a common legal and political framework, and probably within a
reasonably uniform cultural and economic setting as well.

The study of a sub-national government system also offers a much larger
number of observations on which to base generalizations than could possibly be
contemplated for any cross-national comparisons. This is an advantage possessed
by output studies of the kind we have undertaken that is of such profound
importance that it is difficult to exaggerate its worth. For what dogs every
attempt at national level comparisons is the fact that there are always fewer
cases available than the number of plausibly relevant differences between the
cases.[2] Since it is difficult to see how this problem can be overcome and, moreover, because intra-state units, as we have noted, may be assumed to share a
number of constants, intra-state comparison, given the present state of knowledge,
holds the comparative field.

Another advantage of the intra-national approach is that it provides an
accurate statistical profile of the total system — its range of variations, its
extremes, and its averages — and therefore provides the criteria whereby a
number of cases can be selected for detailed investigation on a statistically
rational basis. Comparative macro-studies and case studies can be made thereby
complementary. For all their undoubted refinement, case studies cannot tell
us how statistically representative of the whole they are.

In saying this there is no wish to denigrate the case study which still remains
the most popular mode in the discipline, and which has its own validity.[3]
Moreover, the comparative approach, for all its value in setting the broad contours and general patterns of the system, cannot provide, as the case study can,
a comprehensive account of the policy process that links the independent and
the dependent variables. The case study is particularly popular in the study of
local and urban politics and for those local specialists who may find the output
approach both strange and questionable we would only urge them to persevere.
The output approach, as we freely acknowledge in the ensuing pages, has many
shortcomings, but if it lacks the detailed precision and the certainty of the one-
off study, it does enable us to look at the broad canvas and make statistically
valid generalizations about the local government system as a whole. Both research
modes are, after all, inextricably linked, in the sense that, as one wag has noted,
the plural of anecdote is data.

Output studies also have the advantage of focusing on the distributive and re-distributive aspects of government and thus offer an answer to Lasswell's question, 'Who gets what, when and how?' In doing so they also widen the ambit of research from the Who Governs? question to the equally important one of Who Benefits?[4] The breadth of this question calls for an approach of equally broad scope, and perhaps one of the major qualities of output studies is that they deal with the policy system as a whole, so that we can judge not only the impact of, but also the interplay between, social, economic, and political factors in the determination of government policies. In this sense it is a mode of analysis that may get us closer to comprehending the truly political than any other.

All in all, the output approach has a lot to commend it as a method for elucidating the political process. This study employs it in analysing the possible determinants of the policies and expenditures of English and Welsh local authorities over a sixteen-year period. The period chosen runs from 1957 to 1973 so our findings refer to the local government structure that existed before the 1974 reorganization. This was unavoidable given the need to cover the maximum possible time period, of which more in a moment, for when we began our research the new structure was only a few years old.

The study applies conventional output analysis techniques and these are described together with all the other technical information concerning the research in the Appendices. But the most important part of our study lies in its attempt to widen the range of possible explanatory factors and approaches well beyond the bounds of conventional studies. This it does in three main ways: first, by developing more refined political factors (Chap. 9), especially those relating to party, but also those that reflect the possible consequence for outputs of different party systems. Secondly, the study examines the effect of socio-economic and spatial factors on outputs; not, however, those that are related to the individual characteristics of the population, but rather, the holistic characteristics of urban places — cities and towns. This is the unitary model which assumes that some of the outputs of local government are determined by the role of the local community in a wider subregional, regional, or national system. Two forms of the unitary model are examined; the first is the city's position as a service centre in the urban hierarchy (Chap. 6), and the second (Chap. 7), its role as a city type — county town, manufacturing centre, seaside resort, etc. — in the national urban system. An analogous typology is developed for the counties (Chap. 8).

These are the main themes of the study and we shall return to a more detailed discussion of them later in this chapter. We also analyse our data in relation to some other explanatory theories of resource allocation. These include incremental theory (Chap. 4), which focuses entirely on the budget process and posits that allocations may be explained in terms of the standard operating procedure of regularized increments to the preceding year's allocation. Another theory that purports to explain allocations and which we examine in relation to our data is Tiebout's pure theory of local expenditures (Chap. 3). This interprets local policy outputs almost entirely in terms of consumer demands in a system of local authorities which resembles a market. In this quasi-market system each local government provides a different 'package' of services, and consumers move domicile to that local government which provides the package which comes closest to their own preference for collective services.

One problem that confronts all output studies is their time span. Existing output research, especially that done in Britain, has usually been cross- sectional. That is to say, it is confined to expenditure or real output statistics for one financial year. Yet it is difficult, if not impossible, to conceive of major policy decisions that are not the result of the interplay of factors over much longer time periods than the fiscal year. Moreover, we can never know whether the one year snapshot is typical or aberrant if we do not also know what the expenditure patterns were during the period before and the period after the chosen year. For these reasons, it seems almost axiomatic that output studies must utilize expenditure figures at different points in time and the longer the time period covered the better. It is for these reasons that the present study has taken for analysis a period of approximately sixteen years. Chapter 9 in particular shows just how important a time series study is in unravelling the effects of party politics on total spending patterns.

Another serious difficulty with output studies is that levels and patterns of expenditure may only be crude indicators of service, quality and quantity.[5] Given inevitable variations in the efficiency and costs of local authorities, and the fact that some policy changes may have no expenditure effects, the likelihood that expenditure accurately reflects the quantity of output is, in many cases, inherently implausible. Even where there appears to be a strong prima-facie case for assuming a relationship, it may evaporate on close examination. If measuring quantity presents problems, measuring the quality and impact of a public service is a task of even greater difficulty and complexity,[6] not merely because it is difficult to measure, or to settle upon good indicators, but also because there is often little agreement about what quality actually is.

One way of coping with this problem may be to disaggregate total service expenditures to sub-functions. For such disaggregation may make it possible for the extent of variation to be more closely pin-pointed and it may be possible to assume that some sub-functional expenditures are better measures of output quality. But since it seems unlikely that disaggregation will resolve the quality problem until better techniques are evolved, it seemed prudent to treat the whole matter with considerable caution and to avoid pretending that we can explain it away.[7] For this reason it might seem advantageous to drop the term 'output' from expenditure studies altogether since it connotes a descriptive capacity that expenditure figures clearly do not possess. However, such is its widespread use and its convenience that we have retained it.

Deficient as output studies may be in terms of the quality problem, it ought to be emphasized that for some services, especially the so-called 'personal services', *all* attempts to compare and evaluate must resort to abstractions. Not only are such services produced by the interplay of a multitude of social, physical, and economic factors – the content of which can never be captured by statistics, no matter how elaborate or detailed – but they are ultimately a subjective experience that is not easily amenable to measurement of any kind. Moreover, the more we try to capture service quality by breaking it down into small, manageable, and measurable parts, the more we are forced into dealing with fundamental questions about the goals of social policy. Whereas a broad description of a service and its aims might be agreed, the objectives of each of its component sub-functions will often be the subject of a great deal of disagreement, even among the professionals and the experts. In short, in recognizing that expenditures may be a poor substitute for policy outcomes we must not fall into the error of thinking that the problem of measuring and comparing policies is necessarily resolvable by some other mode of analysis.

It is also important to emphasize that the quality problem should not obscure a cardinal point – that local government in this country now absorbs such a high proportion of the public sector in expenditure terms that its budgetary patterns are worthwhile objects of study in their own right. In 1972/3, the last financial year of the period covered by the present research, local government expenditure in the United Kingdom was in excess of £10,799m., representing almost 14 per cent of GNP and more than a third of public sector expenditure. Local government cost at that time almost two and a half times as much as defence and only marginally less than the nation's annual household food bill. Local government also consumed more than the total amount of tax paid on personal incomes. The expenditure of public money in such gigantic quantities warrants close and careful examination, whatever its bearing on the quantity and quality of public services it buys. There has been some contraction since the mid-1970s, but until then local government's share of total public sector expenditure had been steadily rising over the preceding twenty years as it had in most other Western states.[8] The biggest expansion has been in the fields of education, health, and social welfare.[9] In financial terms local government has, in short, been of increasing importance in the evolution of the modern Welfare State.

The study of local government expenditure also has an intrinsic importance because finance tends to overshadow all other aspects of local government to an extent not usually encountered in national government. This is partly because budget-making and tax setting at the local level have a much greater precision, since the sources of finance — grants, rates, and charges — are all calculable in advance. Moreover, service issues can be brought more closely into focus because the local budget is not an instrument for demand management, and resources are only raised to meet planned service expenditure. The local tax system, at least in Britain, is also considerably more visible to the individual taxpayer than national taxes because the total annual local tax commitment is sent to him in the rate demand. In order to achieve comparable public visibility for national taxation there would need to be a similar statement listing all the taxation paid over the year by individual taxpayers not only via income tax (which is visible but less so than rates because it is extracted by the employer), but also via VAT, National Insurance and the graduated pensions contribution, spirit, wine and tobacco duties, and television and vehicle licences. A moment's contemplation of the effect of such a statement in enhancing the public's awareness of the financial aspects of central government gives some idea of the considerably greater impact of financial considerations in local government.

This higher public visibility of local taxation means that resource questions not only tend to dominate the internal political process to an extent that is unusual in central government, but they also figure much more prominently in local public discussion and debate about local politics. Finally, it must be noted that the continuous publication of annual expenditure statistics for the major services by the Chartered Institute of Public Finance and Accountancy for all local authorities in England and Wales has meant that such statistics have their own significance as performance indicators. They are used, for example, within local authorities with exceptionally high (or low) figures as arguments for policy change.

The Existing Literature

So much for preliminaries. We now turn to a review of the existing literature on output studies in this country. This review will necessarily be fragmentary and to some extent disjointed. This is because there is no uniform general theory or model governing the research. Broadly speaking, British output studies fall into two categories. The first consists primarily of a statistical exercise in which the main object is to 'explain', in a regression analysis sense, as much of the variance in performance, or rather expenditure measures, as possible. Good examples of the genre are Research Studies 4 and 5 published by the Redcliffe-Maud Commission.[10] The regression formula that was used for the allocation of the Rate Support grant before 1982 is another example, as are the econometric studies by Nicholson and Topham,[11] and those for the Layfield Committee by Dawson and by Moore and Rhodes.[12]

Perhaps the best illustration of the considerable advantages and disadvantages of this approach is the Redcliffe-Maud Research Study 5 just mentioned, which was undertaken by Myra Woolf. This investigated, by using factor analysis, the relationship between certain service expenditures in counties and county boroughs and the social, economic, and demographic characteristics of their areas. The results are highly satisfactory in a statistical sense, partly because of the elegance and the precision achieved, and partly because a few factors explain a large proportion of the variance of the dependent variables. But such studies have considerable disadvantages as well. In the first place, it is not always clear what interpretation is to be placed on the components extracted by factor analysis. As Robert Wood put it: 'In factor analysis the labor of giving birth is often easier than naming the baby.'[13] A second deficiency of the approach is that the correlation between the factors and various social, economic, and political variables are often difficult to interpret, and sometimes they appear to be almost wholly devoid of any theoretical significance or meaning.

In this respect the weakness of this type of output study is the strength of the somewhat more theoretical approach which we will now consider. In the British context this more theoretical approach is by far the most popular, being exemplified by the work of Boaden, Davies, Alt, Stanyer and Oliver, Nicholson and Topham, Ashford, Danziger, and Foster et al.[14] This form of analysis is characterized by a concern to develop theoretical propositions against available data.

Although this approach is more satisfactory in terms of understanding the social, economic, and political basis of local government activity, often the results are less satisfying in statistical terms in the sense that correlations are usually low, even when statistically significant, or regression formulae leave a large proportion of the variance unexplained.[15]

In large part the poor explanatory power of any single independent variable, or group of variables, reflects the enormous complexity of performance and expenditure patterns, the possibility of non-linear relationships, and the fairly substantial degree of multicollinearity among groups of independent variables. These complications, in turn, stem from the fact that output research is dealing with the totality of social, economic, and political relationships in whole political systems. This is, as we have already emphasized, one of its great strengths, but it does mean that this relationship is both complex and closely interwoven. Often social research is concerned with a narrower range of relationships where both dependent and independent variables are conveniently abstracted from their environment. In the study of organizations the exclusion of the political environment in which they are immersed provides a good example of this kind of approach.[16]

In any case these problems are not insuperable, although they may well make it more difficult to interpret local authority expenditure patterns than many other social and political patterns. It may be possible to uncover and approximate non-linear relationships by polynomial and multiplicative functions. This is, of course, easier said than done but in principle it is feasible. The problems of multicollinearity are more severe and therefore demand special attention. There seem to be two possible strategies. The first is to process a wide range of intercorrelated variables by multivariate analysis in order to extract orthogonal factors. The drawback of this strategy is that it introduces all the problems of the first kind of output study. For this reason we are unwilling to exchange the statistical strengths of factor analysis for the potentially greater theoretical and explanatory power of other approaches.

The second strategy is to develop theories which explore the causal relationships between variables or clusters of variables, and spending patterns. This is broadly what we have tried to do in this study by developing one old explantory model — the party effect — and introducing two versions of the newer unitary model which is derived from the holistic characteristics of urban local authorities as producers of services within a wider system. The first unitary model is based on the role of cities as central place service centres in the urban hierarchy; the second is based on the economic and social role of cities and counties within the national economic system. We now turn to a detailed introductory discussion of each of these models, beginning with the party model. We have devoted more space to this model, partly because, as a well-tried explanation, there is a great deal more existing research to be discussed than for the other two models, but also because, as will be demonstrated in Chapter 9, the party effect does have a pervasive influence on local expenditure levels.

II   Model 1: The Party and Party System Effect

Party Politics and Expenditure

Economists have taken an interest in the determinants of the level of public expenditure for a very long time, especially in relation to its apparently inexorable growth.[17] In the post-war period, although public sector expenditure growth studies continued,[18] the adoption of multiple regression techniques and the advent of the computer made it possible to examine the causes of expenditure levels in a systematic fashion, applying a range of independent variables to the dependent disaggregated expenditure variables. Many different kinds of political jurisdictions were analysed, including national states, subnational units of federal systems, and units of local government.[19] At this early stage these studies were still almost wholly undertaken by economists and it is important to note that only rarely were they concerned with examining the possible influence of political factors. So, the fact that these studies failed to show that political factors had any bearing on expenditure levels could hardly be said to demonstrate, as some have claimed, that political factors are relatively unimportant as compared with economic factors.[20] Later output studies by economists and sociologists did look at political factors and a notable example at the cross-national level is that by Wilensky who examined the effects of the ideology of ruling parties in twenty-two countries on social security expenditure.[21] Also, it must be recognized that some of these cross-national studies, such as that by Pryor,[22] for example, compare countries with very different political systems, and so inevitably study the effect of political variables on policy outputs.

Political scientists, or rather American political scientists, started to take an interest in output studies somewhat later than their economist colleagues[23] and, as might be expected, the omissions of their predecessors regarding political variables was to some extent repaired. As a result, over a relatively short period a sizeable body of literature emerged on the determinants of service expenditures at both the State and the local level in the United States.[24] Although these studies did not give political attributes as much attention as the economists had given economic and social factors, the same results, broadly speaking, obtained: economic and social characteristics such as urbanization, population density, and, above all, per capita income were more strongly associated with expenditure levels than any other factors.

It is important to note that the political factors that were tested were derived from an earlier phase in the literature of American State government, notably the work of V. O. Key and also Duane Lockard and others.[25] In this literature it was claimed that the key factors affecting the kind of politics pursued were characteristics of the State political system such as the degree of party competition, the level of turnout, and malapportionment. It was assumed that where there was party competition, where turnout was high, and where seats were fairly divided among the electorate, there would be higher levels of State expenditure. We will return to this model of the representative process later. At this stage we may note that one of its implications is that what governments do is a direct reflection of the popular will. According to this view, what is crucial to the effective working of the system is the transmission process between electorate and government. If it is defective because parties do not need to compete, or because citizens fail to exercise their right to vote, or are prevented from doing so, then the interests of the electorate will not be met by government. Especially vulnerable in this model are the poor. If they fail to vote, so the theory runs, or are prevented from voting or participating generally, they will be ignored by the parties when in power, since there will be no incentive to cater for their interests in order to keep or attract their votes.

Few would wish to deny that it is highly likely that if the bulk of the poor opt out of voting or are denied the vote, then the level of redistributive policies is likely to be less than in a system where they *do* participate. Indeed there is a considerable and persuasive body of literature which attributes the emergence of the modern Western Welfare State largely, perhaps decisively, to the enfranchisement of the working class in the closing stages of the nineteenth and the opening phase of the twentieth century.[26] However, it is necessary to distinguish between the way parties behave once the franchise has been established and how they behave in a non-democratic system. So the transmission model seems appropriate for the Deep South before the belated arrival of democracy during the 1960s, but as an interpretation of a working democracy with competing parties the model is too crude: representative government is not merely a transmission process from voter to government. Governments do have and have had autonomy in representative systems,[27] but there is little room in the transmission model for any conception of parties who may act autonomously of the social or the economic structure of the jurisdiction they govern. That is to say, the model does not allow for majority parties which instigate expenditure patterns according to party ideology and only modify their policies in order to attract enough votes to win, or parties which change voters' attitudes by their policies. For such a party the level of participation of any group, including the poor, is unlikely to have any necessary bearing on outputs when they are in government. In other words, one political variable that may be considered as being crucial in other Western countries – party ideology – was largely missing from the research. Curiously enough, as Godwin and Shepard have pointed out, despite the strong assumption in this research that outputs are the direct result of a transmission process from electorate to government (this is what Godwin and Shepard call a linkage model), these same studies in their pursuit of the *independent* effects of political variables assume a *non*-linkage model.[28] In other words, they assume an autonomy for the political factors which their transmission model theory by definition assumes does not exist.

Slowly but surely the various techniques used in the American output studies have been applied to European conditions, and party colour was, as might be expected, a central feature of many of these analyses. In Britain there have been a dozen or so such studies of local government outputs,[29] and in terms of how far they reveal a party effect, results have been mixed. But there has been a clear majority of studies suggesting that party colour does have an effect. This result neatly reflected the extent to which the more traditional literature has been divided between those who have claimed, usually writing in very general terms, that party has little or no effect on policy,[30] and those who as a result of particular case studies have suggested that it has.[31]

If, however, the British research has on balance suggested a party effect, many of the early American and non-American output studies had found little or no relationship between the party variable, or indeed any other political variables, and expenditure patterns. Robert Fried has summarized the findings of almost four dozen such studies covering twelve countries in the following terms:

Political variables have relatively less direct and independent impact than socio-economic variables. In many, probably most, cases some socio-economic variable has been found more useful in explaining the variance in outputs than any political variable. Somehow, the nature of the socio-economic environment seems more important than the nature of community politics in shaping community policies. The implication of these findings is that most forms of political activity are either futile or marginal, whether it be organizing to occupy office or organizing to influence those who occupy office. The socio-economic constraints are such, it would appear, that it makes little difference for urban policy who controls local urban government, what their values are, how many people turn out to vote, what policies the community-at-large or the activists prefer, or how the community is organized for governmental purposes.[32]

If politics is as unimportant as Fried's summary suggests, an enormous question mark is, of course, placed against not just a great deal of political science, but also some of the most cherished assumptions of representative democratic theory. Nevertheless, before European democrats or political scientists surrender to the 'near panic' that Dye claims seized some American political scientists as a consequence of largely the same research Fried was summarizing,[33] it may be a useful exercise to explore some of the reasons why these research findings, important as they undoubtedly are in empirical terms for improving our understanding of how political systems work, ought not to be treated as if they are the definitive answer.

These findings, despite the number of studies on which they are based, ought, for reasons which will become clearer in the next section of this chapter, to be regarded as the beginning rather than the end of the capacity of the technique to tell us what are the determinants of policy. We must be particularly careful not to jump to any arresting conclusions about political determinants, however tempting the prospect may be given the weight of conventional opinion within the political science profession which implicitly assumes the salience of political factors, and in particular party factors. Fried seems to have succumbed to precisely such a temptation:

the weakness of party differences even in apparently more polarised urban party systems seems to suggest that all urban systems are, in effect, non-partisan systems.[34]

So there must be first, caution, and secondly, a frank recognition of the more obvious weaknesses of the existing research on the party effect in telling us anything definitive. One of the reasons why we don't know more about the party effect is the extraordinary, one might almost say bizarre, lack of interest found in the myriad of studies of parties as to whether their central subject, on which so much interest has been lavished, actually does perform what might be supposed is its primary function, namely to affect public policy.[35] As Heclo has remarked, albeit in a footnote, 'The effect of parties on policy making is probably the most poorly investigated topic in the entire vast literature of political parties.'[36] We now turn to a discussion of some of the difficulties and weaknesses of existing research on the party effect.

Deficiencies of Existing Party Effect Research

The first potential weakness of existing research on the party effect is that many of the studies, that is to say those that Fried was summarizing, were comparing total (usually revenue) expenditures. It is possible that total revenue expenditure is a slightly better guide to party effect at the local level than at the central level because local expenditure, unlike national, is more closely tied to what is intended to be spent. As we have noted, this is because local authorities do not indulge in deficit financing as a deliberate act of policy, and therefore only raise what they plan to spend net of transfers and other estimated receipts. But this difference is only likely to be marginal; doubts must remain as to what total expenditure can tell us about the effect of party. Moreover, the case for disaggregation that we have already made has particular force in relation to the party effect, for there is some evidence that the apparent imperviousness of total expenditure to party may be largely a function of the degree of aggregation.[37] The higher the degree of aggregation the lower the likelihood of variation precisely because of the greater impact that such change has on total expenditure and hence tax levels. Since local government systems throughout the West have in the post-war period been required to provide an ever-rising range and quality of services, without in most cases having a commensurate expansion of their tax base, sensitivity to the tax effect of increasing expenditure has been sharpened.[38] It follows that for expenditures for parts of a service and low-spending whole services such tax effect constraints will be weaker, and so the possibility of governing parties raising spending levels correspondingly increases.

Whole-service expenditure totals for the major services are in one sense accounting abstractions: they may have little *operational* meaning for either politicians or bureaucrats except at budget-making, and perhaps none at all for those elements of the general public who count, namely the various 'policy communities'.[39] In order to get to grips with the operational reality of the major services we need to disaggregate to what may be called the bureau or agency level.[40] These are, in British terms, the sub-departments responsible for the sub-functions around which the possible sources of change emanating from decision makers are likely to focus. In the education department, for example, these sub-departments might be further, secondary, primary, and supplies. In housing they might be building and management. For highways, traffic management, public transport, and building and maintenance.

One of the most favoured measures of party impact that has been employed in output studies outside the US is the strength of the Left party: Labour, Social Democrat, or Communist. The reasons why this particular measure has been specially favoured are partly, no doubt, its availability — Left parties almost always identify themselves as such. It is also partly because it is assumed that since they seek to change the status quo via governmental action, Left parties much more than Right parties offer the best prospect of producing measurable policy change. However, like political factors generally, it was found to be wanting as a significant determinant of outputs. As Fried again has it:

It is certainly not clear that the presence of Communist, Social Democratic, or Labourite party majorities in a city make as much difference as might be expected. A direct, independent and strong impact on urban policymaking owing to the leftish party control is quite exceptional, though the aggregate (rather than distributional) performance measures that have been used may mask the true extent of interparty differences and of party control impact.[41]

Fried notes, as we have just said, one exception to this general trend — British local government. Before accepting Fried's general conclusions there are a number of aspects of the research he was summarizing which demand comment.

Size of the Left party majority is one of the most favoured variables used for measuring party effect, yet it is doubtful whether this is the best measure since a large majority may have no more impact on policy than a small majority in systems, like the British, where a simple numerical majority is all that is required to monopolize the reins of power. What is likely to be more important than size of majority in such systems is the length of the Left party's tenure in office. Most major policy change takes time, and only when sufficient time has elapsed can we expect any Left-induced change to reveal itself.

As we noted earlier, it is assumed that Left-controlled councils will spend more in aggregate than anti-Left controlled councils, but a Left party's tendency to spend more is unlikely to operate for all services. Clearly the Left may tend to favour some policies, such as those that have egalitarian objectives, but it may be less favourably disposed than Right parties to other services. It may even favour expenditure cuts for those services. The assumption that Left parties will always spend more in aggregate than its opponents has other deficiencies. Where high local expenditures enhance the overall economy of a community they may be just as favoured by the Right as by the Left. Since a more markedly middle-class population may make more demands on local government for some services (secondary education, police, libraries) than predominantly working-class populations, and since it is in predominantly middle-class areas that bourgeois parties tend to flourish, it is possible that such areas may spend heavily overall. Both Aiken and Martinotti for Italy, and Hansen for Norway have detected this phenomenon.[42] There is also the boosterism of some distinctly non-Left city councils who spend in order to attract industry and promote growth. Given the greater mobility of factors of production in that country, this may be a more likely phenomenon in the United States however.[43]

Also, as we noted earlier, the application of some ideological differences between Right and Left may not have very big, or even any, expenditure effects for certain services. As Irwin has suggested in relation to Dutch local government, 'Many of the desires of the socialist programme cannot be described in monetary terms. Democratization and influence are not matters requiring more money to be spent but on the reorganisation of social and political life.'[44]

Where the Left has come relatively recently to power it will, like all 'new brooms', be searching for policies the effects of which are felt reasonably quickly. In competitive politics there may be little to be gained from changing policy that will bear fruit when you are no longer in power. But, since large items of expenditure are difficult to alter rapidly, the tendency again will be for the incoming party, whatever its colour, to seek out policies with small expenditure effects. It follows that such time considerations also have a close bearing on the assumption that the party effect can be isolated by conventional, one-year, output studies, for if major policy change does take a long time to effect, parties will have to be in power for a long enough time to put their stamp on existing policies. By exactly the same token, where local authorities have changed hands, we will need to know the colour of the preceding regime in order to determine the party effect. Such considerations point very strongly to the need to look most carefully at the party effect over time.

There remains one final point in relation to Fried's summary of the literature on the party effect and this is the possibility that not only were its measures a little crude, but also the coverage of countries was not wide enough. Later research, some of which used more refined measures of the kind we have suggested, has shown that there seems to be a Left party effect operating at the local level. Such research covered countries not covered in the literature summarized by Fried and includes Belgium, Denmark, France, Norway, Sweden, and West Germany.[45] It must be noted, however, that a possible reason for part of this difference may be a shift to more radical policies by the Left in Western Europe in the years since the research Fried was summarizing was completed.[46]

There are two further aspects of the impact of political factors on outputs that should be discussed. The first concerns cross-national output studies, and the second concerns the impact on outputs of party competition. Our foray into cross-national research will be brief. In the first place, it must be emphasized that such research is fraught with even more difficulties than intra-state output analyses if for no other reason than that it is extremely difficult to match policies; that is, to compare like with like between the countries under study.

In many respects the story is the same as for intra-state output studies. That is to say, those studies made in the early phase found little or no party effect,[47] whilst those made later, which tended to cover a more rational group of countries (i.e. only Western states) and used more refined and more precise measures, have found that there is a party effect.[48]

One interesting difference between the inter-state and the intra-state output studies is that among the former those by Castles and McKinlay, and by Borg and Castles, reformulate the party effect measure in terms of Right rather than Left party dominance. This is a persuasive change since it may be hypothesized that, broadly speaking, maintaining the status quo is easier than changing it, and is also less dependent on the vagaries of human volition and local circumstances. Right party ideology is therefore that much easier to translate into policy. It follows that a strong and united Right party may provide a better subject for measuring the party effect than a Left party.[49] A similar pattern of early studies revealing no party effect, and later ones discovering a party effect, is discernible for the more specialized non-statistical comparative studies. Thus Heclo, for example, writing in 1974 is adamant that parties had no effect on pensions policy in Britain and Sweden,[50] whereas Headey, in his study of housing in Sweden, Britain, and the USA claims that 'parties appear to have made a vast difference to housing programmes'.[51] Hjern finds a similar positive relationship between party and social welfare expenditure in Sweden.[52] But, as Stephens[53] has noted, Heclo's definition of what constitutes a party effect is somewhat idiosyncratic, such that some would discount it.

The Party System Effect

So much for the party effect at the cross-national level. We must now turn to another aspect of the impact of politics on outputs — the impact of the inter-relationship between competing parties. The most commonly used measure of this type is the competitiveness of the party system. This is employed by Alt for the British county boroughs, but British studies generally have not paid the same attention to it as has the American literature. The assumption in this literature, as we noted earlier, is usually derived from V. O. Key[54] and others who postulated that the smaller the majority, and therefore the closer the competition, the more likely the incumbents are to increase spending. This assumes a transmission model and is itself a species of the Downsian model.[55]

One problem that underlies such models and all discussions of redistributive expenditure is that of determining what is redistributive and ameliorative and what is not. For example, post-secondary education expenditure is very rarely redistributive despite its almost hallowed place as a measure of egalitarianism in much of the literature on comparative welfare that extends well beyond output studies.[56] These considerations raise important definitional questions which we discuss further in Chapter 9, but a full exploration of which lies outside the ambit of this study.

To return to the party competition effect, although he did use a slightly different measure than that specified on the Key model, Alt found no evidence that more intense party competition led to higher expenditures, and impressionistic knowledge of British local government would suggest that the reverse may be true. That is to say, parties with small majorities facing a single rival tend to pursue budgetary caution because of the impact of increased expenditure on the rates. This type of response also seems to be apparent among parties in Norwegian communes.[57]

The type of parties involved could also affect the extent to which closeness of competition between them affects expenditure. Closeness of competition between two non-class and non-ideological parties as in, say, the Irish Republic or in the United States, may reflect no more than a division of allegiance within an otherwise homogeneous electorate. Alternatively, it may reflect a broad division of the electorate into two relatively distinct sub-national political communities. The division between the bourgeois parties and the socialist Labour parties in Norway and Sweden provides an example of the second type of party system. In the former case, by contrast, increased government welfare may evoke no response from minority party supporters since a change in voting choice may signify something much more fundamental than a mere change in voting habits and would be regarded as tantamount to disloyalty to the voter's group.[58] In other words, we are back to the problem noted at the outset, namely that the conventional party competition explanation for output variation assumes both non-ideological parties and highly volatile voters. It is of some interest that research undertaken since Alt's does suggest that in British local government, at least, it is a competitive system with parties alternating in power, rather than the smallness of their majorities, that affects spending levels.[59]

The distinction between a competitive party and a one-party (or weak party and non-party) system may be the most important affecting expenditure. It could also be that the effect of the closeness of party competition is another reason why the impact of the Left party on outputs has been obscured in past research, since close competition may lead to policy convergence. If such convergence is to the Right, i.e. is anti-redistributive, then it would be the reverse of the Key hypothesis. Here we enter the world of the hegemonic ethos of the polity in question and that lies outside the scope of our study. But suffice it to note that in some Western states — notably Japan, Ireland, and the USA — the hegemonic ethos seems to be clearly to the Right and party competition as such has not produced the extension of welfare expenditure that has characterized most other Western countries. In other words, measuring the party effect in a competitive system is a very complex exercise, as is recognized by Wilensky who is one of the very few students of output analysis to explore the phenomenon in any detail.[60] In a highly competitive party system the impact of party cannot be measured solely by the extent of party policy differences at any point in time. We can only get a complete measure of the party effect if we know what the majority parties would have done had they not had competitors. We have already noted this possibility in relation to overall expenditure patterns, and it is possible to postulate some of the forms of policy convergence in the British party system. Two-party interdependence of this kind has long been recognized and at one stage led to the formulation of Hatschek's law on the inevitability of one party's decline and the other's resurgence.[61]

By convergence is meant first, the moderation effect; that is to say, the tendency for a newly-elected party to preserve the main features of its predecessor's policy, while changing some of the details.[62] This may have a greater relevance in Britain when Conservatives come to power than when Labour does so, since the latter (for the reasons discussed earlier) may be more inclined, other things being equal, to introduce new policies. On these grounds, one would expect the spending patterns of Conservative majorities which supplant Labour majorities to be closer to Labour spending patterns than are those of long-established Conservative majorities, and especially those where the Labour party has never achieved power.[63]

The second form of policy convergence is what may be called the secular Leftward movement. This is the long term tendency for the Left party in some countries to shift the parameters of acceptable public policy and the accepted scope of government Leftward along the Left–Right continuum. This tendency is akin to what Duverger has called the 'contagion from the Left' whereby the emergence of Left parties forces the right to form a party in order to retain its influence.[64] This phenomenon has been clearly apparent in British local government,[65] and it brings us back again to the apparent failure of the Left party effect to show itself in output research to the extent that might have been expected. For it may be that Left parties in some situations, because they are intent on changing the status quo, are more effective in achieving such a shift, and thus, paradoxically, obscuring the Left party impact. It may be that the secular Leftward movement can arise in a given local authority even where the socialists do not actually achieve power,[66] probably because of diffusion – via the 'national local government system'[67] – of the new policies throughout the whole country. All these effects are likely to render the expenditure patterns of authorities operating under a full-blown competitive party system different from those under non-party or one-party systems.

Since the magnitude of correlation coefficients depends upon the range of variability of dependent and independent variables, the relative uniformity of the county borough studies (which tended to be dominated by the two party system) may explain the relatively weak association between straight party strength and expenditure patterns. The conclusion is that output research in Britain needs to be applied also to county councils, for it is only among them that we find a sizeable group of non-party systems.

The inclusion of county councils, incidentally, also makes possible the introduction of a larger range of other non-political variables that could have a bearing on expenditure, such as population density, territorial size, and the agricultural–industrial employment ratio. In any case, as Stanyer has pointed out, counties are important political entities in their own right, and because they have been ignored in much of the general academic literature on local government, they therefore warrant special attention.[68]

Another set of political variables that could repay further investigation are those derived from the interplay of party at local *and* national level, both in a reinforcing and a cross-pressuring sense. Where its parent party is in power nationally, we may expect that the local party's policy preferences will be reinforced. This is likely partly because the centre will be more inclined to aid and abet it in its basic aims than if the opposing party was in power nationally. Party congruence of this kind may also mean that the locality will feel less inhibited about pursuing its favourite policies. A set of such hypotheses in relation to the possible impact of party congruence on local expenditure levels is set out in Fig. 1.1.

| | | CENTRAL GOVERNMENT | |
		Labour	Conservative
LOCAL GOVERNMENT	Labour	High local redistributive expenditures	Medium local expenditures
	Conservative	Medium local expenditures	Low local redistributive expenditures

Fig. 1.1. Possible Impact of Party Congruence on Local Expenditure Levels

Having laid special emphasis on developing new political variables, no claim is being made that they will somehow explain all, or indeed that they can all be operationalized. It must also be stressed that whatever view is taken of some of the earlier research in relation to the misspecification, or non-specification, of political variables there can be no gainsaying that political variables are often likely to be closely connected with economic and social variables. So, no matter what the explanatory power of new political variables may be, there will remain the statistically insoluble problem of sorting out the independent effects of factors which co-vary. Hansen's conception of socio-economic variables as forming part of the *criteria* from which decision makers select before acting, the selection process being 'determined by the political values of decision makers',[69] offers a potentially very fruitful avenue for resolving some of the covariation problem. Hansen's formulation also gives the priority to the political variables that, as we suggested earlier, they ought to be given, and in formal theoretical terms this is the logical way to view the relationship between the two types of variable. For the dependent policy variables are, we can all agree, the product of some kind of political process. They cannot emerge spontaneously from the socio-economic structure. Therefore, whatever the degree of association between service output and socio-economic variables, we cannot say the former was *determined* by the latter, unless we can demonstrate that the given output would have occurred if there was no political mechanism at all. If that cannot be demonstrated then, at the very least, all policy outputs can be assumed, in a formal sense, to be a product of the political process. To return to the Godwin and Shepard terminology, all models of the representative process in a democracy must be non-linkage models.

III   The Unitary Models: The Urban Hierarchy and City Types

Having specified ways in which the orthodox political determinants could be better deployed in order to see that their impact is on outputs, we now turn in this last section of the chapter to the other new approach, the application of the unitary model. Most output studies, as we have noted, utilize a list of independent, socio-economic variables which are derived from the characteristics of the resident population of the jurisdiction in question. The assumption is either that their characteristics somehow get translated into public policies, apparently independently of the political system, or that the government adjusts its service outputs to the needs of the population and that these needs are derived from their socio-economic characteristics. This is, of course, a version of our old friend the transmission model, and, as we have conceded, there will be some relationship between what governments provide and the kind of population they are serving. Rich cities will tend to spend less per head on homelessness and housing than poor cities, and more on selective secondary education. Equally, areas which attract the retired are likely to spend more on services associated with the aged than an area which has a disproportionately large number of young children in its population. Thus, in general, some demographic variables such as social class, population density, and school age population do correlate with certain service expenditures with a degree of consistency. However, this approach has been scarcely more successful in revealing strong associations between socio-economic variables and outputs than it has been with political variables.

This approach's lack of success is particularly evident in Britain. In the most comprehensive of such studies for the county boroughs, which employed twenty-six independent variables and twenty-nine expenditure and output variables, the conclusion was that this technique provided 'a weak and generally unsatisfactory explanation of inter-unit variation in . . . resource allocation'.[70] This conclusion is amply borne out by our own preliminary analysis. It is, in short, difficult to escape the conclusion that this mode of output analysis has come to something of a dead end, and we explore in more detail the limitations of the demographic approach in Chapter 3.

It seems unlikely that the demographic model can be retrieved, for at its very heart is a theoretical void; or rather, the assumptions on which it is based are fundamentally faulty. This is partly because, as we have already emphasized, it assumes that government is mainly engaged in reflecting the objective socio-economic characteristics of its citizens. But democratic governments are not, nor can be, mere reflectors since policies do not spring unaided from objective facts. How we choose to view, and to respond to, objective conditions is in the realm of value. For example, in the field of education it is possible to conceive a situation where the decision makers in a local government area have all the relevant information about its school age population — age and sex distribution, IQ, aptitudes, location, and so forth — yet there would almost certainly be serious disagreement as to the appropriate mixture of private, aided, and maintained schools; or whether the system should be selective or non-selective; and if the latter, the best form of comprehensive system. In order to ascertain what a given socio-ecomonic configuration will 'demand' in terms of public policies, we need to know in what way the principal actors in the decision-making process for the community in question interpret the objective facts before we can know what the relationship is between such facts and public policies.

This is not, however, the only reason why the demographic approach has been relatively unsuccessful, and why we have endeavoured to seek new approaches. Governments, whether local, regional, or national, may have functions to perform; functions that may be only tenuously related to their own population characteristics, and that are derived from the fact that the jurisdictions they govern perform a specialized role as unitary entities within a wider economic system.

It follows that if we are to comprehend one of the influences on the scope and range of public policies in cities we must first discover what its role is *qua* city within a wider system. We must view cities, in short, as systems within systems of cities.[71] The major deficiency of orthodox output studies is that in concentrating almost exclusively on the same battery of individual, socio-economic characteristics they have not only assumed an automatic transmission process, but have also ignored the fact that government policy-making includes those holistic functions just referred to; these require the identification of the individual characteristics of governmental jurisdictions, in this case city governments, and not those of persons or aggregates of persons.

In our research we have focused on two such unitary roles of cities. The first is the role of the city that is derived from its position in the urban hierarchy and the results of our analyses are set out in Chapter 6. This hierarchy is a conceptualization of a country's urban settlement pattern developed by geographers from the theories of Christaller and Lösch.[72] The basis of the theory is a neoclassical economic one based on travel costs for retail shopping and services. The rational consumer, it posits, will usually travel to the nearest shop to buy goods so as to minimize travel costs. Since the travel costs must vary broadly in line with the cost of the good to be purchased and the regularity with which it is consumed, the retail outlets for lower priced and more regularly consumed goods will be more densely distributed than higher priced and more durable goods. In this way a national hierarchical system of shopping and service-providing centres is created, with each rung of the hierarchy providing all the goods and services of the lower rung plus an additional range of outlets for more expensive and occasionally demanded goods and services. At the top of the hierarchy will be the largest centre (possibly the capital city), where will be located, in addition to all other types of shopping and services, the most costly and specialized shopping and services, such as an international opera-house, four-star hotels, consultant physicians, antiquarian bookshops, a stock exchange, and couturier houses. These services will be national in scope and in some cases international. At the bottom of the hierarchy will be the large village where a general store and perhaps a petrol station will be located.[73] A city's place in the system — in effect a nested hierarchy — is determined by the most specialized shopping facilities that locate within its boundaries, but those facilities will also have a strong bearing on what public services the city provides as a government. For example, a third order city may have specialized insurance facilities, a major supermarket, and an imported furniture store. This range reflects the extent of the market from which such shopping facilities attract custom. It is the scale of that market, that is to say the number of consumers prepared to travel to the city's centre, that will also broadly determine what the city's government will provide. In this case a central library, say, a polytechnic, and possibly a civic theatre. The higher up the national hierarchy the city is, the wider the range of public services it is likely to provide and the more specialized these services will be.[74] Also, the higher up the hierarchy, the larger is the population residing in the wider hinterland beyond its political boundaries that the city has to provide services for. Moreover, the fact that a city is a service centre for the population of the wider hinterland means that additional (to the resident population's needs) public services have to be provided to facilitate the service centre function. Such extra support services include highways, public transport, traffic wardens, car parks, police, public cleansing and public health, refuse disposal and sewage disposal services. In short, greater market centrality tends to generate greater demands for public services.

The link between a city's role as a market service centre and a public service centre is not necessarily a close one. The key connection is the demands that the market function places on the public sector for facilitatory services to enable the movement in and out of the city for non-residents who use the city's market and non-market services. There may be additional burdens on the public sector such as vocational education, but they will tend to be minor as compared with the non-resident movement costs. There will be other costs to the public sector the higher the city is in the hierarchy, but these may be a function of scale and increased population density and not of the market.[75]

It follows that a city's position in the hierarchy is likely to be an explicator of some of the policies it pursues. That such a relationship exists between the unitary role of a city as a service centre and its public policy outputs has been demonstrated in a number of studies.[76] Work has also been done as regards ranking county boroughs in England and Wales according to their place in the urban hierarchy.[77]

In addition to being a service centre a city may have any one of a range of specialized roles as a production centre, which, like its service centre role, will affect its public service output. It is this unitary role that is the second focus of our research. Just as a national state may have a comparative advantage within the international market due to its location, natural resources, or topography, or indeed because it has developed such an advantage by conscious choice, so may a city. A city, therefore, has a pattern of public policies designed to maintain and enhance that advantage. The essential point is that such policies would not be found for another city which had no such comparative advantage to maintain and nurture, but was otherwise very similar in terms of conventional population characteristics.

For a local government, a link of this kind with a wider system is likely to be considerably stronger than for individual countries since there will be a much more integrated and unified market — that of the state — to which it is linked. The city thus forms a unit in a spatial division of labour. It follows that towns with precisely the same rank in the urban hierarchy may sometimes be fundamentally different in socio-economic character; Bolton and Bath for example, or Warrington and Canterbury, or Exeter and Sunderland. Some of this difference is obviously accounted for by the fact that these urban centres also specialize in certain activities within the national division of labour.

One major factor influencing the choice of role may be a city's location. Norwich, for example, being out on the East Anglian limb could never have shared in the Victorian industrial expansion to the same extent as, say Manchester, whatever the ambitions of its city fathers. Nor could it have become a major seaport. Similarly we know that a number of industrial centres owe their prominence to the proximity of coal deposits or running water at the time they were first established. But the choice of role may never have been determined by locational considerations of this kind, but may lie in an initial historical accident, such as Lord Nuffield's desire to keep his car manufacturing plant in the same town — Oxford — in which he first began as a bicycle repairer, despite the fact that at the time it was remote from all other major manufacturing centres on which he was dependent for components.

The impact of this specialized productive role on the city's public services will of course vary. For some cities the role will have marked effects on the pattern and the extent of local public expenditure. For others, its impact will be more marginal. One of the most obvious examples of an urban place with a specialized role within the national economic system which markedly affects its public policy outputs is the seaside resort. It needs to ensure, for example, smooth traffic flows during the summer months and this requires more police and a higher than average expenditure on highway maintenance and traffic wardens. Equally it will have to provide much higher than average standards of recreational facilities such as parks, swimming pools, and putting greens. The seaside resort will also want to maintain a generally more salubrious environment, which means more expenditure on public cleansing and environmental health services. As a resort it may also seek to provide a better than average environment for the retired, who require better welfare services, old peoples' clubs, and sun shelters. Another category of specialized urban local authority where expenditure patterns are likely to be influenced by that specialization are county towns and conurbation centres. For each type the city plays a specialized role over and above its role as a service centre in the urban hierarchy, and this has, to some extent, been recognized in the literature on city types. The peculiar patterns of seaside resort expenditure, for example, were first noted nearly forty years ago.[78]

However, the discussion in the city-types literature has lacked the necessary precision so that its categories have been far too heterogeneous in terms of what we already know about the characteristics of cities. It is therefore very difficult to get to grips with the true extent of the impact of its specialized role on local expenditures.[79] Alternatively, where greater care has been taken in refining the typologies, the results have revealed less than might be expected so far as the objectives of the present research are concerned.[80] We therefore decided to start from scratch by creating a classification of cities that followed fairly strict rules, such that each category would be internally consistent in terms of its type, and be exhaustive of that type. We also established three broad criteria of differentiation − centrality, urban environment, and industrial-residential balance. Using in the main these three criteria, we arrive at nine city types and explore their expenditure figures. The results of our analysis are set out in Chapter 7.

Although counties do not form a hierarchy as cities do, and although any given county is likely to be more heterogeneous than any city because of its geographical size and the range of social and economic, urban and rural conditions it covers, counties do have a primary economic function which may serve as a basis for classification. There are those which are primarily agricultural, a few which are mainly working class and industrial, and some which are primarily commuter areas serving the large cities within or near them. Each of these economic and social types has a special pattern of service provision and expenditure, and these are explored in Chapter 8. In addition the chapter considers evidence of regional disparities, and indicators of a special Welsh effect which makes the Welsh counties quite different from their English counterparts.

Before embarking on the detailed analysis of the findings in relation to the new models − party system, urban hierarchy, and city type − it is necessary to counter a possible objection to the whole exercise. This is the claim that, because British local government has such limited autonomy, it is misconceived to look on its policy outputs as being the product of any type of local factors, especially local political factors. If we are to seek the causes of local policy-making, so this objection runs, it is to central rather than local government that we must look, for local government is largely an agent of the centre. Before proceeding to the discussion of our findings proper, it is to a discussion and refutation − at least for the period covered − of the validity of this agency claim that we now turn in the following chapter. The case we make against the agency claim is largely derived from our own data.

NOTES

1. A. Wildavsky, 'Political Implications of Budgetary Reform', *Public Adminis- tration Review*, Autumn (1961), 190.
2. For a discussion of this critical problem for comparative analysis see B. Barry 'Methodology Versus Ideology, the Economic Approach Re-visited', in E. Ostrom (ed.), *Strategies of Political Inquiry* (Beverly Hills, Sage, 1982).
3. The comparative statistical method and the case study method represent two different inferential processes,

... that of statistical inference which makes a statement about the confidence we may have that a surface relationship observed in our sample will in fact occur in the parent population, and that of logical or scientific inference which makes a statement about the confidence we may have that the theoretically necessary or logical connection among the features observed in the sample pertain also to the parent population.

C. Mitchell, 'The Logic of the Analysis of Social Situation and Cases', Mimeo, June 1981.
4. See, for example, T. N. Clark, *Community Power and Policy Outputs* (Beverly Hills, Sage, 1973), p. 53.
5. See N. Boaden, *Urban Policy Making* (Cambridge, Cambridge University Press, 1971), pp. 37–8, and B. Davies, *Social Needs and Resources in Local Services* (London, Michael Joseph, 1968), p. 43.
6. B. Davies, 'Services Provision and Local Needs', in B. Benjamin *et al.* (eds.), *Resources and Population* (London, Eugenic Society, 1972), pp. 153–4.
7. On this see J. Lewis, 'Variations in Service Provision: Politics at the Lay-Professional Interface', in K. Young (ed.), *Essays on the Study of Urban Politics* (London, Macmillan, 1975), pp. 153–4.
8. L. J. Sharpe, 'Is There a Fiscal Crisis in Western European Local Government?', in L. J. Sharpe (ed.), *The Local Fiscal Crisis in Western Europe: Myths and Realities* (London, Sage, 1981).
9. K. Newton, F. Bruun, T. Hansen, F. Kjellberg, G. Martinotti, G. Schaefer, C.-J. Skovsgaard, and L. J. Sharpe, *Balancing the Books: The Financial Problems of Local Government in Western Europe* (London, Sage, 1980), Ch. 3.
10. Royal Commission on Local Government in England, *Performance and Size of Local Education Authorities* (London, HMSO, 1968), and Royal Commission on Local Government in England, *Local Authority Services and the Characteristics of Administrative Areas* (London, HMSO, 1968).
11. R. J. Nicholson and N. Topham, 'The Determinants of Investment in Housing by Local Authorities: an Econometric Approach', *Journal of the Royal Statistical Society*, Series A, 134 (1971), 273–303, and 'Investment Decision and the Size of Local Authorities', *Policy and Politics*, 1 (1972), 23–44.
12. D. Dawson, 'Determinants of Local Authority Expenditure', and B. Moore and J. Rhodes, 'The Relative Needs of Local Authorities', both in the *Report of the Committee of Enquiry into Local Government Finance*, Appendix 7 (London, HMSO, 1976).
13. R. C. Wood, *1400 Governments* (Cambridge, Mass., Harvard University Press, 1961), p. 35. J. Q. Wilson makes a similar point in his introduction to J. Q. Wilson (ed.), *City Politics and Public Policy* (New York, Wiley, 1968), pp. 4–5. For a defence of factor analysis techniques used in conjunction with other methods see T. N. Clark, 'Urban Typologies and Political Outputs', in B. J. L. Berry (ed.), *City Classification Handbook* (New York, Wiley, 1972), pp. 152–78.
14. In addition to those studies already listed in earlier notes, see B. Davies, A. J. Barton, I. S. McMillan, and V. K. Williamson, *Variations in Services*

for the Aged (London, Bell and Sons, 1971); J. E. Alt, 'Some Social and Political Correlates of County Borough Expenditures', *British Journal of Political Science*, 1 (1971), 49–62; F. R. Oliver and J. Stanyer, 'Some Aspects of the Financial Behaviour of County Boroughs', *Public Administration*, 47 (1969), 169–84; D. E. Ashford, 'The Effects of Central Finance on the British Local Government System', *British Journal of Political Science*, 4 (1974), 305–22; P. King, 'Why do Rate Poundages Differ?', *Public Administration*, 51 (1973); D. E. Ashford, 'Resources, Spending, and Party Politics in British Local Government', *Administration and Society*, 7 (1975); R. J. Nicholson and N. Topham, 'Urban Road Provision in England and Wales', *Policy and Politics*, 4 (1975); D. E. Ashford, R. Berne, and R. Schramm, 'The Expenditure – Financing Decision in British Local Government', *Policy and Politics*, 5 (1976); J. M. Danziger, 'Twenty-Six Outputs in Search of a Taxonomy', *Policy and Politics*, 5 (1976); R. R. Barnett and N. Topham, 'Evaluating the Distribution of Local Outputs in a Decentralized Structure of Government', *Policy and Politics*, 6 (1977); J. M. Danziger, *Making Budgets* (Beverly Hills, Sage, 1978); C. D. Foster, R. Jackman, and M. Perlman, *Local Government in a Unitary State* (London, Allen and Unwin, 1980).

15. It is sometimes argued, or assumed, that studies of all county boroughs in England and Wales do not need significance tests since they are based on a total universe and not a sample. It is wrong, however, to assume that significance tests are only useful in order to set the limits of probable sampling error. They are also useful in studies of a total universe in order to set limits around the probability of generating differences on the basis of chance processes. There is, for example, the possibility of generating large correlations between two sets of random numbers. Consequently, it is useful to use significance tests even on figures derived from a total universe.

16. See, for example, P. M. Blau and R. A. Schoenherr, *The Structure of Organisations* (New York, Basic Books, 1971), and P. M. Blau, *The Dynamics of Bureaucracy* (Chicago, Chicago University Press, 1955).

17. One of the earliest students of the causes of state expenditure growth is Adolph Wagner who propounded the so-called 'Wagner's Law'. See R. M. Bird, 'Wagner's "Law" of Expanding State Activity', *Public Finance*, XXVI (1971). For a discussion of those economists who developed and adapted Wagner's thesis see D. Tarschy, 'The Growth of Public Expenditures: Nine Modes of Explanation', *Scandinavian Political Studies*, 10 (1975).

18. For example, S. Fabricant, *The Trend of Government Activity in the United States Since 1900* (New York, National Bureau of Economic Research, 1952), and A. T. Peacock and J. Wiseman, *The Growth of Public Expenditure in the United Kingdom* (London, Allen and Unwin, 1967), 2nd edn.

19. In 1968 Pryor listed 14 'recent' public expenditure studies using long time series for national expenditure levels and 52 studies of the determinants of service expenditures for state and local government. Not all the latter were by economists however. F. L. Pryor, *Public Expenditures in Communist and Capitalist Nations* (London, Allen & Unwin, 1968), Appendix E – 4.

20. T. R. Dye, *Policy Analysis* (Alabama, University of Alabama Press, 1976), p. 29. One study by economists which did look at the effect of political variables and recognize them as such is Peacock and Wiseman, *The Growth*

of Public Expenditure in the United Kingdom.
21. H. L. Wilensky, *The Welfare State and Equality* (Berkeley, University of California Press, 1975), Ch. 2.
22. Pryor, *Public Expenditures in Communist and Capitalist Nations.*
23. There were earlier studies by political scientists on state politics that linked party competition with their economic characteristics. See, for example, A. Ranney and W. Kendall, 'The American Party System', *American Political Science Review*, 48 (1954).
24. One of the most notable of these early studies was R. E. Dawson and J. E. Robinson, 'Inter-Party Competition, Economic Variables, and Welfare Policies in American States', *Journal of Politics*, 25 (1963). There followed R. T. Hofferbert, 'The Relation Between Public Policy and Some Structural and Environmental Variables in the American States', *American Political Science Review*, 60 (1966); T. R. Dye, *Politics, Economics and the Public* (Chicago, Rand McNally, 1966); T. R. Dye, 'Governmental Structure, Urban Environment and Educational Policy', *Midwest Journal of Political Science*, 11 (1967); I. Sharkansky, 'Economic and Political Correlates of State Government Expenditure', *Midwest Journal of Political Science*, 11 (1967). For an assessment of this work see H. Jacob and M. Lipsky, 'Outputs, Structure and Power: An Assessment of Changes in the Study of State and Local Politics', *Journal of Politics*, 30 (1968). Later work which finds political variables to be more important includes C. F. Cnudde and D. J. McCrone, 'Party Competition and Welfare Policies in the American States', *American Political Science Review*, 63 (1969); I. Sharkansky and R. T. Hofferbert, 'Dimensions of State Politics, Economics and Public Policy', *American Political Science Review*, 63 (1969); B. R. Fry and R. F. Winters, 'The Politics of Redistribution', *American Political Science Review*, 64 (1970); R. L. Lineberry and E. P. Fowler, 'Reformism and Public Policies in American Cities', *American Political Science Review*, 61 (1967); and J. W. Clarke 'Environment, Process and Policy: A Reconsideration', *American Political Science Review*, 63 (1969). Also see R. K. Godwin and W. B. Shepard, 'Political Processes and Public Expenditure: A Re-examination Based on Theories of Representative Government', *American Political Science Review*, 70 (1976); and M. S. Lewis-Beck, 'The Relative Importance of Socio-economic and Political Variables for Public Policy', *American Political Science Review*, 71 (1977). Also R. Winters, 'Political Choice and Expenditure Change in New Hampshire and Vermont', *American Political Science Review*, 71 (1977).
25. V. O. Key, *American State Politics* (New York, Knopf, 1956); D. Lockard, *The Politics of State and Local Government* (New York, Macmillan, 1963).
26. For the bare bones of the theory that links the extension of the franchise to the evolution of the Welfare State see T. H. Marshall, *Class, Citizenship and Social Development* (London, Home University Press, 1952); also see S. Lipset and S. Rokkan (eds.), *Party Systems and Voter Alignments* (New York, Free Press, 1967), and P. Flora and A. J. Heidenheimer (eds.), *The Development of Welfare States in Europe and America* (New Brunswick (USA), Transaction Books, 1981); and especially the essay by P. Flora and J. Alber, 'Modernization, Democratization and the Development of Welfare States in Western Europe', in the latter volume.

27. See L. J. Sharpe, 'American Democracy Reconsidered: Part 2', *British Journal of Political Science*, 3 (1973), for a discussion of the necessity for governmental autonomy in a democratic system.
28. Godwin and Shepard, 'Political Processes and Public Expenditures', p. 1131.
29. See note 14.
30. British writers who have argued the relative unimportance of local politics in policy-making include P. Crane, 'Enterprise in Local Government: A Study of the Way in which Local Authorities Exercise their Permissive Powers' (London, Fabian Society Research Series, No. 156), pp. 32–3; W. A. Robson, 'The Central Domination of Local Government', *Political Quarterly*, 4 (1933), 85–104, and *Local Government in Crisis* (London, Allen & Unwin, 1964), especially pp. 51–75; L. P. Green, *Provincial Metropolis* (London, Allen & Unwin, 1959), p. 156; R. M. J. Jackson, *The Machinery of Local Government* (London, Macmillan, 1965), p. 275; and J. G. Bullpitt, *Party Politics in English Local Government* (London, Longman, 1967), pp. 10–19. For commentaries on this literature see J. Dearlove, *The Politics of Policy in Local Government* (Cambridge, Cambridge University Press, 1973), pp. 11–21; Boaden, *Urban Policy-making*, pp. 11–20, and 'Central Departments and Local Authorities: The Relationship Examined', *Political Studies*, 18 (1970), 175–86.
31. See, for example, R. Saran, *Policymaking in Secondary Education* (Oxford, Clarendon, 1975); D. Peschek and J. Brand, *Policies, Politics in Secondary Education* (London, LSE, 1966); and R. Batley *et al.*, *Going Comprehensive* (London, Routledge, 1970).
32. R. C. Fried, *Comparative Urban Performance* (Los Angeles, University of California, Los Angeles, 1972), European Urban Research Working Paper No. 1, p. 71.
33. Dye, *Policy Analysis*, p. 30.
34. R. C. Fried, 'Comparative Urban Policy and Performance', in F. L. Greenstein and N. Polsby (eds.), *The Handbook of Political Science*, Vol. 6, (Reading, Addison-Wesley, 1975), p. 345. Also see Dye, *Policy Analysis*, Ch. 2, who also tends to invest existing output research findings with the definitive accolade somewhat prematurely.
35. Studies of parties, of quite recent vintage, still ignore the output literature. Even David Robertson's admirable analytical treatise on competitive two party systems (*A Theory of Party Competition*, London, Wiley, 1976), has little to say about whether the policies that parties espouse get translated into actual policies. For more conventional studies which ignore what parties actually do when in office, see, for example, R. Rose, *The Problem of Party Government* (Harmondsworth, Penguin, 1974); G. Sartori, *Parties and Party Systems* Vol. 1 (London, Cambridge University Press, 1976); W. E. Paterson and A. H. Thomas (eds.) *Social Democratic Parties in Western Europe* (London, Croom Helm, 1977); and M. Kolinsky, W. E. Paterson and A. H. Thomas (eds.), *Social and Political Movements in Western Europe* (London, Allen & Unwin, 1979). A recent study which still ignores the output literature but does at least attempt to answer systematically the question as to whether parties have any impact on policy is R. Rose, *Do Parties Make a Difference?* (London, Macmillan, 1980). Also see David H. McKay and Andrew W. Cox, *The Politics of Urban Change* (London, Croom

Helm, 1979), which although not a study of parties as such, does attempt to assess the party effect on a specific national policy area.

36. H. Heclo, *Modern Social Politics in Britain and Sweden* (New Haven, Yale University Press, 1974), p. 294.
37. See for example, Danziger, *Making Budgets*, Ch. 5.
38. For a discussion of local finance in a selection of Western states see Sharpe (ed.), *The Local Fiscal Crisis in Western Europe: Myths and Realities.*
39. For a discussion of policy communities see L. J. Sharpe, *The Central Co-ordination of Sub-National Government*, Preprint Series No. 5, Centre for Interdisciplinary Research, University of Bielefeld, 1981.
40. For a fruitful study of budgeting in a large city that adopts the disaggregated agency model see A. Cowart, K. E. Brofoss, and T. Hansen, 'Budgeting Strategies and Success on Multiple Decision Levels in the Norwegian Urban Setting', *American Political Science Review*, 69 (1975).
41. Fried, *Comparative Urban Performance*, p. 74.
42. M. Aiken and G. Martinotti, 'Left Politics, the Urban System and Public Policy', paper given at the Joint Sessions of the European Consortium for Political Research, Florence, Mar. 1980; and T. Hansen, 'Transforming Needs Into Expenditure Decisions', in K. Newton (ed.), *Urban Political Economy* (London, Frances Pinter, 1981).
43. O. P. Williams and C. Adrian, *Four Cities* (Philadelphia, University of Pennsylvania Press, 1963). Also see P. Peterson, 'A Unitary Model of Local Taxation and Expenditure Policies in the United States', *British Journal of Political Science*, 9 (1979). For a study of the British equivalent of a booster-ism city see the study of Croydon by P. Saunders, *Urban Politics: A Socio-logical Interpretation* (London, Hutchinson, 1979).
44. G. A. Irwin, 'Socialism and Municipal Politics in the Netherlands', paper given to the Conference on Parties, Politics and the Quality of Urban Life, Bellagio, June 1975. A similar point is made by H. Trieber, 'Once Again, Does Politics Matter?', paper given at the Joint Sessions, European Consort-ium for Political Research, Florence, Mar. 1980, p. 4.
45. For *Belgium* see M. Aiken and R. Depré, 'The Urban System, Politics and Policy in Belgian Cities', in Newton (ed.), *Urban Political Economy*. For *Denmark* see C.-J. Skovsgaard, 'Party Influence on Local Spending in Denmark', also in Newton (ed.), *Urban Political Economy*. For *France* see J. Kobielski, 'Tendance Politique de Municipalités et Compartements Financiers Locaux', paper given at the Conference on Politics, Policy and The Quality of Urban Life, Bellagio, June 1975; J. L. Becquart, 'French Mayors and Communist Policy Outputs: The Case of Small Cities', paper given at the Joint Sessions, European Consortium for Political Research, London School of Economics, Apr. 1975; and M. A. Schain 'Communist Control of Municipal Councils and Urban Political Change in France', *Studies in Comparative Communism*, 12 (1979). For *Norway* see T. Hansen and F. Kjellberg, 'Municipal Expenditures in Norway: Autonomy and Constraints in Local Government Activity', *Policy and Politics*, 4 (1976); T. Sande, 'The Norwegian Labour Party Policy in City Councils 1913–1923', paper given at the Joint Sessions, European Consortium for Political Research, Strasbourg, 1974; and Hansen, 'Transforming Needs Into Expenditure Decisions'. For *Sweden* see B. O. Birgersson, 'Services in Communes of

Different Types: The Impact of Financial Resources and Political Majority in Swedish Communes', paper given to the Conference on Politics, Policy and the Quality of Urban Life, Bellagio, June 1975; and U. Lindstrom, 'The Swedish Time Series Data Bank: Outline and Possibilities'. For *West Germany* see Treiber, 'Once Again: Does Politics Matter?'. Both of the last two papers were presented to the Joint Sessions of the European Consortium for Political Research, Florence, Mar. 1980.

46. This explanation is suggested by Aiken and Martinotti, 'Left Politics, the Urban System and Public Policy'. A similar trend has been noted in relation to the policy outputs of national systems in F. G. Castles, 'Patterns of Politics and Patterns of Public Expenditure: Some Problems and Speculations', paper given at the European Consortium for Political Research, Joint Sessions, Florence, Mar. 1980.

47. See, for example, P. Cutwright, 'Inequality; a Cross-National Analysis', *Social Forces*, 32 (1967); F. Parkin, *Class Inequality and Political Order* (New York, Praeger, 1971); P. Kaim-Caudle, *Comparative Social Policy and Social Security: a Ten Country Study* (London, Martin Robertson, 1973); R. Jackman, *Politics and Social Equality: A Comparative Analysis* (New York, Wiley, 1975); and Wilensky, *The Welfare State and Equality*.

48. See, for example, B. G. Peters 'Income Redistribution; a Longitudinal Analysis of France, Sweden and the United Kingdom', *Political Studies*, 22 (1974); D. Hibbs, 'Political Parties and Macroeconomic Policy', *American Political Science Review*, 71 (1977); C. Hewitt, 'The Effect of Political Democracy and Social Democracy on Equality in Industrial Societies', *American Sociological Review*, 42 (1977); F. G. Castles, *The Social Democratic Image of Society* (London, Routledge & Kegan Paul, 1978); D. K. Cameron, 'The Expansion of the Political Economy: a Comparative Analysis', *American Political Science Review*, 72 (1978); J. Drysek, 'Politics, Economics and Inequality: A Cross-National Analysis', *European Journal of Political Research*, 6 (1978); F. G. Castles and R. D. McKinlay, 'Public Welfare Provision in Scandinavia and the Sheer Futility of the Sociological Approach to Politics', *British Journal of Political Science*, 9 (1979); J. D. Stephens, *The Transition From Capitalism to Socialism* (London, Macmillan, 1979); E. R. Tufte, 'Political Parties, Social Class, and Economic Policy Preferences', *Government and Opposition*, 14 (1979); S. Stack, 'The Political Economy of Income Inequality: A Comparative Analysis', *Canadian Journal of Political Science*, 13 (1980); J. Kohl, 'Trends and Problems in Postwar Public Expenditure Development in Western Europe and North America', in Flora and Heidenheimer (eds.), *The Development of Welfare States in Europe and America*; S. G. Borg and F. G. Castles, 'The Influence of the Political Right on Public Income Maintenance Expenditure and Equality', *Political Studies*, 29 (1981).

49. F. G. Castles and R. D. McKinlay, 'Does Politics Matter: An Analysis of Public Welfare Commitment in Advanced Democratic States', *European Journal of Political Research*, 7 (1979), and F. G. Castles (ed.), *The Impact of Parties* (London, Sage, 1982).

50. Heclo, *Modern Social Policies in Britain and Sweden*, Ch. 6.

51. B. Headey, *Housing Policy in the Developed Economy* (London, Croom Helm, 1978), p. 235.

52. B. Hjern, 'The Management of Financial Incentives in Social Policy', in K. Hanf and F. W. Scharpf (eds.), *Interorganizational Policymaking* (London, Sage, 1978), p. 281.
53. Stephens, *The Transition From Capitalism To Socialism*, p. 147.
54. V. O. Key, *Southern Politics* (New York, Knopf, 1949), p. 337.
55. A. Downs, *An Economic Theory of Democracy* (New York, Harper, 1975).
56. See Wilensky, *The Welfare State and Equality*.
57. Hansen and Kjellberg, 'Municipal Expenditures in Norway', p. 21.
58. Lewis, 'Variations in Service Provision', p. 76.
59. Ashford, 'Resources, Spending and Party Politics in British Local Government'.
60. See H. L. Wilensky, 'Leftism, Catholicism and Democratic Corporation: the Role of Political Parties in Recent Welfare State Development', in Flora and Heidenheimer (eds.), *The Development of Welfare States in Europe and America*.
61. See C. Friedrich, *Constitutional Government and Democracy* (Boston, Ginn & Co., 1950), p. 417.
62. On this point see Ashford, 'The Effects of Central Finance on the British Local Government System'.
63. For an account of the restricted view of the proper scope of government adopted by a local authority whose overwhelmingly dominant Conservative majority has never been challenged by a socialist opposition, see Dearlove, *Politics of Policy*, pp. 205-25.
64. M. Duverger, *Political Parties* (London, Methuen, 1954), p. xxvii.
65. B. Keith-Lucas and P. G. Richards, *A History of Local Government in the Twentieth Century* (London, Allen & Unwin, 1978), p. 115. Also see J. Gyford, *Local Politics in Britain* (London, Croom Helm, 1976), Ch. 3.
66. Hansen and Kjellberg, 'Municipal Expenditures in Norway', p. 25.
67. P. Dunleavy, *The Politics of Mass Housing in Britain, 1945-1975* (Oxford, Clarendon Press, 1981).
68. J. Stanyer, *County Government in England and Wales* (London, Routledge and Kegan Paul, 1967), pp. 2-3.
69. Hansen, 'Transforming Needs Into Expenditure Decisions', p. 7.
70. J. Danziger, *Budget Making and Expenditure Variations in English County Boroughs*, Ph.D. Dissertation (Stanford, Stanford University, 1974), p. 225.
71. B. J. L. Berry, 'Cities as Systems Within Systems of Cities', *Papers of the Regional Science Association*, 13 (1964).
72. W. Christaller, *Central Places in Southern Germany* (Englewood Cliffs, Prentice Hall, 1966) and A. Lösch, *The Economics of Location* (New Haven, Yale University Press, 1954).
73. K. S. O. Beavon, *Central Place Theory: A Reinterpretation* (London, Longman, 1977).
74. For a discussion of the English and Welsh county boroughs and their position in the urban hierarchy see W. I. Carruthers, 'A Classification of Service Centres in England and Wales', *Geographical Journal*, 123 (1957).
75. Sharpe, 'Is There a Fiscal Crisis'.
76. See for example J. D. Kasarda, 'The Impact of the Suburban Population on Central City Service Functions', *American Journal of Sociology*, 77 (1972); Aiken and Depré, 'The Urban System, Politics and Policy in Belgian Cities';

M. Aiken, R. Friedland, and G. Martinotti, 'The European Urban System: Some Implications For Urban Public Policy', paper to the European Meeting on Applied Urban Research, Essen, 1981; and T. Hansen, 'Urban Hierarchies and Municipal Finances', paper to the European Consortium for Political Research, Joint Workshops, Aarhus, 1982. For a discussion of the unitary model in general terms and the impact of a city's unitary role on its policy-making see, P. Peterson, 'The Unitary Model of Local Taxation and Expenditure Politics in the United States', *British Journal of Political Science*, 9 (1979), 281–314. See also the same author's 'Redistributive Policies and Patterns of Citizen Participation in Local Politics in the USA', in L. J. Sharpe, (ed.) *Decentralist Trends in Western Democracies* (London, Sage, 1979), pp. 157–92.

77. For example W. I. Carruthers, 'Major Shopping Centres in England and Wales, 1961', *Regional Studies*, 1 (1967); by the same author, 'A Classification of Service Centres in England and Wales'; and R. D. P. Smith, 'The Changing Urban Hierarchy', *Regional Studies*, 12 (1968). Also see G. Armen, 'A Classification of Cities and City Regions in England and Wales 1966', *Regional Studies*, 6 (1972).

78. J. R. and U. K. Hicks, *Standards of Local Expenditures: A Problem of Inequality of Incomes* (Cambridge, Cambridge University Press, 1943). Also see C. A. Moser and W. Scott, *British Towns* (Edinburgh, Oliver and Boyd, 1961).

79. For example Moser and Scott, *British Towns*, pp. 84–8.

80. For example Armen, 'A Classification of Cities and City Regions in England and Wales'.

2. BULWARK OF LOCAL DEMOCRACY, OR PUPPET ON A SHOE-STRING?

Introduction

The analysis of the causes of governmental policy variation is, as we have noted at some length in the last chapter, fraught with difficulties. It may be claimed that these difficulties are compounded when the chosen subject for such an analysis is British local government. This is because during the period covered by our research one of the most prominent pieces of received wisdom of the literature, and much of informed opinion generally on British local government in the post-war period, was that the system had been gradually borne down by the weight of central controls. Local government had in consequence, so this view claims, lost most of its autonomy and was so closely controlled by the centre, even over quite trivial matters, that it was little more than an agent of the central government. How, it could be asked, can such a subordinated system be the subject of an output study? We must first answer this question.

More recently these centralization assumptions have been seriously questioned,[1] but until the 1970s they were dominant in the local government literature. Even a cautious and detached standard history published in 1978 has concluded:

If secondary authorities are left with full freedom of action within defined spheres, then something akin to a federal style of government will develop. If local councils are subject to a battery of legal and financial restraints and are left with little opportunity to use discretion or exercize initiative, then local government tends to become local administration of national services. British local government stands at neither of these extremes although the pressures from Whitehall and Westminster push it ever nearer the latter alternative.[2]

Much of the other literature that has discussed central-local relations is rather less hesitant in deciding that local government had indeed become largely the 'local administration of national services'.[3] This conclusion was powerfully reinforced by a series of official reports that appeared during the period, beginning with the Local Government Manpower Committee Reports of 1950 and 1951.[4] The centralization thesis also featured in the Herbert Royal Commission Report on Greater London Government of 1960,[5] and was taken up and made a central feature of the Maud Committee on Management in Local Government which reported in 1967.[6] The Report of the Redcliffe-Maud Royal Commission of 1969 also discerned the growth of central control as being part of the case for reorganizing local government.[7] By creating larger units, it argued, local government would become better fitted to retain its existing powers and attract new ones. This was a theme that was repeated with considerable emphasis by government spokesmen as well during the passage of the 1972 Local Government Act.[8]

The centralization thesis did not rest only on the growth of the instruments of central control but, as Dearlove has pointed out,[9] it also drew strength and plausibility from the steady growth of central grants. The assumption was that as central grants increased so did central control over local government: He who pays the piper calls the tune. It is this version of the centralization thesis which formed the core argument of yet another official inquiry; this was the Layfield Inquiry, which, although it reported in 1976,[10] and thus after our research period, surveyed the whole post-war period.

The third strand in the centralization argument identified growing local subordination with the transfer of powers from local government.[11]

The Loss of Powers

The loss of powers claim is perhaps the weakest element in the centralization case and can be considered first. It is a weak argument because it runs together two quite different things. The transfer of functions from local governmental to central agencies is of course prima facie a loss of power overall but in reality it is not a loss in all cases, as we shall see. Moreover, it tells us nothing about the second thing, namely the degree of freedom which local government exercises over those functions which it retains. Even if it did tell us, it is by no means obvious that local government has, on balance, in fact lost functions over the period under study. Of course, there can be no accurate *net* assessment since public services are not additive, but, in so far as it is possible to judge the relative importance of services (the proportion of the budget they absorb and their political importance), the gains to local government over the period have been at least as significant as the losses. For we need to set against the loss of the hospital service, the electricity and gas supply (by no means a universal service within local government in any case), property valuation, and the trunk roads, the enormous expansion of secondary and further education culminating in the creation of what is in effect a new university system — the polytechnics. Also to be taken into account is the massive expansion of public housing, to the point where local government now owns and manages over 30 per cent of the country's housing stock. Of equal importance is the steady expansion over the period of the local social, health, welfare, and planning services.[12] There is also the steady accretion of minor services such as those for the handicapped, consumer protection, and pre-school education.[13]

Certainly measured in financial terms, as Table 2.1 reveals, local government's share of GNP and of public sector expenditure has grown between 1950 and 1973 by 4.7 percentage points in both cases. Proportionally, the increase in local government's share of GNP was greater during the period 1950 to 1975 than that of the public sector as a whole. Whereas the cumulative annual growth rate for the public sector as a whole was 1.5 per cent, that for local government was 1.9 per cent.

The same picture of growth rather than contraction is evident if the measure is staff. During the second half of the period, that is to say from 1963 to 1973, local authority staff grew by 3.3 per cent as compared with a net loss of 0.3 per cent for central government staff.[14]

Table 2.1 *The Growth of Public Expenditure*

Year	Public expenditure as % of GNP[a]	Local expenditure[b] as % of total public expenditure[c]	Local expenditure as % of GNP
1950	35.3	30.2	10.6
1955	36.4	26.0	9.5
1960	36.5	27.8	10.1
1965	39.4	30.8	12.1
1966	40.3	32.4	13.1
1967	43.2	31.9	13.8
1968	43.7	32.1	14.0
1969	42.8	33.5	14.3
1970	43.2	33.7	14.5
1971	43.3	33.8	14.7
1972	43.3	33.8	14.7
1973	43.8	34.9	15.3

Notes: [a] GNP is total domestic expenditure at market prices.
[b] Local expenditure is total current and capital expenditure. Transfers from central to local government have not been double-counted in the calculations.
[c] Public expenditure includes the total current and capital expenditure of central and local government and public corporations.

Source: Central Statistical Office, *National Income and Expenditure* (London, HMSO, appropriate years).

Another weakness of the loss of functions method of gauging local government autonomy is that it makes no distinction between functions. We have already noted that it is difficult to make satisfactory comparisons because there is no common measure other than finance and, to some extent, staff. Of much greater relevance in this context, however, is the problem of externalities. Some functions that have been transferred to the centre or central agencies have very high externalities in relation to most local government units, such that, not only was it irrational to retain them at the local level, it was also highly inequitable. By centralizing such functions, local government capacity to act was enhanced, since it was relieved of a responsibility that it could neither effectively nor equitably fulfil.

The best example of beneficent centralization of this kind was the transfer of trunk roads in 1936 and 1946. By the mid-1930s these roads were carrying a very high proportion of non-local, interregional traffic and were therefore part of the national traffic system. No individual local authority could, or could be expected to, cope with the maintenance or planning of such roads. Similar considerations apply to the alleged 'loss' of unemployment relief to the centre in the 1930s. With the onset of structural unemployment during the 1920s and the slump in world trade after the Wall Street Crash in 1929, the local authorities with the highest unemployment levels were precisely those whose capacity to meet the increase in relief payments was weakest. Again, shifting the burden to the authority with responsibility for the whole of the national economy — the central government — was a vital gain for the economically-stricken local authorities. Legal power to do the impossible is not *de facto* power.

The Growth of Central Controls

We now turn to the more important arguments of the 'decline of local government' school. The first is that there has been an increase in the number and extent of central controls and directions over local government. According to Keith-Lucas and Richards, the really significant increase in such controls came during the Second World War.[15] They continued to grow after the war, especially during the immediate post-war period, as the central departments were required, under the post-war legislative programme of the Attlee government, to take a much more positive role as promoters of national policies, in particular in the fields of education, water, planning, and child care. The intensity with which the individual departments took up this new more positive role varied considerably,[16] but, in general, the change was sufficiently widespread and deep to constitute an undoubted increase in central supervision and control over the local government system. This change was reinforced during the early part of the post-war period by the need for the centre to ensure a fair distribution of scarce resources among local authorities.

It is important to note that following the two Reports of the Manpower Committee a number of the more detailed central controls were abolished in the early 1950s. Later, more controls were scrapped with the switch from a largely specific grant system to the block grant under the terms of the 1958 Local Government Act. Further relaxation of central financial controls followed in 1963 and 1972.[17]

This decline in central controls must be seen against the growing politicization of central–local relations throughout the period. This took the form of increasing competition between the two major parties at the national level over policies for services that were mainly a local government responsibility, notably housing and education. Ministers therefore sought to supplement their statutory powers by

means of circulars so as to cajole and threaten local authorities in various directions in line with government (party) policy. How far this trend constituted an
increase in central *control* is problematic, for its origin lay in a changing political
climate to which both the local authority and the minister were susceptible.
Compliance by a local authority to a circular may have signified nothing more
than a belated bowing to public opinion, or an anticipation of it, depending on
how far the centre was in line with or ahead of the general drift of public opinion.

The other centralizing trend during the later part of the period that must be
briefly noted is the increasing interest of the Treasury in gaining a grip on what
appeared to be the inexorable growth of local government expenditure noted
earlier (see Table 2.1). But this Treasury intervention did not really come into
full flower until the post-OPEC oil price increase which precipitated the financial
crisis of 1974–5. This undoubted growth in central control therefore lies outside
our period.

Weighing up these various and sometimes contrary trends it is difficult to
come to any final conclusion for the same reason that it was impossible to do so
in relation to functional allocation. An overall conclusion is made all the more
difficult because practice varied considerably between different central departments; on occasion departmental diversity was such as to thwart overall financial
control. In fact it is clear that this diversity was itself a source of local autonomy
since local authorities could claim that it was impossible for them to comply
since separate departmental directives were in conflict.[18] To paraphrase an old
adage, in the interstices of departmental policies local government found at least
some of its freedom.

Perhaps the balance of the various central–local trends lies on the side of an
increase in central controls over the period, especially in finance. But this
conclusion does not in any way validate the local-government-as-agents school
which seems to have exaggerated a quantitative change into a qualitative transformation. Part of the reason for this mistaken interpretation, as we have already
noted, arose out of the need to bolster the case for local government reorganization, and was based on an assumption that subsequent events have proved to
have been false. Probably more powers have been taken from local government
since it was reorganized than in any other comparable period. But that is a story
that lies outside the scope of this study.

In addition to the influence of the reform case on the centralization thesis,
there is also an assumption that the measure of central control is not only (or
even) the importance of the control in question, but how *unimportant* it is.
The irrationality of this assumption is explained by a further assumption that
the centre always seeks powers in an ordered progression from important to
marginal. It follows that if we can find a marginal control, then every other
aspect of the service which is of more importance must be already controlled

by the centre. Typical complaints of this kind might be: 'The Department even controls the level of payments that the local education authority can make in lieu of school transport', or 'Every zebra crossing, no matter how minor, proposed by the local authority has to go to the Minister for approval.'

The undoubtedly detailed character of such controls does not, however, signify the extent of controls over other aspects of policy. In some cases the reverse interpretation could equally plausibly be placed on such controls, i.e. that the concentration on pettifogging detail is a substitute for an inability to exercise control over major policy aspects. It may also reflect the increasing incapacity of the centre to cope in a world that is becoming more complex and interdependent and one which requires it to take on greater and greater burdens. With these increasing responsibilities the centre has less time to devote to any one policy issue so, whereas its reach extends, its capacity to exert its will on any single policy diminishes. An acute awareness of this dilemma produces a further flurry of circulars, instructions, and exhortations thus reinforcing the illusion of increasing central encroachment on the localities.[19]

To return to the dangers of taking the unimportant controls as the measure of overall control, housing provides an excellent example of the relatively marginal being of more concern to the centre than the fundamental. Over the period a number of very detailed central controls and regulations were applied covering housing design and building costs, yet at the same time almost all the major aspects of housing policy, such as how many units should be built, where they should be built, who should be allocated them, on what basis and at what rents, were entirely the responsibility of the local authority. Even where it was clear that local government was acquiescent to central wishes, this may have been a bargaining play to protect local freedom of action in other spheres.[20]

Another reason why central controls were exaggerated is that the general tenor of central–local relations in Britain is usually characterized by order, decorum, and mutual trust; the locality always avoids open revolt, whether or not at the end of the day it does in fact comply. This is mainly because the relationship is conducted by two sets of bureaucrats,[21] and as Keith-Lucas and Richards have rightly asserted, 'It is not in the nature of bureaucracy to promote revolt against properly constituted authority.'[22] Only on very rare occasions did a local authority engage in openly defiant behaviour. Clay Cross was one such example and when it occurred the full majesty of the law was invoked by the centre, and the recalcitrant authority was branded as a deliberate law-breaker who in effect was morally no better than a burglar or a mugger of old-age pensioners. The overriding assumption in central–local relations to which *both* sides feel constrained to pay lip-service is that the centre must prevail – the Queen's government must go on.

Nowhere was this tradition of order, decorum, and apparent hierarchy more marked over the period than in financial relations. As successive Chancellors have wrestled to reduce public sector expenditure, in their attempt to manage a wayward economy when 'overheated', local government has always been regarded as posing a special problem. This was because of the continuous growth of its expenditure that we have already noted. While local government may not have shared the Treasury view that it was a special problem, the long-standing poor performance of the national economy served to reinforce the 'centre must prevail' ethos. Despite much evidence to the contrary, one of the most widely shared and unchanging views in Britain over the post-war period is that central governments can and should have as a primary task the management of the economy. The local government system could never allow itself to be identified by the centre as a saboteur of the economy through non-compliance with a centrally defined remedy. Hence the predisposition on the part of the localities to comply on such financial issues. As Bramley and Stewart have concluded in their study of central–local financial relations, the relationship 'is not so much top-down or bottom-up as all-in-together. Conformance is the pervading mood'.[23]

Such genuine conformity by the localities on certain issues does not, however, reflect their unalloyed subordination to the centre. In the first place, to conform is itself a choice and is therefore a special kind of subordination. A 'slavish free man' is not synonymous with being a slave.[24] Secondly, even if it was, such conformity on financial issues does not mean that local government was willing to bow the knee in other respects.

In short, throughout the period of the study the undoubted co-operation between the localities and the centre on broad financial questions was not an accurate measure of local subordination in general. Conformity was essentially a matter of choice over an issue that all regarded as being of fundamental national importance and remained a choice until the 1980 Local Government and Planning and Land Act. Indeed one of the primary reasons for the introduction of that Act was precisely that even in the financial field local authorities had *not* complied with the centre's wishes, or at least not to the extent required by the Treasury.[25]

The Role of Grants

We now turn to the third and probably the most important indicator cited as evidence that local authorities had become the virtual agents of the centre. This is the financial one and it views the growth of central grants as a direct indicator of the growth of central control.[26] In its extreme form this claim may be dubbed the 'puppets on a shoe-string' argument.

Before examining the validity of this contention it is important to distinguish it from a related but a different set of arguments concerning high central grants which claims, first, that they may blur the local authority's accountability to its own electorate. Second, that given total local dependence on an income-inelastic tax, high central grants render the local government system as a whole vulnerable to irresponsible political manipulation by the centre. Third, it is also argued that high average central grants are bad because those local authorities in receipt of the highest levels of grant will, given the gearing effect, be subjected to disastrous financial instability arising from fairly small reductions in the central grant, again offering the opportunity for political manipulation by the centre.

We have no quarrel with these three claims. Disagreement with the last two would be foolhardy in any case since events since 1979 have shown them to be, regrettably, highly accurate. The contention being examined here is solely the claim that high central grants signify correspondingly strong central control. That, in short, high levels of grant confirm the claim that local government is firmly under the thumb of the centre.

Table 2.2 *Sources of Total Local Government Income in England and Wales*

Year	Rates[a]	Government grants[b]	Other[c]	Total
1950/1	33.9	33.9	32.2	100
1955/6	31.1	37.0	31.9	100
1960/1	33.3	36.2	30.5	100
1965/6	33.3	37.1	29.5	100
1966/7	33.8	37.1	29.1	100
1967/8	32.3	38.8	?38.9	100
1968/9[d]	31.5	38.6	29.9	100
1969/70	26.9	34.7	38.3	100
1970/1	26.2	36.5	37.3	100
1971/2	26.2	36.4	37.4	100

Notes: [a] Rates are net of rate rebates and the domestic element of the Rate Support Grant.
[b] Government grants include the aggregate exchequer grant, housing subsidies, and grants to trading services.
[c] 'Other' includes interest receipts, rents, and trading income, as well as fees and charges on the rate fund account. Since 1969/70, 'Other' also includes transfers from one authority to another, but an attempt has been made to estimate these amounts and to avoid double-counting.
[d] From 1969/70 the data were collected on a revised system of returns and the figures do not necessarily bear direct comparison with earlier years.

Source: *Local Government Financial Statistics, England and Wales* (London, HMSO, annually).

That central grants did grow over the study period is clearly brought out in Table 2.2 which shows that, as a proportion of total local expenditure, grants grew over the twenty-one-year period 1950/1 to 1971/2 from 33.9 per cent to 36.4 per cent. It is very important to emphasize that this growth is in relation to *total* local expenditure because a great deal of the discussion of this strand of the centralization argument is confined to 'rate and grant borne' or 'relevant' expenditure. In this way the growth of 'other' sources of revenue (mainly rents and charges) is ignored and the contribution made by central grants correspondingly exaggerated. Thus for the last year of the study period, 1972/3, a percentage of 38.2 for total expenditure for grants is transformed into a percentage of 56.4 for relevant expenditure.[27] No doubt this makes the centre appear to bulk larger at the local level, but it cannot be justified. The really relevant expenditure is total gross expenditure, and although the grant share of it had risen four percentage points over a twenty-year period this is hardly a cataclysmic change. Very clearly it does not provide a very stout peg on which to hang a convincing case for the centralization argument. It follows that, whatever other faults there may be in choosing English and Welsh local government for analysing the possible determinants of public outputs, it cannot be said that local government had become a system that had lost its freedom of action because it had become a financial prisoner of the centre — a puppet on a shoestring.

But it could be argued on behalf of the centralization thesis that being dependent on the centre for a third of your income, whether matters go much worse or not, is enough to render the notion of local authorities as independent a false one.

This raises a prior question as to what is the relationship between central grants and central control, but, despite the long-standing character of the debate about increasing central financial encroachment,[28] there is very little evidence one way or the other as to what the relationship is.[29] We know, for example, in the field of percentage grants that the proportion of expenditure coming from the centre varies very considerably from service to service. We also know that the total amount of grant that individual local authorities receive varies very considerably. The Layfield Inquiry put the range as being between 30 per cent and 90 per cent.[30]

The claim that this variation is not important since it is the overall effect of the central contribution that counts,[31] can only apply to the former and not the latter case. Even for the former case — the variation in grant for each service — we do know that where the grant was the same for different services and where the function is the same but the grant differs, there is no evidence that central control was related to the level of grant. An example of the same grant for a different service occurs for the police and fire services, which both receive a 50 per cent grant. Yet the Home Office's interest is very considerably greater for the police, in all aspects of the service. There is a similar lack of correspondence between level of grant and central control in the second type of situation, where the service is the same but the grant varies. Up until 1969 classified roads attracted very different proportions of their cost depending on whether they were classified as A, B, or C, yet the Minister of Transport exercised identical controls over all classified roads.

Even if the claim that it is the overall effect which counts is accepted, the

Table 2.3 *County Boroughs: Means and Coefficients of Variation for Expenditure Items in Order of Magnitude (in 1960/1)*

Major services	Selected sub-services	1956/7 Mean £	CV %	1960/1 Mean £	CV %	1964/5 Mean £	CV %	1968/9 Mean £	CV %	1972/3 Mean £	CV %
Total expenditure from rates and grants		n/a		29,710	7	41,260	7	59,310	9	96,410	11
Total education		10,973	11	15,310	10	21,210	9	30,450	10	48,590	10
	Education	n/a		14,928	9	21,046	9	30,425	10	50,944	11
	Education: secondary	3,052	18	4,802	16	6,594	15	8,958	16	15,420	16
	Education: primary and nursery	3,547	15	4,384	14	5,551	13	7,593	12	13,221	14
Police		n/a		2,260	16	3,330	16	4,720	17	7,740	19
Highways		n/a		2,250	20	3,060	21	4,100	21	6,530	20
Housing		n/a		1,850	36	2,320	43	3,450	50	5,610	61
Total health authority services		1,021	22	1,420	17	2,040	16	2,830	17	2,940	16
	Health	n/a		1,379	18	1,948	17	n/a		n/a	
	Education: loan charges	802	28	1,378	26	2,133	22	3,460	23	5,180	23
Sewerage		n/a		860	52	1,120	51	1,670	47	2,880	48
Parks		n/a		850	25	1,150	24	n/a*		1,800	27
Refuse		n/a		780	25	1,040	21	1,400	21	2,500	27
	Welfare	n/a		710	24	1,020	25	1,540	25	**	
Total fire		488	21	647	23	957	23	1,305	24	2,266	22
	Fire	n/a		640	22	940	22	1,270	22	2,060	21
	Fire: pay	482	22	552	22	720	25	1,090	23	1,961	22
Libraries		n/a		500	23	690	25	1,020	26	1,660	26
Children services		n/a		490	23	620	33	990	29	**	
Total public health		n/a		450	26	579	31	2,330*	23	1,890	32
	Education: special education	179	61	414	31	363	22	861	29	1,888	24
	Health: ambulances	200	25	249	22	282	28	511	20	n/a	
	Health: administration	164	31	203	32	n/a		391	30	n/a	

Education: recreation	142	52	193	48	264	50	393	43	730	40
Education: capital from revenue	131	60	183	66	269	70	252	84	241	90
Health: domestic help	117	56	180	48	259	35	386	37	n/a	70
Town and county planning	n/a		170	98			640	71	1,290	
Health: home nursing	123	34	157	33	210	26	273	22	n/a	
Health: mental health	67	38	116	35	241	32	442	33	n/a	
Fire: other expenditure	84	29	113	26	159	26	209	31	328	30
Health: child welfare centres	69	40	92	38	128	40	165	42	n/a	
Health: health visiting	66	34	91	33	129	35	165	36	n/a	
Health: day nurseries	66	94	67	95	73	105	91	104	n/a	
Fire: loan charges	23	68	38	78	58	81	87	75	141	69

* Parks included in public health for this year.
** Children's services and welfare combined in 1972/3: Mean = £6,950, CV = 20 per cent.

Table 2.4 County Councils: Means and Coefficients of Variation for Expenditure Items in Order of Magnitude (in 1960/1)

Major services	Selected sub-services	1956/7 Mean £	CV %	1960/1 Mean £	CV %	1964/5 Mean £	CV %	1968/9 Mean £	CV %	1972/3 Mean £	CV %
Total expenditure from rates and grants		n/a		26,800	20	37,300	20	51,700	20	83,500	17
Total education		n/a		16,880	13	23,420	12	33,300	11	51,470	11
	Education	11,370	16	16,402	17	23,113	13	32,867	12	53,900	11
	Education: secondary	2,931	21	4,950	20	6,784	16	9,112	16	15,601	13
	Education: primary	3,881	19	4,827	20	6,148	19	8,281	15	13,851	15
Highways		n/a		3,750	69	5,020	65	5,740	58	8,520	64
Police		n/a		1,950	13	2,790	14	4,170	12	6,940	13
Total local health authority services		n/a		1,470	15	2,110	19	3,330*	20	3,720*	29
	Health	1,056	22	1,391	19	2,008	19	2,866	18	n/a	
	Education: loan charges	724	37	1,335	27	1,998	25	3,096	28	4,611	28
Welfare		n/a		550	24	830	21	1,260	23	**	
Total fire		n/a		550	17	760	20	1,040	21	1,640	19
	Fire	412	14	531	12	751	14	1,043	15	1,781	14
	Education: capital from revenue	267	41	421	41	622	48	705	55	832	65
Children's services		n/a		400	26	480	26	680	29	**	
	Fire	268	20	344	19	503	17	674	18	1,213	17
	Education: special education	119	76	315	27	453	25	648	30	1,524	24
Libraries		n/a		300	26	450	27	720	20	1,230	20
Town and country planning		n/a		n/a		320	43	500	36	940	36
	Health: ambulances	244	23	293	21	421	21	599	22	n/a	
	Health: administration	160	28	202	23	284	24	389	18	n/a	
	Health: home nursing	151	36	194	37	255	35	321	33	n/a	
	Health: domestic help	130	61	174	55	250	52	368	50	n/a	

Public health

							*		*	
Public health	n/a	18	170	83	280	77	243	17	412	23
Fire: other expenditure	101	58	126	16	174	17	338	47	629	45
Education: recreation	69	38	99	60	188	55	159	35	n/a	
Health: health visiting	69	51	91	41	124	39	428	29	n/a	
Health: mental health	41	50	79	43	202	33	139	48	n/a	
Health: child welfare centres	48		72	48	102	47				
Fire: loan charges	26	63	39	61	63	44	93	46	126	40

* Local health authority services include public health in 1968/9 and 1972/3.
** Children's services and welfare combined in 1972/3: Mean = £5,040, CV = 18 per cent.

Notes for Tables 2.3 and 2.4:

1. Figures for the major services are budgeted expenditure while those for the selected sub-services are actual expenditures. The education, fire, and health figures which appear in the selected sub-services column are net rate and grant borne expenditure per thousand population. For sources and details of expenditure figures see Appendix 1.2.

2. Although detailed expenditure items for education, fire, and health services are available from 1956/7, the data for all service headings are not available for the years before, due to the exclusion of specific grants from the tables produced by the Institute of Municipal Treasurers and Accountants.

3. The number of observations varies from service to service and from year to year because the number of county boroughs and police authorities changes, and because of errors or missing data in the IMTA sources. For the county boroughs the maximum number of observations is 83 and the minimum 74; for the county councils the maximum is 63 and the minimum 43.

post-1979 experience demonstrates as clearly as possible that there is little necessary relationship between control and grant, for central controls have increased sharply whilst. grants have *declined*. All in all, the financial element of the centralization thesis is a weak one and it seems likely that it has been sustained mainly because there has been so little empirical research to test its validity.[32] Yet, as it happens, output studies offer one potentially very fruitful mode for testing the validity of the central dominance thesis. It is to such an exercise that we now turn.

The Centralization Thesis Tested

Certainly, at first blush, it is evident that there is a very high level of variation in service provision as measured by service expenditures. This has been amply demonstrated in a number of earlier studies including those by Boaden,[33] Davies,[34] Boaden and Alford,[35] Danziger,[36] and Ashford.[37] Dearlove also lists a number of other studies that reveal the existence of a high degree of variation among a bewildering variety of local services.[38] Whatever else may characterize local government service provision, it is emphatically not the uniformity one might expect from the claims by the central dominance school. Such extensive variation is confirmed in the results of our own research, which are summarized in Table 2.3 (county boroughs) and Table 2.4 (county councils). These list the coefficients of variation for expenditure items — both whole-sector and sub-sector, in descending order of the means of expenditure magnitude in 1960-1 — for five observation years over the seventeen-year period, 1956-73.

Some of the expenditure items display a striking degree of variation, with day nurseries in the county boroughs having the widest range. In 1964/5 and 1968/9 the coefficient of variation exceeded one hundred per cent. The only other service expenditure to reach comparable levels of variation in the counties was highways, but, nevertheless, expenditure on many other services and sub-services varied considerably in the counties and the county boroughs; for example in the areas of recreation, special education, domestic help, loan charges for the fire service, town and country planning, and capital expenditure from the current account of education departments.

Moreover, there is little indication from the figures in Tables 2.3 and 2.4 that the degree of variation in expenditure was decreasing. There was a marked decline of variation in spending on special education in both the counties and the county boroughs, and a smaller decrease for recreation expenditure in the county boroughs, but, equally, there was a general increase in capital expenditure from the current education account in both types of authorities. On the whole however the extent of variation in expenditures remained fairly constant over the 1956/7-1962/3 period, showing that the local authorities were neither converging nor diverging in the extent to which they varied in their expenditure patterns.

Table 2.5 *Mean Coefficients of Variation for Groups of Expenditure Items, by Size of Expenditure Items in 1960/1*

	Mean CV (%)
County boroughs	
1960/1 For: first 11 items	17
next 12 items	27
last 12 items	53
1972/3 For: first 8 items	15
next 8 items	31
last 9 items	45
County councils	
1960/1 For: first 10 items	23
next 10 items	24
last 9 items	49
1972/3 For: first 6 items	22
next 6 items	21
last 7 items	35

Note: This table is based on the coefficients of variation in Tables 2.3 and 2.4. It groups expenditure items into the largest, medium, and smallest size and gives the mean coefficient of variation for each group.

An equally significant feature of Tables 2.3 and 2.4, however, is not the range of variation, but the unmistakable and consistent tendency for variation to increase as the size of the budget item declines. This trend is confirmed in Table 2.5 which gives the mean of the coefficients of variation for the largest, medium, and the smallest group of expenditure items for two of the observation years. In short, it is clear that variation is a function of disaggregation. This is a phenomenon we will return to at greater length in Chapter 4.

One explanation for this trend could be that central controls lie more heavily on those services that absorb a significant share of the budget; that is to say, in financial terms, the most important services. But such an interpretation raises the crucial question as to what signifies importance in this context. A central department can be very closely concerned with a service even when, as is the case with town and country planning, for example, its share of the budget is very small indeed. More important still is the unresolved problem as to what precisely variation in expenditures of any kind tells us about central control. For it is generally accepted that, although explicit standard setting is rare, one of the motivations for central control is, in broad terms, to maintain minimum national standards. We accept that maintaining a minimum is not in any sense the only motivation of central intervention; ensuring uniformity of provision is also important and there will always be short-term attempts to bring local outputs into line with current departmental policy. However, we may assume with some

Table 2.6 *Coefficients of Variation for Social and Economic Characteristics of County Boroughs*

Variable	CV (%)
% Economically active women, 1971 (log)	3
Population, 1961 (log)	6
Population, 1971 (log)	6
% Retired people, 1961 (log)	7
% Retired people, 1971 (log)	7
% School-aged population, 1960	10
% School-aged population, 1956	11
% School-aged population, 1964	11
% School-aged population, 1968	11
% Manual workers, 1961	12
% Population aged 0–4, 1971	13
% Domestic property with a low rateable value, 1964	13
% Domestic property with a low rateable value, 1968	13
% Domestic property with a low rateable value, 1972	14
% Skilled manual workers, 1961	14
% Skilled manual workers, 1971	16
% Total rateable value made up by domestic property, 1964	17
% Total rateable value made up by domestic property, 1968	17
% Total rateable value made up by domestic property, 1972	17
% School-aged population, 1972	18
% Unskilled manual workers, 1961	18
% Unskilled manual workers, 1971	18
% Unskilled non-manual workers, 1971	19
Rateable value per capita, 1972	20
Rateable value per capita, 1968	21
Rateable value per capita, 1964	22
% Unskilled non-manual workers, 1961	23
% Owner-occupied households, 1971	23
Retail trade turnover per capita, 1961	23
% Retired people, 1971	23
Indictable offences per 1,000, 1968	23
% Non-manual workers, 1971	23
Rateable value per capita, 1960	24
% Skilled non-manual workers, 1961	24
% Domestic property with a low rateable value (1972 log)	24
Low household densities, 1961	25
% Owner-occupied households, 1961	26
Retail trade turnover per capita, 1971	26
% Total rateable value made up of shops, 1964	27
% Total rateable value made up of shops, 1968	28
% Total rateable value made up of shops, 1972	28
Indictable offences per 1,000, 1960	28
Rateable value per capita, 1960	28
% Skilled non-manual workers, 1961	30
% Households rented from local authority, 1961	31
% Households rented from local authority, 1971	31
Indictable offences per 1,000, 1964	31
Population per acre, 1972	32

Variable	CV (%)
% Skilled non-manual workers, 1971	32
Population per acre, 1964	36
Population per acre, 1968	36
Indictable offences per 1,000, 1956	36
% Small, self-employed workers, 1961	41
Population per acre, 1960	41
% Inflow and outflow to work, 1971	41
Population per acre, 1956	42
% Inflow and outflow to work, 1961	43
% Small, self-employed workers, 1971	48
% Total rateable value made up by industry, 1964	49
% Inflow of population to work, 1961	49
% Inflow of population to work, 1971	51
% Total rateable value made up by industrial property, 1968	52
% Total rateable value made up by industrial property, 1972	52
% Agricultural workers, 1961	62
% Total rateable value made up by office property, 1972	67
% Total rateable value made up by office property, 1968	69
% Total rateable value made up by office property, 1964	70
% Agricultural workers, 1971	79
% Agricultural workers, 1961	91

confidence that central equalizing interventions are strongest for those services that are related to personal consumption, i.e. education, personal health, child care, and welfare, for as divisible services they can be specified more precisely in individual terms than can quasi-public-good services such as highways, sewerage, fire, or police. It follows that some of the variation in service provision of the kind revealed in Tables 2.3 and 2.4, at least for this 'personal' group of services, may therefore reflect not so much local autonomy, but the reverse, namely, the exercise of central equalizing controls.

Whether they do or not depends on the extent of the inequality of conditions that such central controls are seeking to rectify, conditions which are usually called, rather loosely, 'need'. For only if the socio-economic conditions within a local authority fall below the average will a corresponding difference in service provision, designed to rectify the below average conditions, be revealed.

There is another possibility of cost variation not reflecting local autonomy. This is where the costs of service production vary from locality to locality. Thus a uniform service may be induced by central controls, but because local costs vary, the amount spent on these services may differ. However, variation in local costs is highly unlikely to be a major cause of variation in local spending because wage bargaining in local government is highly centralized and wage costs form a large proportion of local service costs. In any case it is impossible to pick up this kind of effect from our data, although it is possible to relate variation

Table 2.7 *Coefficients of Variation for Social and Economic Characteristics of County Councils*

Variable	CV (%)
% Population at school, 1968	7
% Population at school, 1972	7
% Population at school, 1964	8
% Population at school, 1960	8
Population, 1971 (log)	8
Population, 1961 (log)	9
% Population at school, 1956	9
% Economically active married women, 1971	9
% Population aged 0–4 years, 1961	10
% Owner occupied households, 1971	12
% Total rateable value made up by domestic property, 1968	12
% Total rateable value made up by domestic property, 1972	12
% Population aged 0–4 years, 1971	12
% Domestic property with low rateable values, 1968	13
% Manual workers, 1971	13
% Manual workers, 1961	14
% Domestic property with low rateable values, 1964	14
% Domestic property with low rateable values, 1972	14
% Owner-occupied households, 1961	15
% Total rateable value made up by domestic property, 1964	15
Indictable offences per thousand population, 1968	15
% Unskilled manual workers, 1971	15
% Unskilled manual workers, 1961	16
% Population over retirement age, 1961	18
Non-manual workers, 1971	19
Unskilled non-manual workers, 1971	19
Skilled manual workers, 1971	20
Skilled non-manual workers, 1971	20
% Population over retirement age, 1971	20
Rateable value per capita, 1960	21
Rateable value per capita, 1972	21
Skilled non-manual workers, 1971	21
Skilled non-manual workers, 1961	22
Skilled manual workers, 1961	22
% Total rateable value made up of shops, 1968	22
% Total rateable value made up of shops, 1972	22
Unskilled non-manual workers, 1961	23
% Households rented from local authority, 1971	23
Rateable value per capita, 1968	23
Low household densities, 1961	24
Rateable value per capita, 1956	24
% Households rented from local authority, 1961	24
Rateable value per capita, 1964	25
Indictable offences per thousand population, 1956	25
Indictable offences per thousand population, 1960	25
Indictable offences per thousand population, 1964	25
% Economically active married women, 1961	25
% Total rateable value made up by offices, 1968	49
% Total rateable value made up by offices, 1972	52

Variable	CV (%)
% Total rateable value made up by industry, 1972	54
% Total rateable value made up by industry, 1968	55
% Small, self-employed workers, 1971	57
% Small, self-employed workers, 1961	65
% Agricultural workers, 1961	75
Population per acre, 1968	75
Population per acre, 1972	75
% Agricultural workers, 1971	83
Population per acre, 1964	85

in local conditions to differences in spending. It is, of course, not an easy task, since obtaining the necessary information is extremely difficult, even supposing the information was susceptible to clear definition and measurement. But our research has revealed that there is a high degree of variation in many of the social and economic characteristics of local authority areas that may be related to inequalities of need. This is clearly evident in Tables 2.6 and 2.7 which list the coefficients of variation for a series of socio-economic variables in ascending order of magnitude.

Whatever the degree of social and economic homogeneity of British cities by comparison with cities in other countries in the Western world, Tables 2.6 and 2.7 suggest that they were not becoming any more homogeneous over time. Most variables changed their coefficient of variation only slightly between 1961 and 1971 (the two census years) or between 1956/7 and 1972/3 (the first and last of our financial years). In the county boroughs (Table 2.6), it is true, the percentages of the agricultural workers, population densities, crime rates, and rateable values per capita did narrow their distributions quite considerably (i.e. by five percentage points or more), but, on the other hand, there were also significant increases in the percentage for self-employed workers and the proportion of the population which is of school age. In the counties (Table 2.7), variations in population per acre, indictable offences, and working wives also dropped considerably, but, on the other hand, the distribution of agricultural workers increased its variability. The counties, like the county boroughs, generally display the same degree of variability over time, a clear indication that both types of authority were not becoming more homogeneous in any marked way.

So far the evidence is reasonably clear: there is a considerable degree of variation in expenditure on different services and sub-services in both the counties and the county boroughs. There is also a considerable degree of variation in the social and economic characteristics of these authorities. The range of these variations did not decrease in most cases for either type of authority during the sixteen-year period covered. But the key question raised by these conclusions is, as we have already noted: what is the precise relationship between the socio-economic variables and the expenditure variables? We turn to this question in the next set of tables which list the results of regressing the social, economic, and political variables on the expenditure variables for the county boroughs and counties. Table 2.8 shows the proportion of the variance in spending which is explained by the regression equations.

Table 2.8 *Percentage of the Variance* (R^2) *in Per Capita Service Expenditures explained by local Social, Economic, and Political Variables, 1972/3*

County boroughs Service	R^2	Service	R^2
Housing	63.4	Refuse	29.6
Education	61.0	Sewerage	29.2
Total	53.9	Highways	27.0
Police	46.9	Parks	18.5
Libraries	33.3	Local health	11.7
Fire	31.3	Planning	11.0
Social services	30.1	Public health	10.5
County councils Service	R^2	Service	R^2
Highways	80.0	Social services	33.2
Total	75.9	Planning	32.7
Education	65.8	Libraries	32.0
Health	47.4	Fire	27.9
Police	43.0		

The figures show that a large proportion of the variance is explained for some services but not for others. The figures are usually higher for the counties than the county boroughs, although from the point of view of the centralization thesis it is difficult to see why this should be. Is there some qualitative difference in central government's control over the two types of authority which accounts for the different R^2 in Table 2.8? It seems highly unlikely. On the contrary, the explanation is more likely to lie at the local level; that is to say in differences in the nature of the two kinds of authority, and in their social, political, and economic characteristics, rather than in any variation in the incidence and effect of central control.

For example, only 27 per cent of highways spending is explained by local variables in the case of the county boroughs, but the figure is 80 per cent for the counties. In order to explain this remarkable difference between the two types of local authority the centralization thesis would have to argue that central control is much stronger in one case than in the other. However, it seems simpler, and much more plausible, to argue that the different results for the two types are best explained by the broad differences in their socio-economic character-istics. The county boroughs are, for example, wholly urban, whereas counties range from the predominantly agricultural and sparsely populated to the very mixed suburban, quasi-rural, and rural such as Surrey or Lancashire. It is not the impact of the centre which explains local variability but, on the contrary, the range of socio-economic variation within the counties and county boroughs.

Turning to differences within the two types of authority, Table 2.8 shows that some service spending is quite well explained by local variables while other spending is not. Highways, education, and police appear high up on the list, and planning, social services, and fire towards the bottom. The significant fact about these figures is that they show little rhyme or reason so far as the central dominance theory is concerned. Services which are generally thought to be of great importance to central government are mixed in with those which are almost the exclusive preserve of local interests. For example, in the case of the county boroughs, libraries, fire, social services, refuse, sewerage, and highways all fall within the 27–33 per cent bracket, and yet fire, social services, and highways are all services in which central government has a considerable interest in maintaining minimum standards, while refuse and libraries are entirely 'local' services. Similarly, in the counties, social services, planning, libraries, and fire all fall within the 27–33 per cent range, but whereas three of them (social services, planning, and fire) are of some concern to central government, libraries are of very little interest. At the same time, a service like highways in the county boroughs, which is of considerable national interest, is weakly related to local circumstances, while housing and education, of no less importance nationally, are strongly related. In other words, services which have in common the fact that they are usually supposed to be fairly highly controlled and regulated by central government do not differ from services which are usually supposed to be the main, or sole, concern of local authorities. The former are no more divorced from local circumstances than the latter, and the latter are no better or worse explained by local conditions than the former.

This is certainly not consistent with the central dominance theory, if only because the theory would lead one to suppose that the services which are centrally determined would behave in a roughly similar way such that they would be distinguished from the services which are governed to a much greater extent by local policies and priorities. Social and economic circumstances seem to have as much influence over spending on services in which central government takes a keen interest, as they do over spending on services which are left to local initiatives and preferences.

So far we have been examining in the light of our data the validity of the central dominance thesis in terms of both of its strands, the increase in central controls and directions, and the increase in central grants. However, our data

Table **2.9** *Zero-order Correlations Between Per Capita Grants and Per Capita Service Expenditures, County Boroughs and Counties, 1972/3*

Service	County boroughs	County councils		
		England and Wales	England	Wales
Total	0.48***	0.84***	0.37**	0.83**
Local health	0.10	0.83***	0.28*	0.85***
Highways	0.12	0.82***	0.33*	0.83***
Police	0.02	0.68***	0.18	0.77***
Education	0.37**	0.63***	0.04	0.78***
Planning	−0.16	0.47***	0.04	0.36
Libraries	−0.18	0.34**	−0.09	0.36
Social services	0.28*	0.27*	−0.07	−0.07
Fire	0.31**	0.11	−0.25*	−0.16
Housing	0.57***			
Public health	0.25*			
Sewerage	−0.23*			
Refuse	0.20*			
Parks	0.01			
(N)	(83)	(58)	(45)	(13)

Note: ***, **, * indicate significance at 0.001, 0.01, and 0.05 respectively using a one-tailed test. The same convention to indicate significance levels is used in all other tables in this volume.

also enable us to examine the possible independent effect of grants and it is to an examination of this effect that we now turn.

The Role of Grants

Table 2.9 summarizes the analysis which correlates per capita grants in the county boroughs and in the counties with per capita spending. The table shows that the relationship varies from one service to another, from one type of authority to another, and from one part of the country to another. In other words, the relationship is highly varied, suggesting overall a rather mixed, but on balance, somewhat weak relationship between grants and spending. This finding is broadly in line with Ashford's conclusions from his study of the relationship between expenditure patterns for services and grants over a twenty-year period.[39]

As might be expected, there is a consistently significant statistical association in the case of total spending. This relationship seems to be especially strong among English and Welsh counties taken together and among Welsh counties on their own.

For the individual service expenditures, again, the influence of grants seems to be quite strong in the Welsh counties, but otherwise there is no discernible overall consistency in the figures. Significant correlations are found among the county boroughs for eight services, but not for the other six. In the case of sewerage the figure is actually negative. The figures are uniformly significant and sometimes very strong for the counties, suggesting a clear tendency for high grants to be associated with high spending. This positive relationship between central intervention and local action being more evident in the counties than in the county boroughs is broadly in line with one of the rare output studies that has attempted to assess the impact of grants on local expenditure.[40]

It must be emphasized that if the high correlations for individual services do indeed reflect the influence of grants, a major puzzle needs to be solved. For the high correlations for the county borough services are not for the same services that have high correlations in the counties. More puzzling still is the fact that the Welsh county service correlations are markedly different from the English counties. The most important message that emerges from Table 2.9 is that grants may be a significant influence on service expenditures in Wales but not in England. Why, we are forced to ask, does the influence of grants suddenly take effect when we cross the border from Gloucestershire to Glamorgan? We will return to this puzzle in Chapter 8.

Summarizing the results set out in Table 2.9, we may say that there is very meagre evidence that grants convert local authorities into the agents of the centre. There may be some effect on total expenditure, and there is fairly strong evidence that grants have a consistently direct impact on some Welsh county service expenditures. Perhaps the only sure conclusion to be drawn from Table 2.9 is that if grants are important in influencing local policies, their influence is mediated by a further set of factors which operate for some services but not for others.

Before leaving the possible centralizing effect of grants it ought to be emphasized that since 1965 the distribution of the needs element of the Rate Support Grant (RSG) has itself come to be determined by existing local authority spending levels: so that the causal relationship between grants and spending had become throughly confused in the later part of the study period, such that the revelation of a close connection between the two does not necessarily mean that grants determine spending levels any more than it argues for the reverse.

Conclusion

Viewing the preceding discussion and analysis as a whole, the claim that local authorities are little more than agents has little support from either our data, or what may be reasonably deduced from what we know from other sources. Those who have argued that the local government system had become beholden to the centre no doubt did so from the best of motives, but they obviously had a somewhat shaky grasp of what a real agency relationship would be like. It may be helpful in this summarizing discussion to specify very briefly what such a relationship would entail. In the first place, the centre would be the statutory service provider and as such would specify precisely what it wanted to its agents. It would also be in a position to exercise powers over them in order to ensure that these objectives were fulfilled. The grant system would in turn be transformed from a combination of both resource equilizer and makeweight for an inadequate local tax base, into purely a payment for services rendered. It is difficult to envisage such a system continuing for very long without the centre demanding some say in the appointment of those running the agencies, rather in the same way that they do with the boards of the nationalized industries or hospital boards. The point hardly needs labouring that agencies of this kind would be very different animals from the present local authorities.

If the agency claim has always been far-fetched, what of the more limited claim that local authorities are not agents, but are still sufficiently lacking in real freedom of action as to render them inappropriate for an output study of the kind we have undertaken? The imprecision of this conception of local government makes it a difficult claim to counter. Nevertheless, we suspect that it too underestimates the power of the localities, since it is based on a misconception that is derived from the way in which so much of central–local relations is presented on the public stage. The star of the drama is always the minister and the drama's climax is his announcement of his new policy, the rest – the crucial translation of the brave intentions into reality – is always denouement. The form in which the drama is performed, with its imagery of a military command structure – 'I will do "X" and then I will ensure "Y" – so dear to British executive government, merely serves to reinforce the impression that the whole of the apparatus of government – the central department or agency, NHS, central field agencies, quango, public corporation, or local authority – are all merely line regiments in the minister's army.

Local government is not, however, part of the minister's army. If anything it is a separate army with a focus and a role that is remote from the central department. It is, to continue the analogy, an army that has, above all, a monopoly of executant expertise and information about the conditions in which the new policies have to be implemented. It is a remarkable fact that in the many discussions in the literature on central–local relations the actual conditions which face the centre are seldom spelt out. Yet these conditions provide considerable handicaps for the kind of central government that even the moderate centralization school seems to envisage. It is the very pith and essence of the separation of roles between centre and locality in the implementation process that severely limits the power of the centre to command where the locality resists but stays overtly within the law. As Stanyer has pointed out,[41] the centre can with some effort stop something happening, but it has great difficulty in spurring the local authority to act against its own wishes.

We have already noted one link between the claim that local authorities are little more than agents, and local government reorganization. There is also another more important link which arises directly from the rigid division of roles between centre and locality in the British system, and which, paradoxically, underlines the limits of the centre's capacity to prevail over the localities. The increasing difficulty the centre experienced in achieving its aims at the local level concerning a widening range of complex and politically sensitive policies was undoubtedly an influential factor in getting reorganization on to the statute book. For with reorganization, the number of localities with which the centre had to deal was drastically reduced.[42] It is the very extreme quality of the reorganization, which has given Britain possibly the largest local units in the Western world, that underlines the limitations on the centre's capacity to exercise effective control in day-to-day relationships with the localities.

It is this conception of the centre, as having far more limits on its ability to impress its will on the localities than the centralization thesis admits, that, in our view, emerges from the preceding discussion and analysis in this chapter and which fully justifies the application of output analysis to English and Welsh local government. In his summary of the Layfield Inquiry's conclusions, G. W. Jones comes closest, we feel, to capturing in summary form the reality of central–local relations during the study period:

Most mandatory obligations laid on local authorities are vague and general leaving scope for local discretion. The Committee found that most local expenditure was determined neither by central requirement nor by totally free choice, but fell between the two and was the outcome of a complex mixture of pressures, such as advice and urging from government departments, inspection, circulars and letters, accumulated past practice, professional attitudes, political influences, and the activities of various pressure groups both local and national, and competition and emulation amongst local authorities themselves.[43]

We conclude, finally, that the British local government system is sufficiently autonomous to warrant an output study, and we now proceed in the next two chapters to an examination of some alternative theoretical constructs for explaining public policy variation.

NOTES

1. The four most important books to question the centralization assumption are N. Boaden, *Urban Policy-Making: Influences on County Boroughs in England and Wales* (London, Cambridge University Press, 1971); J. Dearlove, *The Politics of Policy in Local Government* (London, Cambridge University Press, 1973); J. Stanyer, *Understanding Local Government* (London, Fontana/Collins, 1976); and R. A. W. Rhodes, *Control and Power in*

Central–Local Relations (Farnborough, Gower, 1981). Also see G. W. Jones (ed.), *New Approaches to the Study of Central–Local Relationships* (Farnborough, Gower, 1980). Boaden's study is of particular importance since it is rooted in an analysis of local government outputs of the kind undertaken in this study.

2. B. Keith-Lucas and P. G. Richards, *A History of Local Government in the Twentieth Century* (London, Allen & Unwin, 1978), p. 159.
3. The centralization thesis is widespread in the local government literature, but for typical examples see D. N. Chester, *Central and Local Government* (London, Macmillan, 1951); W. A. Robson, *Local Government in Crisis* (London, Allen & Unwin, 1966), p. 67; R. M. Jackson, *The Machinery of Local Government* (London, Macmillan, 1965), p. 275; West Midland Study Group, *Local Government and Central Government* (London, Routledge, 1956), *passim*; and R. J. Buxton, *Local Government* (Harmondsworth, Penguin, 1970), Ch. 3. Also see J. A. G. Griffith, *Central Departments and Local Authorities* (London, Allen & Unwin, 1966).
4. Local Government Manpower Committee, *First and Second Reports*, Cmnd. 7870 and Cmnd. 8421 (London, HMSO, 1951 and 1952).
5. *Report of the Royal Commission on Local Government in Greater London*, Cmnd. 1164 (London, HMSO, 1960).
6. Maud Committee, *Management of Local Government* (London, HMSO, 1967).
7. *The Royal Commission on Local Government in England – Report* (Redcliffe-Maud), Cmnd. 4040 (London, HMSO, 1969).
8. B. Wood, *The Process of Local Government Reform 1966–74* (London, Allen & Unwin, 1976).
9. Dearlove, *The Politics of Policy in Local Government*.
10. *Inquiry into Local Government Finance – Report* (Layfield), Cmnd. 6453 (London, HMSO, 1976).
11. See, for example, Robson, *Local Government in Crisis, passim*.
12. W. A. Robson, one of the most trenchant advocates of the theory that local government had been undermined by a loss of functions, did recognize that local government had acquired new powers (*Local Government in Crisis*, p. 29), but, as Stanyer has pointed out, Robson takes little or no account of the enormous expansion of existing local services. See Stanyer, *Understanding Local Government*, Ch. 10.
13. For a list of the new functions acquired by local government over the post-war period, see K. Newton *et al.*, *Balancing the Books: The Financial Problems of Local Government in West Europe* (London, Sage, 1981), pp. 207–8.
14. K. Newton, 'The Local Financial Crisis in Britain: A Non-Crisis Which is Neither Local Nor Financial', in L. J. Sharpe (ed.), *The Local Fiscal Crisis in Western Europe: Myths and Realities* (London, Sage, 1981).
15. Keith-Lucas and Richards, *A History of Local Government*, Ch. VIII.
16. Griffith, *Central Departments and Local Authorities, passim*.
17. Keith-Lucas and Richards, *A History of Local Government*, p. 171.
18. A. Alexander, *Local Government in Britain Since Reorganization* (London, Allen & Unwin, 1981), Ch. 7.
19. For a perceptive discussion of this problem, see C. D. Foster, R. Jackman,

and M. Perlman, *Local Government Finance in a Unitary State* (London, Allen & Unwin, 1980), p. 342.

20. See M. Laffir, 'Professionalism in Central–Local Relations' in Jones (ed.), *New Approaches to the Study of Central–Local Relationships*.
21. R. Greenwood, 'Fiscal Pressure and Local Government in England and Wales', in C. Hood and M. Wright (eds.), *Big Government in Hard Times* (Oxford, Martin Robertson, 1981).
22. Keith-Lucas and Richards, *A History of Local Government*, p. 176.
23. G. Bramley and M. Stewart, 'Implementing Public Expenditure Cuts', in S. Barret and C. Fudge (eds.), *Policy and Action: Essays on the Implementation of Public Policy* (London, Methuen, 1981), p. 60. Also see Greenwood, 'Fiscal Pressure and Local Government'.
24. Foster, Jackman, and Perlman, *Local Government Finance in a Unitary State*, p. 355.
25. Alexander, *Local Government in Britain Since Reorganization*, Ch. 7.
26. Although in no sense supporting the extreme centralization claim, the most recent protagonist of this view is the Layfield Report (see note 10). Also see Jones, 'Central–Local Government Relations: Grants, Local Responsibility and Minimum Standards', in D. Butler and A. H. Halsey (eds.), *Policy and Politics* (London, Macmillan, 1978).
27. Layfield *Report*, p. 385, Table 26.
28. See, for example, Chester, *Central and Local Government*, which was published in 1951. Foster, Jackman, and Perlman give a reference for 1928. See their *Local Government Finance in a Unitary State*, p. 365, footnote 3.
29. For a very useful discussion of the possible impact of grants on local authorities see E. Page, 'The New Gift Relationship: Are Central Government Grants Only Good for the Soul', paper given at the Annual Conference of the Political Studies Association, Hull, April 1981.
30. Layfield, *Report*, p. 216.
31. Jones, 'Central, Local Government Relations: Grants, Local Responsibility and Minimum Standards'. Also see E. Page, 'The New Gift Relationship', E. Page, 'The Measurement of Central Control', *Political Studies*, XXVIII (1980), and J. C. Gibson, C. H. Game, and J. D. Stewart, 'The Measurement of Central Control in England and Wales', *Political Studies*, XXX (1982).
32. The rare exceptions include Ashford, 'Resource Spending and Party Politics in British Local Government'; Page, 'The New Gift Relationship'; and Foster, Jackman, and Perlman, *Local Government Finance in a Unitary State*, pp. 356–62.
33. Boaden, *Urban Policy-making*.
34. B. Davies, *Social Needs and Resources in Local Services* (London, Michael Joseph, 1968).
35. N. Boaden and R. Alford, 'Sources of Diversity in English Local Government Decisions', *Public Administration*, 47 (1969).
36. J. Danziger, *Making Budgets: Public Resource Allocation* (Beverly Hills, Sage, 1978), Ch. 3.
37. D. E. Ashford, 'Resources, Spending and Party Politics in British Local Government', *Administration and Society*, 7 (1975).
38. Dearlove, *The Politics of Policy*, Ch. 1.
39. D. E. Ashford, 'The Effects of Central Finance on the British Local

Government System', *British Journal of Political Science*, 4 (1974).
40. Foster, Jackman, and Perlman, *Local Government Finance in a Unitary State*, pp. 356–62.
41. Stanyer, *Understanding Local Government*, Ch. 10.
42. For further discussion of the link between reorganization and an easing of the management task of the centre see L. J. Sharpe, '"Reforming" the Grass Roots: An Alternative Analysis', in Butler and Halsey (eds.), *Policy and Politics*, pp. 104–6. Also see Foster, Jackman, and Perlman, *Local Finance in a Unitary State*, p. 342.
43. Jones, 'Central–Local Government Relations: Grants, Local Responsibility and Minimum Standards', p. 75.

3. CONVENTIONAL APPROACHES

Introduction

In this and the following chapter we will discuss the strengths and weaknesses of various alternative approaches to the study of why local policies and expenditures vary, with a view to picking out those aspects of these approaches which might contribute to a more satisfactory explanation. The next chapter will consider incrementalist theory, and the present one will examine three other approaches which are used in the current literature. These are:

(1) The Tiebout hypothesis
(2) The demographic approach
(3) Factor and cluster analysis.

The Tiebout Hypothesis

The American economist Charles M. Tiebout explains local policy and service provision in terms of the movement of population in search of local costs and benefits which suit their preferences. Tiebout argues that local authorities are unable to adapt to the demands of their residents because revenue and expenditure patterns are more or less fixed, at least in the short to medium term. Instead of municipalities adapting to their residents, however, residents ('consumer-voters', as Tiebout calls them) move between municipalities in search of their optimal package of public services and taxes. 'The consumer-voter', Tiebout writes, 'may be viewed as picking that community which best satisfies his preference for public goods ... at the local level various governments have their revenue and expenditure patterns more or less set. Given these revenue and expenditure patterns, the consumer-voter moves to that community whose local government best satisfies his set of preferences. The greater the number of communities and the greater the variance among them, the closer the consumer will come to fully realizing his preference position.'[1]

The Tiebout hypothesis, either in its original form, or in one of its many amended·forms, has been widely accepted by economists, and also by some sociologists and political scientists, particularly in the United States, where it has been used to explain and justify the highly fragmented form of government found in the typical metropolitan area. Whereas many commentators have found such balkanization to be a root cause of many of the ills of the American metropolis, the Tiebout approach has been used to justify the system in terms of the economy and efficiency with which such a quasi-market is supposed to produce and allocate public goods.[2] There are few empirical tests of the Tiebout hypothesis but one such study concludes:

These results appear consistent with a model of the Tiebout variety in which rational consumers weigh (to some extent at least) the benefits from local public services against the cost of their tax liability in choosing a community of residence: people do appear willing to pay more to live in a community which provides a high-quality program of public services (or in a community which provides the same program of public services with lower tax rates).[3]

The approach also has its advocates on this side of the Atlantic, mainly among economists but also in other social science fields. For example, Foster, Jackman, and Perlman in their monumental work *Local Government Finance in a Unitary State* make quite extensive use of the hypothesis, and the assumptions underlying it, in their chapter on local taxes. They also use it (among other arguments) to support their case for small units of local government, suggesting that a public goods equilibrium can be achieved by the mechanism of consumer-voter migration between small and competing municipalities.[4] The same point is made repeatedly by Richardson, who quotes the results of American work on the assumption that it applies to Britain, and who extends the whole agrument to cover not just individuals and households, but also business firms in their search for optimum conditions.[5] Two other economists, Barnett and Topham, give the Tiebout hypothesis 'a central role' in their analysis of locally provided public goods, and write that 'the attractions of Tiebout's market analogue are both obvious and compelling'.[6]

Empirical tests of the Tiebout hypothesis, however, are rather few and far between, particularly in the United Kingdom, but one such test by Aronson deserves close attention.[7] Aronson writes: 'It is conceivable that migration induced by fiscal factors (i.e. public services provided and taxes payable) will produce a stable population distribution among towns of a metropolitan area. Each town offers a different mix and quantity of public services, and residents of the area can be thought of as "voting with their feet"; that is, they move to the town that best satisfies their preferences.'[8] He then compares population movements within local government jurisdictions in the metropolitan areas of Harrisburg (Pennsylvania), Leeds, and Manchester, and concludes that his evidence shows Tiebout-type mobility, though less in England than the United States because there is less fiscal variation between local authorities in England.

In spite of its widespread acceptance as a fact of local life in both Britain and the USA, the Tiebout hypothesis has some severe problems, and some American and British critics have questioned its relevance to the American situation on both theoretical and empirical grounds.[9] Its use as a theory explaining variations in local government outputs in Britain is all that concerns us here, however, although much of what follows may apply to the USA as well.

Perhaps the first thing to be said is that the approach does have some relevance to some people and some local authorities: tax exiles choose to live in Liechtenstein or the Canary Isles for Tiebout-type reasons; the affluent sometimes choose to retire to the south coast, partly for its weather and scenery, but also, perhaps, for local services and tax levels; the movement from the big cities to the suburbs and the outlying villages may have been induced, partly, by the wish to escape from big city taxes. On the other hand, even if such moves are made mainly for public goods and tax reasons, the numbers involved are relatively small, and the theory runs into considerable empirical and theoretical problems so far as the great bulk of the British population is concerned. We will deal with the theoretical problems first.

The Tiebout article is entitled 'A pure theory of local expenditures', and is intended to apply to all local authorities. Yet the theory depends upon a fairly large number of local authorities existing within a fairly small geographical area (without this there will not be adequate choice for consumer-voters), and since only a fairly large metropolitan region can sustain this large number, the theory deals not so much with rural or small town areas as with metropolitan areas. Tiebout's is not a general theory, but a more specific one of metropolitan spending. Even so the theory has limited application to the UK where all but the very largest and most heavily populated metropolitan regions have relatively few local authorities by comparison with the USA, where one region may contain hundreds, or even a thousand, municipalities. In addition, the theory assumes that local authorities are largely responsible for financing their own services from their own taxes, thus giving the consumer-voter a choice of trading off local taxes against local services. In the UK, of course, a large proportion of local spending (about 40 per cent of current income) is derived from central government grants. The national funding of local services reduces the importance of purely local revenues, and, therefore, reduces the importance of the tax-service calculations made by consumer voters.[10]

Local services may still play a part, however, in determining where people buy a house. It is well known, for example, that middle-class parents often make careful enquiries about local schools before buying a new house. But it is important to note that this may provide little evidence whatsoever for the Tiebout hypothesis, since, given the size of local authorities in Britain, the choice is often between different schools in one and the same local authority. In other words, the choice may not be between different authorities with different tax levels and different educational qualities, but between different areas within the same authority, with different educational standards but the same tax level. Thus citizens may well take local services into account when deciding where to live, but this may have no relevance to the Tiebout hypothesis.

The last major theoretical objection to the Tiebout hypothesis concerns its assumption that those who consume local public services will live in and pay taxes to, the municipality which provides them. It assumes a world in which there are no, or only negligible, economic externalities, and no 'free-rider' problems.[11] This is entirely necessary to the approach since it will not work in a situation where people are able to consume but not pay for services. Such complete self-containment is a reasonable assumption in the private sector where only theft gets a free lunch, but it is entirely unrealistic within an urban agglomeration where local authorities abut on each other. Within such areas the services of one authority (roads, police, fire services, public health, etc.) may be consumed by people who pay their taxes to another authority. This is the basis of what has been termed 'the city-suburb' exploitation thesis whereby suburbanites may use, but do not pay for, some services provided by the central city.[12] It is also the basis for the finding that the costs of central city services in the USA are determined as much by the number of people living just outside the city, as by the number and type of residents it has within its boundaries.[13]

One major reason for the creation of large local authorities in the UK is to avoid the worst free-rider and externality problems. Nevertheless, as later chapters will show, local costs are quite heavily determined by the number of people living outside an authority but using some of its services. Meanwhile it is enough to note that the Tiebout hypothesis is caught on the horns of a dilemma:

Either, (1) the larger the number and the smaller the population of authorities in a single area, the more the area fulfils the conditions for the Tiebout hypothesis, but the more likely the Tiebout effect will be undermined by externality and free-rider problems;

Or, (2) the smaller the number and the larger the population of authorities in a single area, the smaller the externality and free-rider problems, but the less the area fulfils the conditions for the Tiebout hypothesis.

This suggests, at the very least, that the Tiebout hypothesis should be modified to take account of spill-over, positive and negative externality, and free-rider effects. More seriously for the theory, it suggests that the very basis of a fragmented system of metropolitan government is incompatible with the high degree of mobility of consumer-voters necessary for the theory to work in the first place.

These theoretical arguments suggest that the Tiebout effect in Britain is likely to be weak and restricted to a small number of metropolitan areas, and special cases such as the south coast retirement areas. The empirical evidence suggests that even this puts the case for the Tiebout effect rather strongly. Empirically, the Tiebout hypothesis is based upon what the author himself calls 'an extreme model',[14] which rests upon a set of assumptions which are difficult to swallow. One of these states that: 'Restrictions due to employment opportunities are not considered. It may be assumed that all persons are living on dividend income.'[15] This assumption is entirely necessary to the theory since it guarantees a mobile population unrestricted by job location and so capable of moving from one municipality to another.

The mobility of the population is dealt with in another assumption which states: 'Consumer-voters are fully mobile and will move to that community where their preference patterns, which are set, are best satisfied.' Now, of course, even people living on investment income are not fully mobile because they usually take into account the costs of moving house, these being both financial and social — moving away from friends, neighbours, and perhaps dependent relatives, plus the psychological upheaval of moving. Those who work for a living must also take into account the costs and convenience of travel to work, although it should be said that Tiebout published his article in 1956, long before the energy crisis. At the root of the theory, however, is the assumption that the world is populated by rational, profit/income maximizing individuals who base their life decisions upon a careful calculus of economic gains and losses.[16] Tiebout's theory does not allow for the intrusion of irrational or non-rational behaviour including laziness or restlessness, snobbishness or community attachment, nor does it allow for social pressures and processes, such as racism or class prejudice, which are important influences on residential patterns.

Tiebout also states that: 'Consumer-voters are assumed to have full knowledge of differences among revenue and expenditure patterns and to react to these differences.' In the market economy it may sometimes be safe to make assumptions about a good knowledge of the market, but it is dangerous to do so where British local government is concerned. The most exhaustive study of citizens' knowledge of local government in England and Wales summarizes its findings in the following way: 'There seems to be a certain level of general public ignorance concerning local government and the services provided by the council. For instance, 20 per cent of our informants were unable to name a single service provided by their council at either the local or the county level.'[17] Ignorance on this scale suggests that local taxes and service provision can play no more than a minor role in decisions about where to live. Besides, whereas the consumer *may* make a rational economic choice between soap powders or motor cars, the whole issue of taxes and public services is so clouded by emotion, ignorance, and ideology that it is difficult to make any assumptions about full knowledge and rational appraisal of alternatives. This is particularly true of local government taxes and services in the UK where all sorts of misconceptions and prejudices are rife.[18]

Another of Tiebout's assumptions concerns that of an optimal community size — the optimum number of residents for which a given bundle of services can be produced at the lowest average cost. Here, again, there is a marked difference between the private and public sectors, with the former generally producing one, or only a fairly small range of products, and the public sector covering a wide range of services. Because these services vary so much in type and nature, the notion of an optimal size for units of local government has been firmly rejected by some writers, one likening the search for an optimal size to the search for the philosopher's stone.[19] This criticism does not, it should be said, deal with the nub of Tiebout's assumption, which concerns the optimal size for a given authority delivering a particular range of services, and not the optimum size for units of local government in general. Nevertheless, the job of deciding whether any given authority is approaching optimality is an enormous one which no economist has satisfactorily accomplished even for one service, never mind a package of them. What proportion of the 80,000 units of local government in the USA, or of the 410 in England, achieve anything approaching optimality is anyone's guess, and to make assumptions about it is to introduce an entirely unknown quantity into the discussion.[20]

The assumptions underlying Tiebout's work are so much at variance with the real world that they are enough to raise a serious set of objections to his theory,[21] but there is another, and possibly more serious, set of objections. In spite of the widespread acceptance of the theory, there are few attempts to test it. At the same time, the considerable amount that is known about the key element in his theory, namely, the reason why people move location, suggests that the Tiebout hypothesis is largely an irrelevance. We will deal, first, with one attempt to test the theory, before briefly considering the literature about why people move house.

An adequate test of the Tiebout hypothesis requires studying the geographical movement of 'consumer-voters' in order to find out why they move house, and what importance they attach to local government taxes and services. The results would then have to be compared with a control group of immobile citizens in order to show that they did not move because of a general satisfaction with local taxes and services. In other words, the Tiebout hypothesis deals with the mobility of individuals and households, and requires testing at the individual and household level. Aggregate data about residential movement is not enough, and can constitute, at best, only circumstantial evidence for the theory. Unfortunately, the best-known attempt to test the Tiebout hypothesis in the UK — that by J. Richard Aronson — uses aggregate data.[22]

Aronson argues that a population shift between 'origin towns' and 'destination towns' is to be expected, when destination towns offer either higher per capita expenditures at no higher tax rate, or at least the same per capita expenditures at a lower tax rate, to every resident of the origin town. (He does not consider the possibility that consumer-voters might prefer to pay higher taxes in return for better services, although this is also a real possibility). He then compares the population changes of origin and destination towns in order to show that the former have generally lost, and the latter generally gained, population. In order to carry out this analysis he specifies many of the assumptions already discussed (perfect mobility, perfect knowledge of local taxes and expenditures, costless commuting, no spill-overs, externalities, or free-riders, and a dependence of each local authority on its own revenues, i.e. no central government grants), but he also makes a further set of assumptions which are not discussed.

(1) Tax rates are expressed in terms of rate poundages as a percentage of local rateable value. This fails to distinguish between domestic rates (of importance to the Tiebout hypothesis) and non-domestic rates (of no direct importance to the movement of households), and it further compounds the error by confusing total rateable value with the value of domestic property.

(2) Aronson assumes that net population changes between 1965 and 1972 are due to migration. In other words, births and deaths in these authorities are assumed to cancel each other out exactly during the eight-year period.

(3) He assumes population changes are due to the Tiebout effect, but makes no attempt to go to the heart of the matter by uncovering the causes and motives prompting residential mobility.

(4) Like Tiebout, Aronson assumes that those who wish to move to another municipality are free to do so, and that those who stay are living where they wish. In other words, the assumption about perfect mobility assumes that there is a single and unified housing market to which all have equal access. The existence of a large public sector in the housing stock, and of a wide variety of social and economic exclusionary mechanisms in the housing market, raises questions about this assumption.[23]

What Aronson's figures *do* show is that large central cities are losing population, while outlying smaller towns and suburbs are gaining. He shows that Leeds, as an 'origin town' lost, while Bingley, Harrogate, Pontefract, and Wetherby, as 'destination towns', gained population. The hypothesis that Leeds would serve as a destination town for Bradford, Halifax, and Huddersfield, was, not surprisingly, unsupported by the data. Similarly, the hypothesis that Manchester would serve as a destination town for Salford was not supported. However, the conclusion that large industrial cities are tending to lose population to small towns and suburbs is scarcely new, and it certainly fails to constitute an empirical demonstration of the Tiebout effect. To claim it as an adequate test is to assume the very thing the research sets out to test in the first place.

This brings us to the question of why people *actually* move – a question which is crucial to the Tiebout hypothesis, but rarely, if ever, asked in the literature. Fortunately, there is a large amount of good research on this matter, and while space permits only a brief summary here, it is clear that rather little of it supports the proposition that citizens move in order to maximize their preference for public goods. The decision to move, and the choice of house and location once

the decision has been made, is based predominantly upon:
   (1) the cost, quality, type, and size of house and garden,
   (2) the need to be near a job,
   (3) a change in family circumstances,
   (4) a wish to be near friends, family, and neighbours.[24]
About one in twenty people move to be nearer to 'public' facilities such as
schools, social facilities, or shops, or to be in a better neighbourhood,[25] and
among all the reasons given for wishing to move only one in seven concern
neighbours, neighbourhood, and environment.[26] This is scant support indeed
for the Tiebout hypothesis, especially when one takes into account the fact
that many aspects of shops, social facilities, neighbourhood, and environment
are relatively independent of local authority policy, and have only tangential
bearing upon local taxes and services.

It is difficult to avoid the conclusion that the wish to move, and the choice
and location of a new house, is only marginally affected, for the majority of
people, by the considerations which Tiebout concentrates upon. It is highly
likely that population movements will have their effect upon local taxes and
services, and that local authorities will try to make adjustments accordingly,
but the suggestion that local authorities adapt, however slowly, to their populations is the converse of the Tiebout hypothesis. In short, the whole approach,
in spite of its general acceptance among economists and among many other social
scientists in the USA, has little to recommend it to a study of local authority
expenditures in England and Wales. It may explain why tax exiles live abroad,
and it may help to explain why some wealthy people retire to tastefully modern-
ized thatched cottages on the south coast, but it does not explain why the
remaining fifty million citizens of England and Wales live in places like Norwich,
Gateshead, Derbyshire, or Somerset.

The Demographic Approach

Whereas the Tiebout hypothesis argues that citizens respond to local policy,
rather than vice versa, the demographic approach makes no claim of this sort,
but assumes only that there will be a correspondence of some kind between
local policy and the residents of any given local authority. Thus, for example,
it might be suggested that the more affluent the residents of an authority, the
more likely it is to spend on such things as education, parks, libraries, police,
fire, and roads, whereas poorer communities are likely to concentrate their
efforts on such things as housing, social services, and health services. Hence the
demographic composition of authorities is assumed to determine or influence
local spending patterns in one way or another.

The standard technique for this kind of research is to compile a list of dependent variables, usually per capita expenditures for a range of local services and

sub-services, and a further list of independent variables which describe the social, economic, and political characteristics of the populations of these authorities. It then tries, usually by means of correlation and regression analysis, to establish a fit between service expenditures and population characteristics. Sometimes propositions relating particular sets of independent variables (which may be grouped according to their 'need, resources, and disposition' characteristics)[27] are explored, but more usually a likely-looking set of independent variables is run against expenditure figures to see if anything statistically significant comes out. It is not too much to say that many of the studies of this kind are a trawling exercise in which as large a net with as fine a mesh as possible is thrown out, and the catch then inspected for things of interest.

The largely atheoretical nature of the demographic approach is the first of its two major problems, but since this weakness has already been dwelt on by other writers, it is enough to produce two short quotations to make the point. Robert Fried has written: 'Rather than a comparative theory of performance, we seem to be laying the foundations for another monument to "adhockery".'[28] And James Danziger, in one of the best studies of local spending carried out in Britain or elsewhere, writes that: 'The broadest criticism of the approach has argued persuasively that it lacks any theory of linkages which explicates the relationships between policy outputs and characteristics of the environment . . . In general, it seems fair to say that demographic-approach studies have been prone to the sins of barefoot empiricism.'[29]

Lack of theory to explain interesting results would be a severe fault, but, unfortunately, the approach also lacks interesting results. Although it works in some countries better than others, its empirical findings are often disappointing in the sense that correlations and the percentage of the variance explained (in the statistical sense) are generally quite low. There are exceptions, but even the largest bank of carefully selected, defined, and measured variables are usually unable to explain more than half the variance, and this is particularly true of British studies.[30] Hence Danziger concludes: 'the demographic approach provides a weak and generally unsatisfactory explanation for the variation in county borough resource allocation . . . the demographic approach has minimal explanatory power for most allocation measures.'[31] In fact, Danziger is more critical than need be of some of his own results: he is able to explain between fifty and eighty per cent of the variation in police, housing, education, and total expenditure, although it is true that the majority of services do not respond nearly as well.

Danziger's conclusions are supported by the results of the present study, where correlation and regression analysis produced mixed but generally rather poor results. (For details of the methods used to produce these results see the Appendices.) In spite of a long and detailed list of independent variables describing the social, economic, and political characteristics of local authorities, the correlations produced were few and far between, and even when they were statistically significant, most were not of much substantive significance. Little theoretical sense could be made of the whole correlation matrix, with positive and negative, significant and insignificant figures scattered in what seemed to be a more or less random manner. Variables which were significant for some services were insignificant for others, and though some services correlated with a fairly long list of community characteristics, others were associated with very few. The percentages of per capita service expenditures explained by the regressions were similarly disappointing, as Tables 3.1 and 3.2 show. By and large, the results for the counties are better than for the county boroughs, but many of the county services fail to respond readily to the demographic approach. In most cases the regressions account for less than half the variance, and in many cases they account for less than a third.

Table 3.1 *Percentage of the Variance (R^2) in Per Capita Service Expenditures explained by selected Demographic Variables, County Boroughs, 1960/1 and 1972/3*

Service	1960/1	1972/3
Housing	60.2	63.4
Education	55.1	61.0
Total	43.1	53.9
Police	40.8	46.9
Children	33.9	–
Highways	31.4	27.0.
Libraries	31.7	33.3
Social services	–	30.1
Fire	29.0	31.3
Refuse	27.4	29.6
Sewerage	25.8	29.2
Parks	20.5	18.5
Local health	20.5	11.7
Public health	16.6	10.5
Planning	11.8	11.0

It is not clear why the county results are better, although the greater variations among them, mentioned in earlier chapters, probably has something to do with this, and underlines the need to include counties in the analysis. It is also notable that political variables appear as statistically significant in quite a number of the equations for both counties and county boroughs, but especially the former. In other words, there is some evidence in these preliminary results to show that politics does indeed matter in setting levels of public expenditure, even when allowance is made for social and economic variables.

The figures in Tables 3.1 and 3.2 suggest something which throws some light upon the strengths and weaknesses of the demographic approach: the method appears to work somewhat more satisfactorily for the divisible as opposed to the indivisible services. That is, services such as education, social services, and housing, which are provided for particular people or families, have a higher R^2 than general community services such as planning, police, fire, parks, refuse, and libraries.[32] There are exceptions to this observation, but, nevertheless, it may be that divisible services are more strongly related to the characteristics of resident populations (age, class, wealth, etc.), while the indivisible, or general community, services may be more closely tied to features of the local authority as a whole, rather than to the characteristics of its individual residents. This suggestion will be picked up and developed in the following chapters.

Table 3.2 *Percentage of the Variance (R^2) of Per Capita Expenditures explained by selected Demographic Variables, County Councils, 1960/1 and 1972/3*

Service	1960/1	1972/3
Highways	82.3	80.0
Total	74.9	75.9
Education	62.3	65.8
Local health	39.1	47.4
Welfare	37.7	–
Police	35.4	43.0
Libraries	35.1	32.0
Social services	–	33.2
Planning	–	32.7
Public health	29.1	–
Fire	20.9	27.9
Children	12.0	–

Nevertheless, it must be acknowledged that the demographic approach is not particularly successful for the general run of services, although, by and large, the British results are not much worse than those for other Western countries where the approach has been tried. There are possibly two main reasons for this; the size and nature of British local authorities, and the size of central government grants. British local authorities are quite possibly the largest (in terms of population size) in the Western world, and certainly the largest of the major nations of Western Europe.[33] Consequently, any given authority is likely to cover a fairly wide range of social and economic conditions – industrial, commercial, residential, inner city, outer suburb, middle class, and working class – hence, authorities tend to be internally heterogeneous in composition, and similar to each other in their heterogeneity, at least in comparison to other local authorities in many Western states. This makes the demographic approach less powerful than in, for example, the United States, where the poor and wealthy authorities tend to be separated out in the same metropolitan area.[34] The fact that central government grants make up a large proportion of income further irons out differences and makes local authorities less dependent upon their own resources. The fact remains, however, that there are still considerable variations in local authorities and their spending, but that the demographic approach is not conspicuously successful in explaining them.

Factor and Cluster Analysis

The third possible approach to the question 'why do local outputs vary?' involves the use of factor analysis and cluster analysis. In effect, this is a version of the demographic approach which uses factor or cluster analysis to reduce the amount of data for analysis. Since there are many social, economic, and political variables which might have a relationship to expenditures, and since many of these variables are themselves closely related, they do not lend themselves easily to regression analysis. In the absence of guiding theory, what variables should be included in the regressions, and what is to be done when, as invariably happens, the analysis runs headlong into the problem of multicollinearity? One solution to these problems is to use factor analysis on either the independent or the dependent variables in order to simplify the vast quantity of data, and in order to produce a set of statistically unrelated factors which might then be used to some effect in explaining spending patterns. The general techniques of factor and cluster analysis have been tried with varying degrees of success in many branches of urban studies, and perhaps this could be repeated in an output study.[35]

Factor analysis was tried on expenditure data for English and Welsh counties and county boroughs, but the results were either poor or difficult to interpret, or both. They were poor because the components extracted accounted for only a small proportion of the total variance, particularly of expenditures, where five main components accounted for less than forty per cent of county borough variation, and where four main components accounted for less than thirty-five per cent of the county variation. A factor analysis of social, economic, and political characteristics fared better than this (78 per cent), but in all cases the factors extracted were difficult to interpret and label.[36]

For example, the first expenditure factor, which accounted for only 18 per cent of the variance in county boroughs, had strong negative loadings with total, personal health, education, children, and welfare expenditure, but no significant and positive loadings on any service. The best we can do, therefore, is to label this factor as an absence of high spending in total, and on children, personal health, education, and welfare. This is clumsy, and adds nothing to our understanding of local spending patterns. The labelling and interpreting problem was encountered at almost every turn in the analyses, and it is small wonder that another attempt to derive a typology of county borough expenditures was largely unsuccessful.[37]

Table 3.3 *Simple Correlations between Per Capita Service Expenditures, County Boroughs, 1972/3*

	Hous.	Pol.	Fire	H'ways	Plan.	S.S.	L.H.	P.H.	Parks	Ref.	Sew.	Libs.	Ed.
Total	0.75***	0.61***	0.38***	0.24*	0.22*	0.66***	0.28*	0.38***		0.37***		0.47***	0.53***
Education	0.25*							0.25*					
Libraries	0.24*	0.36***		0.29**	0.33**	0.48***				0.23*			
Sewerage	−0.33**	−0.24*											
Refuse	0.39***	0.36***		0.22*		0.24*							
Parks					0.24*	0.35***							
Public health	0.31**												
Social services	0.51***	0.31**		0.22*									
Planning													
Highways	0.26*		0.24										
Fire	0.26*	0.36***											
Police	0.45***												

Note: This table shows only the statistically significant figures using a two-tailed test.

A quick look at the correlation matrices between service expenditures makes it clear why no general factors emerge from the data. Table 3.3 presents figures only for the county boroughs and only for one year, but tables for other years, and also those for the counties, show much the same, that is, a rather feeble set of figures with more holes than substance, and little of any great substance at that. In other words, a tendency to spend heavily on any one service, or set of services, is not notably associated with a tendency to spend heavily or lightly on any other service or set of services. Faced with the motley array of figures available, any grand design involving typologies of public policies, whether devised by Lowi, by Adrian and Williams, or by Sharkansky and Hofferbert, wilted rather quickly.[38]

Our analysis ran up against even more trouble when it tried to group local authorities according to their values for the principal components. Group one covered a multifarious assortment of cities, including very large and small ones (Manchester and Bury), grimy industrial towns and well-tended seaside resorts (Halifax and Bournemouth), ports and inland county towns (Liverpool and Exeter). Groups two and three showed no more rhyme or reason, clustering together such ill-assorted places as Bath and Blackburn, Canterbury and Cardiff, Gateshead and Gloucester, and Leicester and Lincoln.[39] These places appear to have little in common other than distantly related spending patterns, and so it was decided on theoretical and empirical grounds that factor analysis and cluster analysis of this kind had little to recommend it.

Before abandoning the approach altogether, however, one last method was tried — that of hierarchical clustering in order to produce groups of authorities (in the form of a dendrogram) according to their spending patterns.[40] This method is ideally suited to the grouping of geographical units, whether nation states or local authorities, and if successful, could tell us not only which local authorities are most alike, but also, perhaps, indicate why they are so.[41] Unfortunately, the technique was not successful for, once again, it grouped together places which seem to have little in common, other, that is, than a vague similarity in their spending. Bolton and Canterbury end up cheek by jowl. York is closely matched with Wolverhampton, as is Doncaster with Eastbourne. Leicester appears alongside Dewsbury, Bootle, Worcester, and East Ham. Such strange alignments of urban disparates suggests that hierarchical clustering techniques are not suited to the job in hand. Certainly no typology or taxonomy of authorities suggested itself, and no pattern with a meaning emerged. The logic of hierarchical cluster analysis and its statistical basis is not in question; the problem arises only in the attempt to understand, interpret, and explain the results of the technique in this case. After puzzling over the results, they still appeared to produce an apparently random list of cities.

Quite possibly the only lesson to be learned from the failure in this case of factor and cluster analysis is that urban spending patterns are so complex, and vary along so many different dimensions, that they cannot be understood in these terms, no matter how complex the computer program and no matter how much detailed evidence it can take into account. Another approach to the whole question is necessary.

Conclusion

This chapter has considered three fairly orthodox and conventional approaches to output studies, of which two, the Tiebout hypothesis, and factor and cluster analysis turn out to be of little use. The Tiebout hypothesis, however well it might fit the situation in metropolitan areas of the USA, has limited relevance to Britain, and cannot help us much in the search for an explanation of why different local political systems vary in the public policies they adopt. Factor and cluster analysis, as a technical way of proceeding with large data sets similarly offers little help, mainly because local authorities seem to vary so much, or to vary in so many different ways, so far as their service expenditures are concerned, that it is impossible to pick out any strong underlying trends, or to group authorities in a way which helps us toward an understanding of why they spend different amounts on their services.

This leaves the demographic approach, which, though generally unsuccessful and lacking in both compelling theory and satisfactory empirical results, does offer something in the way of acceptable results for what has been termed divisible services. These are the local services which have specific and clearly defined consumers such as school-aged children, or children in need of care, old people, or those in substandard housing. Indivisible services, in contrast, are community-wide, and available in theory to all residents of a local authority. In the case of such things as highways, they are available to others also. By and large, divisible services are better explained by the demographic approach, which is to say that the amount a local authority spends on such things as education and housing is closely associated with the social, economic, and political charac-teristics of its resident population. Indivisible services, on the other hand, are generally less closely associated with community characteristics, and clearly need another sort of approach.

Though it is more successful than the other approaches, the demographic approach still leaves a lot to be desired, in that even when its empirical results are good, it still fails to explain. It can produce significant correlations or regres-sion coefficients, but little more. This might possibly serve as a place to begin, but it cannot be the place to end an output study.

NOTES

Grateful thanks are due to David Heald for his kind help with the first section of the chapter. His extensive comments on a draft have resulted in many changes, although not nearly as many or as drastic as he would have liked.

1. C. M. Tiebout, 'A pure theory of Local Expenditures', reprinted in M. Edel and J. Rothenberg (eds.), *Readings in Urban Economics* (New York, Macmillan, 1972), pp. 513–23.

2. See, for example, V. Ostrom, C. M. Tiebout, and R. L. Warren, 'The organisation of government in metropolitan areas: a theoretical enquiry', *American Political Science Review*, 60 (1961), 831–42; R. L. Bish, *The Public Economy of Metropolitan Areas* (Chicago, Markham, 1972); J. M. Buchanan, 'An economic theory of clubs', *Economica*, 32 (1965), 1–14; R. A. Musgrave and P. B. Musgrave, *Public Finance in Theory and Practice* (Tokyo, McGraw-Hill, 1976), p. 619; V. Ostrom and E. Ostrom, 'A behavioural approach to the study of inter-governmental relations', *The Annals*, 359 (1965), 137–46; R. O. Warren, 'A municipal services market model of metropolitan organization', *Journal of the American Institute of Planners*, 30 (1964), 193–204; R. O. Warren, *Government in Metropolitan Regions: A Reappraisal of Fractionated Political Organisation* (Davis, Calif., Institute of Governmental Affairs, University of California, 1966).

3. W. E. Oates, 'The effects of property taxes and local public spending on property values; an empirical study of tax capitalization and the Tiebout hypothesis', *Journal of Political Economy*, 77 (1969), 969. For similar studies reaching the same general conclusions see B. W. Hamilton, 'Property taxes and the Tiebout hypothesis: some empirical evidence', in E. S. Mills and W. E. Oates (eds.), *Fiscal zoning and Land Use Controls* (Lexington, Mass., Lexington Books, 1975), pp. 12–29, and B. Hamilton, E. Mills, and D. Puryear, 'The Tiebout hypothesis and residential income segregation', in E. S. Mills and W. E. Oates (eds.), (Lexington, Mass., Lexington Books, 1975), pp. 101–18.

4. C. D. Foster, R. Jackman, and M. Perlman, *Local Government Finance in a Unitary State* (London, Allen and Unwin, 1980), pp. 218–41, 566–7.

5. H. W. Richardson, *Urban Economics* (Harmondsworth, Middx., Penguin Books, 1973), pp. 151–2; H. W. Richardson, *The New Urban Economics* (London, Pion, 1977), pp. 37 and 142; H. W. Richardson, *Regional and Urban Economics* (Harmondsworth, Middx., Penguin Books, 1972), p. 160; and H. W. Richardson, *The Economics of Urban Size* (Farnborough, Hants, Saxon House/Lexington, 1973), pp. 91 and 186–7. Most American research on the subject suggests that local taxes and fiscal incentives play little or no part in the choice of regional location, although they may have a secondary importance in determining location within regions; see M. Wasylenko, 'The location of firms: the role of taxes and fiscal incentives', in R. Bahl (ed.), *Urban Government Finance: Emerging Trends* (Beverly Hills, Calif., Sage, 1981), pp. 155–90.

6. R. R. Barnett and N. Topham, 'Evaluating the distribution of local outputs in a decentralized structure of government', *Policy and Politics*, 6 (1977), pp. 56 and 67. For a British geographer who also uses the Tiebout approach

see B. Goodall, *The Economics of Urban Areas* (Oxford, Pergamon, 1972), p. 160.

7. J. R. Aronson, 'Financing public goods and the distribution of population in metropolitan areas: an analysis of fiscal migration in the United States and England', in A. J. Culyer (ed.), *Economic Policies and Social Goals* (London, Martin Robertson, 1974), pp. 313–41.

8. Aronson, 'Financing public goods', p. 314.

9. See, for example, the highly critical comments in H. E. Brazer, 'Some fiscal implications of metropolitanism', in B. Chintiz (ed.), *City and Suburb* (Englewood Cliffs, NJ, Prentice-Hall, 1964), pp. 132–3. For the views of a British geographer see R. J. Bennet, *The Geography of Public Finance* London, Methuen, 1980), p. 37.

10. Aronson gives this as a reason to explain the weaker results in Britain compared with the USA; Aronson, 'Financing public goods', p. 338.

11. Tiebout's assumption that 'The public services supplied exhibit no external economies or diseconomies between communities' contrasts strongly with a large body of writing which discusses externality and free-rider problems. See, for example, K. R. Cox, *Conflict, Power and Politics in the City* (New York, McGraw-Hill, 1973), pp. 2–15; R. Vernon, 'The myth and reality of our urban problems', and L. C. Fitch, 'Metropolitan financial problems', both in Chinitz, *City and Suburb*, pp. 100–3 and pp. 115–19.

12. One study which discusses the exploitation of the central cities is J. Heilbrun, 'Poverty and public finance in the older central cities', in Edel and Rothenberg, *Readings in Urban Economics*, pp. 523–45.

13. J. D. Kasarda, 'The impact of suburban population growth on central service functions', *American Journal of Sociology*, 77 (1972), 1111–24.

14. Tiebout, 'A pure theory . . .', p. 516.

15. The assumptions of the Tiebout model are spelt out by the author in 'A pure theory . . .', pp. 516–17.

16. Few political economists of the Tiebout type discuss their working assumptions, and only one, R. L. Bish, lays them out: 'Four basic assumptions of economic analysis are common in the recent applications of economics to political phenomena. They will be discussed in detail at this point, being essential throughout this study. They are the assumptions of scarcity, methodological individualism, self-interest, and individual rationality in the use of scarce resources', Bish, *The Public Economy*, p. 3. With the exception of scarcity (which is not an assumption but a fact of social existence), these assumptions are highly questionable, to say the least.

17. Committee on the Management of Local Government, Volume 3, *The Local Government Elector* (London, HMSO, 1967), p. 5.

18. See, for example, K. Newton *et al.*, *Balancing the Books: The Financial Problems of Local Government in West Europe* (London, Sage, 1980), pp. 125–60.

19. H. W. Richardson, 'Optimality in city size, systems of cities and urban policy', in G. C. Cameron and L. Wingo (eds.), *Cities, Regions, and Public Policy* (Edinburgh, Oliver and Boyd, 1973), pp. 29–48.

20. Jerome Rothenberg suggests that the 'balkanized' structure of metropolitan government in the United States is likely to result in suboptimality; J. Rothenberg, 'Local decentralization and the theory of optimal government',

in Edel and Rothenberg (eds.), *Readings in Urban Economics*, pp. 545–68.

21. According to Harvey Brazer, Tiebout's assumptions cause him not merely to throw out the baby with the bath water, but to throw away the bath as well; Brazer, 'Some fiscal implications . . .', p. 133.

22. Aronson, 'Financing public goods . . .', pp. 313–41.

23. As Brazer puts it: 'Even if individuals had full knowledge of differences among communities in revenue and service patterns and were willing to move in response to them, their own tastes, income, zoning, racial and religious discrimination, and other barriers to entry to various communities would restrict their mobility'; Brazer, 'Some fiscal implications . . .', p. 133. See also E. S. Mills's telling one-page commentary, in C. S. Russell (ed.), *Collective Decision Making* (Baltimore, Johns Hopkins University Press, 1979), p. 83.

24. For evidence on these points see J. B. Cullingworth, *Problems of an Urban Society*, Volume 1: The Social Framework of Planning (London, Allen and Unwin, 1973), p. 35; M. Woolf, *The Housing Survey in England and Wales* (London, HMSO, 1967), p. 103; P. Hall, R. Thomas, H. Gracey, and R. Drewett, *The Containment of Urban England*, Volume 2: The Planning System (London, Allen and Unwin, 1973), pp. 146–62; A. Murie, P. Niner, and C. Watson, *Housing Policy and the Housing System* (London, Allen and Unwin, 1976), pp. 53–6; L. S. Bourne, *The Geography of Housing* (London, Edward Arnold, 1981), pp. 133–7; D. V. Donnison, 'The movement of households in England', in *Essays on Housing*, Occasional Papers on Social Administration, No. 9 (Welwyn, Herts., Codicote Press, 1964), pp. 51–4; J. B. Cullingworth, *English Housing Trends*, Occasional Papers in Social Administration, No. 13 (London, Bell, 1965), pp. 59–65; and Office of Population Censuses and Surveys, *General Household Survey 1978* (London, HMSO, 1980), p. 56.

25. Bourne, *The Geography of Housing*, p. 134.

26. *General Household Survey 1978*, p. 56.

27. This useful classification was devised by N. T. Boaden and R. R. Alford, 'Sources of diversity in English local government decisions', *Public Administration*, 47 (1969), 203–23.

28. R. C. Fried, 'Comparative urban performance', in F. I. Greenstein and N. W. Polsby (eds.), *The Handbook of Political Science* (Reading, Mass., Addison-Wesley, 1976, Vol. 6), p. 320.

29. J. N. Danziger, *Making Budgets* (Beverly Hills, California, Sage, 1978), p. 83.

30. There are some forty British studies which use the demographic approach in one form or another. Most of them are in the notes to Chapter 1, and their general results are summarized in K. Newton, 'Community performance in Britain', *Current Sociology*, 26 (1976), 49–86.

31. Danziger, *Making Budgets*, p. 113.

32. While divisible goods are targeted at specific people, households, or groupings — those of school age, those in need of housing, children in need of local authority care — indivisible goods are similar to what economists call 'pure public goods', which are available to any member of the community. A public library is, in theory, available to all citizens, though in practice it is likely to be more accessible to those living nearby, whereas a council house

or a place in a primary school, is available only to certain clearly specified people.

33. L. J. Sharpe, '"Reforming" the grass roots: An alternative analysis', in D. Butler and A. H. Halsey (eds.), *Policy and Politics* (London, Macmillan, 1978), p. 95.

34. See, for example, T. R. Dye, *Politics in States and Communities* (Englewood Cliffs, New Jersey, Prentice-Hall, 1969), p. 290, and R. C. Hill, 'Separate and unequal: governmental inequality in the metropolis', *American Political Science Review*, 68 (1974), 1557-68.

35. There is a huge literature which groups or clusters British towns and cities according to various characteristics, starting with the pioneering study of C. A. Moser and W. Scott, *British Towns* (Edinburgh, Oliver and Boyd, 1961), and including more recent work, such as G. Armen, 'A classifcation of cities and city regions in England and Wales, 1966', *Regional Studies*, 6 (1972), 149-82; H. F. Andrews, 'A cluster analysis of British towns', *Urban Studies*, 8 (1971), 271-84; R. Webber and J. Craig, 'Which local authorities are alike?', *Population Trends*, (1976), 13-19; P. L. Knox, 'Spatial variations in level of living in England and Wales in 1961', *Transactions of the Institute of British Geographers*, 62 (1974), 1-24; D. Donnison and P. Soto, *The Good City* (London, Heinemann, 1980); D. Byrne, B. Williamson, and B. Fletcher, *The Poverty of Education* (London, Martin Robertson, 1975); S. Sacks and R. Firestine, 'Dimensions and classification of British towns on the basis of new data', in B. J. L. Berry (ed.), *City Classification Handbook* (New York, Wiley, 1972); and J. H. Johnson, J. Salt, and P. A. Wood, *Housing and the Migration of Labour in England and Wales* (Farnborough, Hants, Saxon House, 1974), pp. 62-7. For a refined version of the cluster analysis developed by Moser and Scott, see Scientific Control Systems Ltd., *Cluster Analysis* (London, Scientific Control Systems Ltd., 1970). Aiken and Depré use factor analysis to extremely good effect in their study of communal expenditures in Belgium, see M. Aiken and R. Depré, 'The urban system, politics, and policy in Belgian Cities', in K. Newton (ed.), *Urban Political Economy* (London, Frances Pinter, 1981), pp. 85-116.

36. As Robert Wood puts it: 'In factor analysis the labor of giving birth is often easier than naming the baby'; R. C. Wood, *1400 Governments* (Cambridge, Mass., Harvard University Press, 1961), p. 35.

37. See, J. N. Danziger, 'Twenty-six outputs in search of a taxonomy', *Policy and Politics*, 5 (1976), 201-12.

38. T. Lowi, 'American business, public policy, case studies, and political theory', *World Politics*, 16 (1964), 677-715; I. Sharkansky and R. I. Hofferbert, 'Dimensions of state politics, economics, and public policy', *American Political Science Review*, 63 (1969), 867-79; and O. P. Williams and C. R. Adrian, *Four Cities* (Philadelphia, University of Pennsylvania Press, 1963), pp. 187-267.

39. In fact most attempts to cluster or group urban places or local authorities in Britain produce some rather strange results. For example, Moser and Scott isolate a group of towns (Group 5) which they label or describe as 'including many of the large ports as well as two Black Country towns'. The group does not include all the large ports, the remainder being found in two other groups, nor all the Black Country towns, the rest being located

in three entirely different groups. Group 5 also includes some of the smaller ports, the rest of these ending up in a set of still different groups; see Moser and Scott, *British Towns*, pp. 84–6.

40. B. Everitt, *Cluster Analysis* (London, Heinemann, 1974), pp. 8–24.
41. This method has been used in some British urban studies; see, for example, D. Byrne, B. Williamson, and B. Fletcher, *The Poverty of Education* (London, Martin Robertson, 1975); D. Donnison and P. Soto, *The Good City* (London, Heinemann, 1980); and P. Knox, *Social Well-Being: A Spatial Perspective* (Oxford, Clarendon Press, 1975).

4. INCREMENTALISM AND OUTPUTS

Introduction

This study is set firmly in that part of the literature on public policy — that concerned with the output approach — which operationalizes outputs largely in terms of financial statistics and usually attempts to explain output variation by the variations in economic, social, and political characteristics of each unit of analysis, in our case the top-tier local authorities in England and Wales. There is, however, another approach which attempts to explain policy variation as the product of the application of regularized decision-making routines. This is a form of what Allison has called the 'organizational process approach'.[1]

Whereas in the output approach policy is assumed to be the product of factors both external and internal to the decision-making process, the organizational approach seeks explanation wholly from within the organization. Another key difference between the two modes of analysis is that the organizational process mode is usually confined to examining one institution over time, whereas the ecological mode compares the behaviour of different but comparable institutions either at one point in time, or in time series.

In the particular form of the organizational process approach that we are to examine, the dominant focus is on the budget, and the assumption is that its composition (i.e. the distribution of cash between items) is very largely the product of regularized decision rules or 'standard operating procedures'.[2] This is the theory of incremental budgeting.

According to this theory, the budget neither reflects the resolution of a full-dress conflict over allocations of the competing public services as expressed in agency bids, nor is it the product of a rational maximizing decision-making process. Rather, it consists largely of a repetition of the budget which preceded it a year earlier. The budgetary process mainly comprises the standard operating procedure of adding a marginal and regularized increase (or decrease) — the increment — to the preceding year's allocation. The underlying assumptions of the incremental theory of decision-making, from which the budget-making theory is derived, has been most precisely stated by Dahl and Lindblom:

Incrementalism is a method of social action that takes existing reality as one alternative and compares the probable gains and losses of closely related alternatives by making relatively small adjustments in existing reality, or making larger adjustments about whose consequences approximately as much is known as about the consequences of existing reality, or both. Where small increments will not achieve desired goals, the consequences of large increments are not fully known, and existing reality is clearly undesirable, incrementalism may have to give way to calculated risk.[3]

The best known propagator of that aspect of incremental theory which concentrates on the budget is Aaron Wildavsky. As we shall see, the theory as he and his colleagues have propounded it has a number of ambiguities, but its essence has been stated by Wildavsky thus:

Budgeting is incremental not comprehensive. The beginning of wisdom about an agency budget is that it is almost never actively reviewed as a whole every year in the sense of reconsidering the value of all existing programmes as compared to all possible alternatives. Instead it is based on last year's budget with special attention given to a narrow range of increase or decreases. Thus the men who made the budget are concerned with relatively small increments to an existing base.[4]

It must be emphasized that the size of the increase is not the only criterion; also to be considered are the regularity of changes in allocations, the extent to which the preceding year's allocations dominate the decision process, and the number of alternatives that are considered. Wildavsky again:

The key terms are 'existing base', 'small number of items', and 'narrow range of increases or decreases'. One knows whether a method of budgetary problem-solving is or is not incremental, then, by whether or not decision-making focuses around the existing base (which may be approximated by last year's amount) and by whether the number of alternatives considered by decision-makers is small or large (or, in budgetary terms by the regularity of the size of the increase or decrease). The number of alternatives considered and the distance from existing levels, e.g. the size of increases or decreases, are the key criteria.[5]

Wildavsky's budgetary incremental theory, which has spawned a sizeable literature,[6] was initially based on a study of the budgetary procedures of the US federal government and especially the procedures of the House Appropriations Committee. He has since broadened his purview to include the budget-making process in other democratic countries.[7] In co-operation with O. A. Davis and M. A. H. Dempster he has also refined the incrementalist thesis and by means of econometric analysis provided further evidence in support of the thesis's relevance to the American federal budgetary process.[8]

Wildavsky asserts the theory's inherent plausibility on the familiar grounds that such is the complexity of the issues at stake, decision-makers have only very limited time, and even more limited knowledge and intellectual capacity, to do anything more than consider procedures such as standardized but marginal increase, or, but less likely, decreases, to last year's allocation:

There are cases in which one might do better if we had endless time, and un-limited ability to calculate. But time is in terribly short supply, the human mind is drastically limited in what it can encompass, and the number of budgetary items may be huge, so that the trite phrase 'A man can only do so much' takes on real meaning.[9]

It is important to recognize that Wildavsky is not only concerned to describe the budgeting process. As Danziger and many others have pointed out, the incrementalist thesis is not merely descriptive and explanatory but prescriptive as well.[10] For example, Wildavsky is always anxious to assert that the essential nature of the budgeting process in a democracy renders any notion of rational budgeting, of the kind conventionally preferred by administrative reformers, as being impossible and unnecessary. Rational budgeting is impossible because of its necessarily all-embracing character, since every major item has to be scrutinized from the bottom up, as it were. It is unnecessary because, in any case, normal budgeting achieves the objectives of co-ordination and priority-setting — in so far as they can be achieved — that rational budgeting seeks to achieve.[11] We may define rational budgeting procedures, broadly speaking, as comprising some form of specification of expenditure allocations on the basis of a policy-preference hierarchy that is related to expected resources. Such is the all-pervading logic in incrementalism, claims Wildavsky, that even where such a system is introduced — such as PESC and PAR in British central government — it becomes incrementalist in practice.[12] This is because the rational system raises the visibility of the allocative process, making each spending department more conscious of who is getting what, and especially where it occurs. It also highlights which department is getting *more* than the predicted resource increase. What might have been settled quietly by back-stair deals under the old order becomes every spending agency's most urgently sought-after information. There is corroboration of Wildavsky's claim that the adoption of synoptic budgeting only serves to enhance the likelihood of incrementalism. This corroboration is of particular importance for the present discussion since it is derived directly from two empirical studies of English local government.[13] However, confirmation does prompt the question as to why such vast amounts of ink have been spilt by the incrementalists in attacking the iniquities of synoptic budgeting. For it should be noted, the introduction of erstwhile rational and synoptic procedures, claims Wildavsky, actually *enhances* incrementalism.

Wildavsky's claim that rational budgeting procedures are inappropriate in a democratic system is perhaps less explicit than his other prescriptive arguments, but it is clearly discernible where he draws parallels between 'normative' budgeting and totalitarianism.[14] Although Wildavsky denies any direct influence,[15] the prescriptive aspect of his theory of incremental budgeting has direct links with the branch of the more general literature on decision-making which also argues that, because we cannot accurately predict the future, or because of cognitive and time limitations, all decision-making — both public and market — is incremental and sequential rather than all-embracing and rationally maximal in character.[16] Wildavsky's prescriptive arguments on behalf of incrementalism, especially his constant reference to synoptic budgeting entailing the centralization of power within the system — as if such a conjunction automatically rules it out of court for a democracy — also has links with that more general clutch of theories, concepts, and assertions that have come to be known as pluralism,[17] and which are so closely identified with the American democratic tradition.[18]

Defects of Incremental Theory

This more general incremental theory has serious shortcomings as a theory of decision-making, not least because it assumes that a marginal change in policy always has a marginal outcome, but also because it assumes that all new policies can be tackled by a process of cumulative change over time, however 'lumpy' those policies may be. Moreover, general incremental theory seems to assume that the arrival at the desired destination by a series of *ad hoc* hops is achieved without the benefit of any preconceptualization of such a process by the decision-makers.[19] These are all dubious assumptions, but they need not detain us since our principal concern is not with the general incrementalist theory but the theory of incremental budgeting.

There is an important aspect of incremental budgeting theory that must be noted before proceeding to the analysis of our data. This is the ambiguity surrounding the meaning of incremental as used in the theory. In Wildavsky's original formulation it is clear that the *scale* of each year's change in allocation is regarded as an inverse measure of its incremental character, as well as the regularity with which the given increase occurs. For example, in his earliest statement of the theory he provides a table giving the percentage annual increases in the appropriations for thirty-seven federal agencies dealing with domestic services, over a twelve-year period. The only purpose such a table could conceivably serve is to illustrate the scale of annual budgetary change and Wildavsky clearly indicates that the scale of the increase is what the table is designed to illustrate. He ends his discussion of the table with the following:

Just under three quarters of the cases (326) occur within 30 per cent, less than 10 per cent (31) are in the extreme range of 50 per cent or more.[20]

His use of incremental as reflecting the scale of change also concurs with normal usage. However, in later statements and especially in an article in which he and his colleague M. A. H. Dempster answer some of those who have criticized the incremental theory, he denies that the scale of the change from one year to the next does denote the existence of incrementalism, and all the emphasis is on regularity of change as the primary indicator. Even a 300 per cent increase in one year can be incremental: in fact, under this new definition, incrementalism becomes merely a synonym for regularity.

An incremental process refers to the relationship between the participants, not to the method of calculation. Whether or not a process can be so described depends on the regularity of the relationships between congress and agencies acting through the Office of Management and Budget. A process may be regular if appropriations and requests increase at 300 per cent a year every year, or it may be regular if the request increases 100 per cent and the appropriation reduces it by 95 per cent. If Congress follows a regular 100 per cent annual increase in requests by cutting 50 per cent in one and adding 200 per cent in the next, the budgetary process is still incremental, that is, regular. By a non-incremental process then, we mean irregularity in the pattern of mutual relations. Showing that any specified proportion of organizational output is larger or smaller than a size arbitrarily determined to be 'incremental' does not say anything about the nature of a budgetary process; that can only be determined by a study of the interaction between participants.[21]

There is no need to pursue this change of heart here, or to speculate on its causes, but it seems to us that such a redefinition drains the incremental thesis of much of its status and interest as an explanatory theory. Moreover, the redefinition came rather late in the day. So we make no apology for sticking to the original — and accepted — meaning of incremental. Thus the ensuing analysis will be based on the assumption that the scale of annual changes as well as their regularity are indicators of incrementalism. In making this interpretation we take comfort not merely from the fact that such an assumption accords with normal usage, but also from the fact that such an assumption seems also to have been made by most of those who have tried to apply the incremental theory.

As we have noted, the incremental budgeting theory has attracted considerable academic attention and is probably the most influential of all the organizational process theories of policy-making. It is, however, not without weaknesses in addition to those already noted. In the first place it runs together a plausible explanation of the problems that budget-makers must face and the claim that budget-making, except in exceptional circumstances such as war or perceived economic and social crisis, must therefore be incremental. It may be true that no budget process does, or can, start with a *tabula rasa* each year for all the reasons that incremental theory asserts. Significant elements of expenditure, for example, are likely to be mandatory. Equally, there will always be severe time constraints operating which rule out fundamental reappraisals, even supposing sufficient information could be marshalled to make such reappraisals effective. Finally, the incommensurability of various policies and the lack of knowledge about their precise consequences, render any rationally maximizing calculus difficult and probably impossible. Few, in other words, can deny the validity of the incrementalist's attack on the more extreme theories of comprehensive programme and target budgeting. But ill-conceived as these theories may be for the real world of democratic government, it does not follow that budget-making must therefore be incremental. Indeed, it is equally plausible to assume that the very limitations on knowledge, time, and mental capacity that it is asserted make legislators cautious, could make them bold. If decision-makers are as likely to be bold as they are cautious, the model that is more likely to fit the facts is a random rather than an incremental one. The necessary simplification of the process of determining allocations has, in short, nothing necessarily to do with the scale of change,[22] nor with its regularity. As Danziger has noted, an explanation of a *process* is not necessarily an explanation of output.[23] In other words, in order to link, firstly, the undoubtedly persuasive case that incremental theory makes for denying the possibility of root-and-branch budgeting with, secondly, the actual allocations, another factor must be introduced. Although it is seldom mentioned by incremental theorists, and in some cases actually ruled out,[24] there is an obvious candidate. This is the fiscal constraint derived from the usual desire of decision-makers to keep down tax increases; or, if possible, avoid them altogether. Where a deficit is ruled out as well, as is the case in local government, this constraint is, of course, all the stronger. The crucial importance of the fiscal constraint has been pointed out by others who have tried to apply incrementalist theory, notably Crecine and Wanat,[25] and it is our contention that the fiscal constraint is just as vital in limiting the manner in which allocations are made as are the cognitive, information, and time constraints that figure so prominently in incrementalist theory.

It follows that where the revenue constraint is weakened, incrementalism will be less likely. Such a situation occurs where decision-makers *are* willing to increase taxes; that is to say where their desire for policy change outweighs their fear of electoral retribution. Equally, at the local level, the fiscal constraint will be weaker where the cost of the change will be met wholly, or in part, by a transfer from senior government, and thus will not evoke an unfavourable electoral response.

If the fiscal constraint assumption is broadly correct, it also follows that the less impact that a given public service expenditure has on the total budget, the less inhibited will politicians be about behaving non-incrementally when they desire to expand a service. Where the desire is to cut expenditure then the reverse may apply: cuts in a service which absorbs a major part of the total budget will be much closer to the overall cut in total expenditure sought than will cuts in services that absorb only a fraction of total expenditure. To put it another way, incrementalism may be a function of the unit, or level, chosen for analysis. The larger the budget of the chosen unit or level is, proportionately to the total budget, the greater the tendency to act incrementally; and the smaller the unit is proportionately, the greater the tendency to act non-incrementally.

However, if there is such a relationship between scale and incrementalism, does this mean that only the most detailed line items ought to be examined? Clearly not; the system itself provides levels and units — departments, agencies, etc. – which the student may legitimately take as given, although it must be emphasized that agency, or departmental, budgetary behaviour may be of fairly limited relevance to output analysis. It is even possible that, as Natchez and Bupp argue in relation to the research of Wildavsky and colleagues into federal agency budgeting, 'The reason for the greater statistical success of the quantitative budget studies lies in the fact that agencies were taken as the unit of analysis.'[26]

If we are to discover whether incrementalism under the terms of the theory is taking place, the object should not be to achieve the maximum disaggregation of expenditure items before analysis begins, but rather to decide what is the most appropriate level at which to make the analysis, given that the higher the level of aggregation the greater the fiscal constraint. Fortunately, it is possible to define a level of administration which is the most appropriate for applying not just incremental theory, but any other theory that seeks to uncover the determinants of public policy outputs. This level is the sub-departmental or agency level, for this is the level at which, as we noted in Chapter 1, decision-makers, and in particular, parties, are likely to focus their main interest. By sub-department or agency is meant, for example, the primary, secondary, and special education sub-services of an education department; or the ambulance, home nursing, and mental health sub-services of a health department. These sub-departments are also the level at which the public is more likely to focus its interest. Whereas departmental expenditures may, in political terms, be largely abstractions that arise because cognate public functions are usually more efficiently exercised under a single administrative umbrella, the sub-departmental, or agency, level defines fairly precise, largely homogeneous, and therefore more immediately comprehensible, activities. For similar reasons, in the competition for resources as the budgetary buildup proceeds, it is at these operational levels that bureaucratic allegiances are likely to form. Above all, this is the level where actual policies or programmes arise. Thus we may say that it is this operational level that has not only greater political relevance, but is, in fact, the level at which any analysis that seeks to discover the determinants of policy change should focus. As Natchez and Bupp have put it:

The first step, then, in untangling information on policy choices from data on the administration of government is to shift the level of analysis from agencies and departments to programmes. This is to say that in the context of the budgetary process, programmes are the operating units of public policy, that they provide categories that are closer to being true outputs of government than the older categories.[27]

Of course, disaggregation down to the programme or operational level is not absolutely essential for testing the proposition that there is a negative relationship between proportional size of the expenditure item and the tendency to incrementalism. Some departments (i.e. the planning department or that for

Table 4.1 Cross-year Correlations of County Borough Expenditure Items, by Size of Expenditures in 1960/1

Major services	Selected sub-services	Mean expenditure per thousand 1960/1 (£m.)	Correlations between expenditure in: 1960/1 and			1956/7 and
			1964/5	1968/9	1972/3	1968/9
Total expenditure		29.71	0.76	0.60	0.45	n/a
Total education		15.31	0.87	0.78	0.62	n/a
	Education	14.93	0.89	0.79	0.56	0.70
	Education: secondary	4.80	0.89	0.73	0.54	0.45
	Education: primary and nursery	43.84	0.89	0.73	0.66	0.66
Police		2.26	0.88	0.68	0.56	n/a
Highways		2.25	0.84	0.69	0.49	n/a
Housing		1.85	0.81	0.61	0.40	n/a
Local health services		1.42	0.85	0.68	0.21	n/a
	Health: total	1.38	0.80	0.66	n/a	0.51
	Education: loan charges	1.38	0.72	0.47	0.18	0.22
Sewerage		0.86	0.80	0.69	0.55	n/a
Parks		0.85	0.88	n/a	0.59	n/a
Refuse		0.78	0.88	0.76	0.51	n/a
Welfare		0.71	0.83	0.58	n/a	n/a
Total fire		0.65	0.88	0.81	0.81	0.78
	Fire	0.64	0.89	0.80	0.58	n/a
	Fire: pay	0.55	0.93	0.82	0.81	0.78
Libraries		0.50	0.87	0.69	0.64	n/a
Children's services		0.49	0.80	0.64	n/a	n/a
Public health		0.45	0.76	0.47	0.29	n/a
	Education: special	0.41	0.85	0.65	0.57	0.51
	Health: ambulances	0.25	0.81	0.65	n/a	0.61
	Health: administration	0.20	0.85	0.70	n/a	0.45
	Education: recreation	0.19	0.54	0.36	0.34	0.24
	Education: capital from revenue	0.18	0.69	0.61	0.39	0.44
	Health: domestic help	0.18	0.88	0.66	n/a	0.54
Town and country planning		0.17	0.78	0.61	0.53	n/a

Health: home nursing	0.16	0.89	0.72	n/a	0.70
Health: mental health	0.12	0.55	0.37	n/a	0.30
Fire: other expenditure	0.11	0.68	0.63	0.59	0.48
Health: child welfare centres	0.09	0.81	0.69	n/a	0.56
Health: health visiting	0.09	0.89	0.82	n/a	0.71
Health: day nurseries	0.07	0.93	0.92	n/a	0.88
Fire: loan charges	0.04	0.57	0.21	0.08	0.06

Notes:

1. Figures for the major services are budgeted expenditure while those for selected sub-services are actual expenditures. The education, fire, and health figures which appear in the selected sub-service column are net rate and grant-borne expenditure.

2. Although detailed expenditure items for education, fire, and health services are available for 1956/7, the data for all service headings are not available for years before 1959/60 due to the exclusion of specific grants from the IMTA tables. Consequently, it is only possible to correlate across the years 1960/1 to 1972/3. However, correlations between 1956/7 and 1968/9 are given wherever possible because this provides another long time span of twelve years against which the figures for 1960/1–1972/3 may be compared.

3. The number of observations varies from service to service and from year to year, because the number of county boroughs and police authorities changes, and because of errors or missing data in the IMTA sources. Rather than producing a figure for each service in each pair of years, the following gives the minimum and the maximum number of observations in each column:

	Minimum	*Maximum*
Column 1	73	81
Column 2	70	79
Column 3	69	77
Column 4	70	77

Table 4.2 *Cross-year Correlations of County Council Expenditure Items, by Size of Expenditures in 1960/1*

Major services	Selected sub-services	Mean expenditure per thousand 1960/1 (£m.)	Correlations between expenditure in:			
			1960/1 and		1972/3	1956/7 and
			1964/5	1968/9		1968/9
Total expenditure from rates and grants		26.80	0.96	0.95	0.94	n/a
Total education		16.88	0.95	0.87	0.84	n/a
	Education	16.40	0.88	0.83	0.76	0.86
	Education: secondary	4.95	0.93	0.90	0.79	0.84
	Education: primary	4.83	0.97	0.92	0.84	n/a
Highways		3.75	0.94	0.94	0.96	n/a
Police		1.95	0.85	0.57	0.40	n/a
Local health authority services		1.14	0.88	n/a	n/a	n/a
	Health	1.39	0.89	0.73	n/a	0.67
	Education: loan changes	1.34	0.79	0.62	0.40	0.41
Welfare		0.55	0.77	0.60	n/a	n/a
Total fire		0.55	0.86	0.78	0.79	0.30
	Fire	0.53	0.64	0.54	0.55	0.05
	Education: capital from revenue	0.42	0.64	0.40	0.41	n/a
Children's services		0.40	0.86	0.71	n/a	n/a
	Fire: pay	0.34	0.85	0.81	0.72	0.72
	Education: special education	0.32	0.80	0.68	0.56	0.14
Libraries		0.30	0.85	0.58	0.32	n/a
	Health: ambulances	0.29	0.83	0.72	n/a	0.52
	Health: administration	0.20	0.78	0.52	n/a	0.66
	Health: home nursing	0.19	0.91	0.83	n/a	0.73
	Health: domestic help	0.17	0.91	0.71	n/a	0.58
Public health		0.17	0.65	n/a	n/a	n/a
	Fire: other expenditure	0.13	0.70	0.47	0.64	0.23
	Education: recreation	0.10	0.70	0.67	0.61	0.65
	Health: health visiting	0.09	0.87	0.70	n/a	0.72
	Health: mental health	0.08	0.60	0.24	n/a	0.02

| Health: child welfare centres | 0.07 | 0.86 | 0.74 | n/a | 0.69 |
| Fire: loan charges | 0.04 | 0.75 | 0.31 | 0.32 | 0.16 |

Notes:
1. Notes 1 and 2 for Table 4.1 apply also to this table.
2. For reasons given in note 3, Table 4.1, the number of observations varies from service to service and from year to year. The minimum and maximum number of observations for each column is as follows:

	Minimum	*Maximum*
Column 1	43	58
Column 2	42	56
Column 3	41	56
Column 4	42	56

recreation and leisure) do not break down into agency-type sub-departments, but each constitutes as a whole department the operational level around which political and bureaucratic budgetary competition focuses. Since the expenditure of these smaller homogeneous departments tends to be substantially smaller than that of the large heterogeneous departments like education, transport, or health, their respective expenditures over time may be compared to see whether there is a scale effect.

Disaggregated large-sector expenditures and the whole-sector expenditure of the more homogeneous and smaller departments, then, provide a useful basis for assessing the validity of the incremental thesis. Moreover, and most important of all, a local government system provides sufficient observations over time of such expenditures as to render the exercise meaningful. Surprisingly, although some research has been undertaken on incrementalism in British local government,[28] such a full-scale assessment has not been undertaken. It is to such an assessment of the incremental thesis in the light of our data that we now turn.

Analysis of Data

The data to be analysed are derived from the expenditure on fourteen major services and twenty sub-services for English and Welsh counties and county boroughs, for five separate financial years over the period 1960/1 to 1972/3. Tables 4.1 and 4.2 set out the findings for each service and sub-service in terms of the mean expenditure for 1960-1 in descending order of magnitude (the first column). The second, third, and fourth columns give correlations for each expenditure item in each observation year with the 1960-1 figure. In addition, the last column gives the correlations for 1968/9 in relation to the financial year 1956/7, this being the largest time span that the data will permit (see note 2 for Table 4.1), and it provides further confirmation for the trends observable in the preceding columns.

It will be seen that the incremental theory holds up very well for total expenditure in the counties, but clearly does not apply in the county boroughs. A similar difference is discernible for most of the other whole-sector items, and the counties emerge as undoubtedly more incremental than their urban counterparts for the larger expenditures. Incrementalism clearly did not occur, however, for the smaller items, all of which in both types of authority show wide variations between years. In short, in both county boroughs (Table 4.1) and county councils (Table 4.2), the correlations for each service and sub-service tend to decline with the decline in the size of the expenditure item (in 1960/1) for each observation year for both types of authority. This relationship is not consistent throughout, but the trend is unmistakable. It is further confirmed in Tables 4.3 and 4.4 which list the mean cross-year correlations for the four observation years by size of expenditure item. Only for two sets of correlations for the county boroughs (in Table 4.3), 1960/1-1964/5 and 1960/1-1972/3, is there not a consistent decline in the correlations with a decline in the mean of expenditure size, and even then the inconsistency is very marginal.

Table 4.3 *Mean Cross-year Correlations between Expenditure Items by Size of Expenditure Items (County Boroughs)*

	Mean correlations for:
1960/1-1964/5	First eleven expenditures = 0.83 Next twelve expenditures = 0.85 Last twelve expenditures = 0.76
1960/1-1968/9	First twelve expenditures = 0.68 Next eleven expenditures = 0.69 Last eleven expenditures = 0.60
1960/1-1972/3	First eight expenditures = 0.54 Next eight expenditures = 0.53 Last eight expenditures = 0.43
1956/7-1968/9	First six expenditures = 0.55 Next seven expenditures = 0.51 Last seven expenditures = 0.53

Note: This table is based on the correlations in Table 4.1. It simply groups expenditure items into the largest, median, and smallest size and gives the mean cross-year correlations for each group.

To summarize, Tables 4.1 to 4.4 amply confirm the hypothesis adumbrated earlier, that incrementalism, as measured by the extent of expenditure change for budget items, may be a function of the proportionate share of the total budget absorbed by the budget item. And, further, that this inverse relationship between the scale of expenditure items and the scale of change may be caused by fiscal constraint rather than the inherent difficulty, or unlikeliness, of budgeting on a rational basis as is claimed by incremental theory.

As we have noted, the findings in Tables 4.1 to 4.4 suggest that counties may be more incremental than county boroughs. For example, the cross-year correlations for total expenditure for counties (line 1, Table 4.2) hardly change for the three observation years that are correlated with 1960/1, and even some twelve years later total expenditure has a coefficient of 0.94 for counties as compared with 0.45 for county boroughs (line 1, Table 4.1). A similar difference between the two types of authority is observable for some of the expenditures for whole sectors such as education, police, highways, fire, and libraries. We can only speculate as to why the counties seem to be more incremental, but one strong possibility is the greater insulation of counties from external factors. Incremental theorists accept that the incremental tenor of budgetary change can be disrupted by external effects — what are called 'shift points'. These effects are usually modelled 'by a series of exogenous variables representing the intrusion of the outside world'.[29] There are certain characteristics of the county's links with the 'outside world' which suggest that it may have been better placed to insulate itself from such intrusions than the county borough.

Table 4.4 *Mean Cross-year Correlations between Expenditure Items by Size of Expenditure Items (County Councils)*

	Mean correlations for:	
1960/1–1964/5	First nine expenditures	= 0.92
	Next ten expenditures	= 0.79
	Last ten expenditures	= 0.77
1960/1–1968/9	First nine expenditures	= 0.81
	Next nine expenditures	= 0.65
	Last nine expenditures	= 0.58
1960/1–1972/3	First five expenditures	= 0.84
	Next six expenditures	= 0.59
	Last six expenditures	= 0.53
1956/7–1968/9	First seven expenditures	= 0.57
	Next six expenditures	= 0.56
	Last six expenditures	= 0.41

Note: This table is based on the correlations in Table 4.2. It is the county council equivalent of Table 4.3.

In the first place, the county's election cycle was triennial, whereas the county borough's was annual. It may be argued, therefore, that the county could, other things being equal, ignore external public pressure longer than the county borough, since the consequences of doing so were less immediate. Secondly, one of the county's primary links with the outside world – the council members – was more remote from the decision-making process. This was partly because the council and the committees met less often than those of the county boroughs, and partly because the seat of county government was decidedly more remote on average from the homes of the council members and their constituencies. For similar reasons it may be argued that county bureaucracy was equally more insulated from the external world than its counterparts in the county boroughs. The absence of competitive party systems in the counties, as compared with the county boroughs, may also have insulated counties from important aspects of their environment more effectively than was possible in the county boroughs. This is because the absence of a party system tends to make it difficult for the average elector to focus on his government around the issues that are likely to affect the distribution of major expenditures. Where, on average, more than half of the seats were never even contested – which was the case for the counties during the study period – this aspect of insulation may be expected to have been further enhanced.

Supposing that our assumptions about the nature of the revenue-expenditure relationship in local government are broadly correct, Tables 4.1-4.4 also suggest that the fiscal constraint seems to operate in the counties more than in the county boroughs. Again we can only speculate on why that may be, but one answer could be that rural areas are more sensitive to local tax increases. This is because there tends to be a smaller proportion of the tax base derived from industry and commerce; moreover, farming is largely absolved from rates. It follows that any increase in expenditure is likely to have a more direct effect on how much domestic ratepayers have to pay — all of whom have the vote — than in urban areas.

Also, in a competitive party system, party ideology will certainly count for more in the policy-making process and will thus be more likely to override the more normal operating procedures of incremental budgeting. Our research, then, strongly suggests that incremental theory does seem to apply to these policies that are to some degree insulated from the direct effects of the democratic process and in particular do not operate under a competitive party system. To put it in another way, incrementalism is a stable form of budgeting that is the product of a stable form of decision-making.[30] In competitive party systems where the electorate also has greater purchase on the decision-making process, incrementalism does not seem to apply. Above all, it does not apply in either type of system for the small budget items. All the evidence suggests that incrementalism is an increasing function of aggregation. In short, parties do seem to matter, and so does scale.

We return to a more detailed and sustained discussion of the impact of parties on outputs in Chapter 9, and in particular the possibility that was first raised in Chapter 1 in relation to output research proper, namely that American parties in terms of their ideological consistency and internal coherence are of a fundamentally different kind to those usually found in other Western countries. The decision-making process within which American parties operate is also more conducive to blunting rather than reflecting what ideological consistency and cohesion American parties do have. In other words, the failure of American output research to find that politics does matter, which we discussed in Chapter 1, is on all fours with the discovery that all political change is incremental. Like the transmission model of policy-making, incrementalism assumes that the political process is essentially an epiphenomenon of something else; and both perhaps are profoundly influenced by ideological preconceptions about both the proper limits of governmental action and the proper limits of governmental power.

Before proceeding to Chapter 5 it is important at this point to draw together some of the threads of the discussion in the preceding chapters. In Chapter 3 we saw that despite some modest success, there were serious defects in the conventional ecological approach, since it assumes some sort of transmission process whereby the socio-economic character of the population of the political units gets automatically translated into public policy. Also in Chapter 3 we saw that the Tiebout thesis is substantially more deficient as an explicator of public policy variation. Although a decided improvement on the Tiebout thesis, the third conventional mode for explaining policy variation – incrementalism – clearly does not operate for relatively small budget items, and more decisively for our main theme, incrementalism does not occur where there is a thorough-going party system.

Having examined some of the principal explanatory constructs and found them wanting, we now turn to some alternatives. The first set are geographical and take as their unit of analysis not the internal socio-economic composition of cities, but cities' role as holistic entities within a wider national or regional economic system.

NOTES

1. G. Allison, *Essence of Decision: Explaining the Cuban Missile Crisis* (Boston, Little Brown, 1971), p. 67.
2. R. Cyert and J. March, *A Behavioural Theory of the Firm* (Englewood Cliffs, Prentice Hall, 1963).
3. R. A. Dahl and C. Lindblom, *Politics, Economics and Welfare* (New York, Harper and Row, 1953), p. 82.
4. A. Wildavsky, *The Politics of the Budgetary Process* (Boston, Little Brown, 1974), 2nd edn., p. 15. That this quotation does provide the best synopsis of the theory is suggested by the fact that it is the one chosen by the author and his collaborator to describe incrementalism in M. A. H. Dempster and A. Wildavsky, 'On Change: Or, There is No Magic Size for an Increment', *Political Studies*, XXVII (1979), 372.
5. Dempster and Wildavsky, 'On Change: Or, There is No Magic Size . . .', 372.
6. The more notable contributions to this literature, in addition to Wildavsky's own, include: T. J. Anton, *The Politics of State Expenditure in Illinois* (Urbana, University of Illinois Press, 1966); J. Barber, *Power in Committees: An Experiment in the Governmental Process* (Chicago, Rand McNally, 1966); J. P. Crecine, *Governmental Problem Solving: a Computer Simulation of Municipal Budgeting* (Chicago, Rand McNally, 1969); T. R. Dye, *Politics, Economics and the Public* (Chicago, Rand McNally, 1966); R. F. Fenno, *The Power of the Purse: Appropriations Politics in Congress* (Boston, Little Brown, 1966); J. R. Gist, *Mandatory Expenditures and the Defence Sector: Theory of Budgetary Incrementalism* (Beverly Hills, Sage, 1974); I. Sharkansky (ed.), *Policy Analysis in Political Science* (Chicago, Markham, 1970); and I. Sharkansky, *The Routines of Politics* (New York, Van Nostrand, 1969).

7. H. Heclo and A. Wildavsky, *The Private Government of Public Money* (London, Macmillan, 1973), and A. Wildavsky, *Budgeting: A Comparative Theory of Budgetary Processes* (Boston, Little Brown, 1975).

8. O. A. Davis, M. A. H. Dempster, and A. Wildavsky, 'A Theory of the Budgetary Process', *American Political Science Review*, 60 (1966); O. A. Davis, M. A. H. Dempster, and A. Wildavsky, 'On the Process of Budgeting: An Empirical Study of Congressional Appropriations', in G. Tullock (ed.), *Papers on Non-Market Decision-Making* (Charlottesville, University of Virginia, 1966); O. A. Davis, M. A. H. Dempster, and A. Wildavsky, 'On the Process of Budgeting II: An Empirical Study of Congressional Appropriation', in R. F. Byrne *et al.* (eds.), *Studies in Budgeting* (Amsterdam, North-Holland, 1971); and O. A. Davis, M. A. H. Dempster, and A. Wildavsky, 'Towards a Predictive Theory of Government Expenditure', *British Journal of Political Science*, 4 (1974). For another example of applying predictive incremental models to actual budget data, see A. Cowart, K.-E. Brofoss, and T. Hansen, 'Budgeting Strategies and Success at Multiple Decision Levels in the Norwegian Urban Setting', *American Political Science Review*, LXIX (1975).

9. Wildavsky, *The Politics of the Budgetary Process*, p. 10.

10. J. N. Danziger, 'Assessing Incrementalism in British Municipal Budgeting', *British Journal of Political Science*, 6 (1976), 336. For other critics of incrementalism who base their criticism at least in part on the prescriptive nature of incrementalism, and in particular its inherently conservative bias, see Y. Dror, *Public Policy-making Re-examined* (Scranton, Chandler, 1968), and A. Etzioni, *The Active Society: A Theory of Societal and Political Processes* (New York, Free Press, 1968). For a spirited defence of incrementalism against such criticisms by someone who must be regarded as the nearest thing to the founding father of incrementalism in its broadest sense, see C. E. Lindblom, 'Still Muddling, Not Yet Through', *Public Administration Review*, 39 (1979).

11. Wildavsky, *The Politics of the Budgetary Process*, see especially Ch. 5.

12. Wildavsky, *Budgeting*, Ch. 19.

13. Danziger, 'Assessing Incrementalism in British Municipal Budgeting'; and R. Greenwood, C. R. Hinings, and S. Ranson, 'The Politics of the Budgetary Process in English Local Government', *Political Studies*, XXV (1977). It is essential also to see J. N. Danziger, 'A Comment on "The Politics of the Budgetary Process in English Local Government"', *Political Studies*, XXVI (1978), for it is there, and not in the article by Greenwood *et al.* about which it comments, that the link between synoptic policy-making and incrementalism is brought out. This is conceded by Greenwood and his colleagues in 'A Rejoinder to Danziger's Comment' in the same issue of *Political Studies* as Danziger's article.

14. Wildavsky, *The Politics of the Budgetary Process*, p. 129.

15. Wildavsky, *The Politics of the Budgetary Process*, p. 61, footnote 33.

16. See, for example, H. Simon, *Administrative Behaviour* (Glencoe, Free Press, 1945); H. Simon, *Models of Man* (New York, Wiley, 1957); J. March and H. Simon, *Organizations* (New York, Wiley, 1958); Cyert and March, *A Behavioural Theory of the Firm*; and D. Braybrooke and C. Lindblom, *A Strategy of Decision* (New York, Free Press, 1963).

17. This aspect of Wildavsky's incremental theory is most clearly evident in

his 'Political Implications of Budgetary Reform', *Public Administration Review*, XXI (1961). Also see Dahl and Lindblom, *Politics, Economics and Welfare*; Braybrooke and Lindblom, *Strategy of Decision*; and C. Lindblom, *The Intelligence of Democracy* (New York, Free Press, 1965). For one of the earliest claims for the essentially democratic character of incrementalism, see K. Popper, *The Poverty of Historicism* (London, Routledge, 1957), and *The Open Society and Its Enemies*, Vol. 1, (London, Routledge, 1945).

18. L. J. Sharpe, 'American Democracy Reconsidered: Part II and Conclusions', *British Journal of Political Science*, 3 (1973).

19. R. E. Goodin and I. Waldner, 'Thinking Big, Thinking Small and Not Thinking At All', *Public Policy*, XXVII (1979).

20. Wildavsky, *The Politics of the Budgetary Process*, p. 14.

21. Dempster and Wildavsky, 'On Change: Or, There is No Magic Size', p. 374. For a discussion of what constitutes an acceptable incremental change, see J. Bailey and R. O'Connor, 'Operationalizing Incrementalism: Measuring the Middles', *Public Administration Review*, 35 (1975).

22. Bailey and O'Connor, 'Operationalizing Incrementalism: Measuring the Middles'.

23. J. N. Danziger, 'Comparing Approaches to the Study of Financial Resource Allocation', in C. Liske, W. Loehr and J. McCamant (eds.), *Comparative Public Policy: Issues, Theories, and Methods* (Beverly Hills, Sage, 1975), p. 81. The same point is also made by J. Wanat, 'Bases of Budgetary Incrementalism', *American Political Science Review*, LXVIII (1974).

24. In Crecine's study of US local authorities, for example, the available revenue is assumed to be fixed in the model. See Crecine, *Governmental Problem Solving*, p. 68.

25. J. P. Crecine, 'A Simulation of Municipal Budgeting: The Impact of the Problem Environment', in W. Coplin (ed.), *Simulation in the Study of Politics* (Chicago, Markham, 1968); and J. Wanat 'Bases of Budgetary Incrementalism'. Also see D. E. Ashford, R. Berne, and R. Schramm, 'The Expenditure-Financing Decision in British Local Government', *Policy and Politics*, 5 (1976), which also makes a strong plea for considering expenditure and revenue together.

26. P. B. Natchez and I. C. Bupp, 'Policy and Priority in the Budgetary Process', *American Political Science Review*, LXVII (1973), 955. J. Danziger makes a similar point in relation to incremental analysis for British local government in 'A Comment on the Politics of the Budgetary Process', p. 113.

27. Natchez and Bupp, 'Policy and Priority in the Budgetary Process', 956.

28. See note 13.

29. Dempster and Wildavsky, 'On Change: Or, There is No Magic Size', p. 376.

30. This conclusion is broadly in line with the other studies that have analysed British local government expenditures in terms of incremental theory, namely: Danziger, 'Assessing Incrementalism in British Municipal Budgeting'; Greenwood *et al.*, 'The Politics of the Budgetary Process'; 'Chronic Instability in Fiscal Systems', in R. Rose and E. Page, (eds.), *Fiscal Stress in Cities* (Cambridge, Cambridge University Press, 1982). Similar conclusions for Swedish local government are reached by J.–E. Lane, A. Westlund, and H. Stenlund, 'Analyses of Structural Variability in Budget-Making', *Scandinavian Political Studies*, 4 (1981).

5. LEAGUE TABLES

Introduction

The last two chapters have shown that the main conventional approaches toward the explanation of local variations in policy and spending achieve no more than modest success at best, even though some of them call upon the most complex methods of statistical analysis. Their relative failure to help us to understand and explain, throws us back to square one, and forces us to retreat to the most basic and simple of methods. This entails nothing more than ranking authorities from the highest to the lowest spenders on each service, and puzzling over the resulting league tables to see what they can tell us about the causes of variations in local spending. Do local authorities of a similar kind tend to cluster together in the league tables, or are they distributed randomly, with no apparent rhyme or reason? This is the simplest of string-and-sealing-wax methods, it is true, but the results suggest some more fruitful lines of development which will be taken up in subsequent chapters. In other words, the chapter is mainly, but not wholly, of a preliminary nature. It will proceed by examining the league tables for each local government service in turn, starting with the four (parks, sewerage, refuse, and housing) which are the responsibility of county boroughs but not counties, and then going on to the remaining services which are handled by both kinds of top-tier authority.

Parks

Although parks consume a small proportion of the local authority budget, they are as good a place as any to start, because this item has, as an earlier chapter shows, firmly resisted satisfactory analysis in the past. The hypothesis that wealthier authorities spend more on parks, in the absence of more pressing demands, is barely supported by the British evidence; but most of the variance remains unexplained.

However, two explanations for high expenditure on parks jump out of the league table. At the top comes a group of seaside resorts — Eastbourne, Great Yarmouth, Bournemouth, and Brighton; with Southend, Blackpool, and Hastings not far behind them. The reasons for high parks expenditure in these cases scarcely needs comment — seaside resorts need their parks and gardens to attract visitors. At the same time, a completely different group of cities also spends heavily on parks. These are the capitals of large urban agglomerations, including Manchester, Birmingham, Liverpool, Bolton, Sheffield, and Newcastle, which need parks and open spaces because they are surrounded by large urban areas. In contrast, the county towns such as Ipswich, York, Exeter, Gloucester, and

Norwich spend little, presumably because they are surrounded by open space and natural parkland.

Table 5.1 *Per Capita Parks Expenditure (£), by Type of Authority, County Boroughs, 1960/1 and 1972/3*

Type of authority	1960/1	(n)	1972/3	(n)
Conurbation	0.956	(17)	1.881	(14)
Semi-urban	0.834	(18)	1.822	(18)
Semi-rural	0.826	(22)	1.838	(23)
Rural	0.797	(26)	1.699	(28)
Seaside resorts	1.167	(8)	2.240	(9)
County towns	0.661	(12)	1.510	(12)
County borough mean	0.846	(83)	1.795	(83)

Evidence for these relationships is presented in Table 5.1, with data for two years presented to show consistency over time. The table shows how much the seaside resorts spent compared with the county towns, and how much urban authorities spent compared to rural ones. In order to make this point, the 83 county boroughs were divided into four groups, as follows:

(1) *Conurbation authorities*: those which were at least 75 per cent sur-surrounded by other authorities with a population density of at least five people per acre.

(2) *Semi-urban authorities*: those which were mainly (75 per cent) surrounded by other authorities with a population density of between three and five people per acre.

(3) *Semi-rural authorities*: those which were mainly (75 per cent) surrounded by other authorities with a population density of between three and one person per acre.

(4) *Rural authorities*: those which were mainly (75 per cent) surrounded by authorities with a population density of less than one person per acre.

As the figures show, there is a fairly strong relationship between high spending and an urban or semi-urban environment. If the seaside resorts are removed from the rural category, the relationship is stronger. The relationship holds irrespective of the social class of local authority populations, as Table 5.2 shows. Urban authorities, both middle and working class, spend relatively heavily on parks compared with rural ones.

Two general points emerge from these findings. First, when looking for factors which might explain expenditure variations it is not enough to deal only with the characteristics of resident populations, for the figures show that factors which are not simply aggregates of individual characteristics can be important — in this case, the economic function of the city (the seaside resorts), and the nature of the city's physical environment (urban and rural). The Tiebout hypothesis makes explicit assumptions about (economic) individualism, and the demographic approach assumes the importance of resident population characteristics. Consequently, both lack explanatory power.

Table 5.2 *Per Capita Parks Expenditure (£), by Social Class and Urban-Rural Dichotomies, County Boroughs, 1960/1*

	Urban		Rural	
Middle Class	Croydon	1.555	Ipswich	0.502
	Wallasey	1.059	York	0.556
Working Class	Salford	1.201	Burton	0.505
	Oldham	1.003	Barrow	0.605

Second, it is clear that different kinds of cities can spend similar amounts on a given service but for different reasons, just as similar types of cities can spend different amounts on the same service for their own reasons. This greatly complicates the picture, and, in addition, limits the use of cluster and factor analysis computer programs. For example, both the seaside resorts and the county towns are wealthy, residential, commercial, and small to medium sized, but their parks expenditure fell at the extremes of the distribution. In contrast, the seaside resorts have little in common with the conurbation capitals, but both had a high parks expenditure. Thus when the computer searches for significant correlations, or for common dimensions on which to base its cluster, it finds little to go on — there are at least two sets of correlations to be sorted out, and at least two dimensions to be distinguished. It is not enough to be multivariate; analysis must be multivariate *and* multidimensional. Analysis may start with simple distinctions in order to elaborate powerful theory, but it cannot start with nothing but a computer and elaborate statistical methods.[1]

Having investigated parks expenditure in some detail, and drawn out the general implications of the results, we can proceed with the analysis of other services at a greater pace.

Sewerage

Sewerage expenditure is another which resists satisfactory analysis in conventional demographic studies. However, a casual inspection of the league table (Table 5.3) shows that the geographical location of the authority is crucial: very simply, those on the coast spent less than inland authorities. Of the twenty-five at the bottom of the table in 1972/3 seventeen were coastal cities, and of the twenty-five at the top, twenty-one were inland.[2] There seems also to be a regional variation in that in 1960/1 and 1972/3, all the Tyneside authorities (West Hartlepool, Newcastle, Tynemouth, South Shields, Gateshead, and Sunderland) were among the nine lowest.

Table 5.3 *Per Capita Sewerage Expenditure (£), by Coastal and Inland Cities, County Boroughs, 1960/1 and 1972/3*

Type of authority	1960/1	(n)	1972/3	(n)
Inland	0.971	(57)	3.183	(56)
Coastal	0.619	(26)	2.247	(27)
Seaside resorts	0.667	(8)	2.523	(9)
Others	0.597	(18)	2.109	(18)
County borough average	0.801	(83)	2.878	(83)

Among the coastal cities, the seaside resorts are notable for their relatively high spending, no doubt because they invest in treatment plant to keep their beaches pollution-free, whereas other coastal authorities may simply opt for the cheaper solution of pumping sewage out to sea.

Refuse

Refuse is another service which has weak associations with population characteristics, and which responds poorly to the demographic approach. However, common sense and a little knowledge suggest that, since transport costs are a high proportion of total spending, refuse costs will be highest where refuse has to be carried long distances to rubbish dumps. Authorities which are in the middle of large conurbations, therefore, are likely to have higher costs than rural or free-standing authorities.[3]

Table 5.4 *Per Capita Refuse Expenditure (£), by Urban and Rural Authorities, County Boroughs, 1960/1 and 1972/3*

Type of authority	1960/1	(n)	1972/3	(n)
Conurbation	0.810	(17)	2.909	(14)
Semi-urban	0.843	(18)	2.740	(18)
Semi-rural	0.759	(22)	2.324	(23)
Rural	0.730	(26)	2.270	(28)
County borough average	0.779	(83)	2.495	(83)

Note: Authorities are classified in the same way as in Table 5.1.

The figures in Table 5.4 show that urban authorities did spend more than rural and free-standing ones. At the very top of the league tables in 1960/1 came Birmingham, Manchester, Leeds, and Liverpool, and at the bottom were Bristol, Reading, Wakefield, Newport, Dewsbury, Gloucester, and Plymouth. Some of the seaside resorts are also high spenders, presumably because they maintain high public health standards, and also because they have to empty the dustbins of hotels, restaurants, and guest-houses, all of which throw away relatively large quantities of food which have to be moved quickly. Perhaps more important than either of these explanations is the fact that seaside resorts have large summer-time populations, compared with their relatively small resident population, and, therefore, their per capita (resident population) costs are high. The same sort of effect is likely to apply to seaside-resort spending on police, highways, public health, and parks.

These figures suggest that it is not population size and diseconomies of scale which cause high spending, but rather the geographical scale of urban settlements in England and Wales. It is notable, for example, that Bristol, a large but free-standing city, was at the very bottom of the table in 1960/1, and Leicester, Nottingham, and Stoke also spent relatively little. Conversely, relatively small authorities located in the middle of conurbations, for example St. Helens, Barnsley, Stockport, Wigan, and Halifax, were high spenders.

Housing

Housing is the first divisible service discussed in this chapter, and it will be remembered that such a service generally responds quite well to the demographic approach, because it correlates strongly with a wide range of local authority population characteristics. Housing — defined as the size of the rate fund contribution to the housing revenue account — is no exception. In stepwise regression analysis, six variables retain their statistical significance, as follows:

Variable	*Beta*
Years of Labour control	0.44***
Overcrowding	0.42***
Absence of hot water	0.28**
Percentage of local authority housing	−0.15**
Standardized male mortality rate	0.21**
Percentage of school-aged population	0.21**

Together these variables explain 70 per cent of the variance in 1960/1. A slightly different combination of variables appears in the 1972/3 regression, but the results are essentially similar, and show that high housing expenditure is a function of Labour control, poor housing conditions, low-income populations, and a relatively large proportion of old people.

The league table approach can add little to this, other than to illustrate. At the top of the table appear a series of poor, industrial cities such as Bootle, Gateshead, Warrington, and West Ham, while more affluent commerical and residential places like Blackpool, Southport, Croydon, Bath, and Oxford, are at the bottom. In 1960/1, seven of the eight seaside resorts were in the bottom ten.

Libraries, Museums, and Art Galleries

In the majority of authorities, expenditure on libraries is included with museums and art galleries, but for the sake of brevity all three will be called library expenditure. As with other indivisible services, library spending has resisted satisfactory explanation. A ranking of county boroughs, however, shows that the most important conurbation capitals, such as Liverpool, Manchester, Newcastle, Birmingham, and Leeds, have rather high figures. At the other extreme, many of the smaller industrial cities which exist in the shadow of the major capitals spent the least on libraries — places such as Dewsbury, East and West Ham, South Shields, and Bootle.

This raises the distinct possibility that library expenditure is closely connected, not with the size or nature of the resident population of a city, but with the size and nature of the population for which that city is a regional capital. Fortunately, the geographer, Carruthers, has ranked and grouped cities in England and Wales (excluding London) according to their importance as service centres, and the average library expenditure for each group in the hierarchy shows clearly enough that spending does decline as the importance of the city as a service centre declines (see Table 5.5).

Table 5.5 *Per Capita Library Expenditure (£), by Importance of Service Centres, County Boroughs, 1960/1 and 1972/3*

City rank[a]	Examples	1960/1	1972/3	(n)
Group 2B	Manchester	0.667	2.424	(5)
Group 2C	Cardiff	0.590	1.703	(4)
Groups 3A/3a	Bradford	0.530	1.777	(31)
Groups 3B/3b	Halifax	0.472	1.493	(27)
Groups 3C/3c	Burton	0.421	1.427	(7)
County borough mean		0.503	1.672	(74)[b]

Notes: [a] The ranking is that of W. I. Carruthers, 'Major shopping centres in England and Wales', *Regional Studies*, 1 (1967), 56–81. For some details of this study see Appendix 3.
[b] The total number of observations is 74, both because Carruthers does not classify all county boroughs, and because, for comparative reasons, the analysis is limited to boroughs which existed in both 1960/1 and 1972/3.

This approach does not lend itself to the counties, but a league table of high and low spenders reveals that the former category consists mainly of the wealthier, larger, and rather more urban authorities, while the latter includes mainly poorer, smaller, more remote, and rural counties. Four of the top ten are home counties (Essex, Surrey, Buckinghamshire, and Kent), which are not only large, but also wealthy and fairly urban, whereas the low spenders include many of the poorer and more agricultural counties, like the Isle of Ely, Holland and Kesteven in Lincolnshire, Anglesey, Pembrokeshire, and Caernarvon.

The common thread in counties and county boroughs seems to be neither the population size nor the density of the spending authority, but the number of people within regular using distance of libraries, which is in turn a function of absolute numbers and density. Among the county boroughs the capitals of the largest conurbations spent the most, and among the counties the highest spenders were the largest and most urbanized authorities. In short, spending seems to be a function of the total number of people who are within reasonable travelling distance of the libraries. This spatial element has rarely been considered in previous studies of local government outputs.

Town and Country Planning

Planning expenditure constitutes a small part of local authority budgets (less than half a per cent), and, of course, a good deal of planning work can be done without spending much. It is also notable that there is a greater variation in planning expenditure than any other service. In 1960/1 the highest per capita figure was £0.901 (Exeter), and the lowest (Sunderland) was £0.001. Little of the variance in county borough or county spending, however, is explained by the conventional approaches.

Yet the league tables show up something of interest, for it is clear that cities which suffered from heavy bombing during the war are grouped at the top. In fact, of the twelve county boroughs listed as having had major air attacks and at least 150 tons of high explosives dropped on them, ten are in the top twenty in 1960/1 for planning expenditure − these being East and West Ham, Birmingham, Plymouth, Bristol, Coventry, Portsmouth, Southampton, Hull, and Sheffield.[4] If one adds to these the cities of Exeter, Great Yarmouth, Hastings, Southend, Eastbourne, and Birkenhead, because they were also attacked by air at least fifty times and suffered great damage, then there are few county boroughs among the twenty highest spenders which did not suffer from extensive wartime damage.[5] The high spending authorities had not changed much by 1972/3. It seems that cities which had to set to work planning and rebuilding on a large scale in 1945 were still spending relatively heavily on planning twenty-five years later. By comparison places such as Chester, Carlisle, Blackpool, and Solihull, which received no more than the odd stray bomb, spent well below the national average.

This is not the whole story, however, because some high spenders, such as Bath and Worcester, had little bomb damage, whereas two cities which suffered moderately (Cardiff and Nottingham) are near the bottom of the table. Another part of the explanation seems to lie in the difference between the smallest and poorest industrial cities, and the smaller, richer, and historic ones. The former monopolize the bottom places (Sunderland, Oldham, Walsall, South Shields, Wakefield, and Barrow), while the latter (Bath, Worcester, Norwich, Canterbury, Oxford, and Gloucester, for example) spend above the average. In other words, high planning expenditure is found among many of the cities which had to be reconstructed after extensive bomb damage, and also among the older and more historic cities which have spent on conservation. There are many exceptions, however, and it is clear that these generalizations take us only part of the way to an adequate explanation.

Patterns are even more difficult to discern among the counties. There was a tendency for the home counties and for some of the other wealthier authorities to spend above the average — Kent, Buckingham, Berkshire, Essex, Oxfordshire, and Sussex, for example — perhaps because their conservation programmes are also relatively expensive. More notable is the high proportion of Welsh counties among the top spenders. In 1972/3 they fill seven of the top ten places. Beyond this, though, little sense can be made of the league tables, and planning expenditure remains something of a mystery.

Police

The study of police spending is complicated by the amalgamation of many of the counties and county boroughs to form a much smaller number of police authorities. In 1972/3 there were only forty-four police authorities in England and Wales, and many of these covered two or more counties and/or county boroughs, although per capita expenditures are given for individual authorities as if they were separate. This means that conclusions drawn from these figures must be treated with great caution.[6] Nevertheless, police spending shows some fairly clear uniformities.

The league tables reveal that the major capitals (Liverpool, Manchester, Newcastle, Birmingham, and Leeds) spent the most, followed by less important centres like Hull, Bristol, and Nottingham. Bottom of the list were the small cities on the industrial periphery — Smethwick, Sunderland, and Dewsbury, for example. It seems, that police spending may be strongly influenced by whether or not a city is a regional or metropolitan capital — by its importance as an urban area.

Cutting across this trend, however, are the seaside resorts, which were high spenders. Presumably their pubs, clubs, casinos, dance halls, summer crowds, and traffic densities all require police attention, besides which, a visible police presence may be good for a sense of security and for tourist business. These factors will be intensified by the fact that relatively small resident populations support police services for large tourist populations.

If seaside resorts are removed — as special cases — from the list of county boroughs, and if the remainder are grouped, as they were in Table 5.5, according to the Carruthers urban hierarchy, it can be seen (Table 5.6) that police spending is associated with the importance of a city as a service centre. The most important provincial capitals have the highest figures, and the figures gradually decline as one goes down the hierarchy, although the curve turns up again at the very bottom. Nevertheless, police and library spending appear to follow the same general pattern.

Table 5.6 *Per Capita Police Expenditure (£), by Importance of Service Centre, County Boroughs, 1960/1 and 1972/3*

City rank	Examples	1960/1	1972/3	(n)
Group 2B	Manchester	3.12	10.856	(5)
Group 2C	Cardiff	2.34	8.102	(4)
Groups 3A/3a	Gloucester	2.103	7.493	(27)
Groups 3B/3b	Rochdale	2.148	7.016	(24)
Groups 3C/3c	Merthyr Tydfil	2.198	7.920	(6)
County borough average		2.271	7.715	(66)

Note: The total number of observations is 66, because the seaside resorts have not been included, because Carruthers does not classify all county boroughs, and because, for comparative reasons, the analysis is limited to authorities which existed in both 1960/1 and 1972/3.

It is more difficult to discern trends or patterns among the counties, partly, no doubt, because quite a large proportion of the smaller ones are amalgamated into larger police authorities, together with the county boroughs within them. The Welsh authorities appear among the high spenders, with nine of the counties making up the four Welsh authorities in 1972/3 being at the top of the list, and only two at the bottom. There is also some evidence that population sparsity makes a difference.[7] Among the English counties in the top twenty spenders, 16.4 per cent of their total geographical area is classified as urban, compared with 10.8 per cent among the bottom twenty. The top group have a population density of 1.25 per acre, compared with 1.08 at the bottom. Yet these differences are small, and there are many exceptions, so the generalization cannot take us as far as we would wish.

Fire

Fire and police services are often grouped together, and yet correlation analysis suggests that they have rather little in common.[8] Neither is at all satisfactorily explained by the regression models of demographic studies, and in so far as they correlate with anything, they are not correlated with the same set of social, economic, and political variables. The picture is further obscured by the existence of joint fire authorities, especially among the smaller counties, which makes the figures difficult to interpret in some cases.

Fire service expenditure is influenced by Home Office standards of fire cover, which are based on four categories of fire risk.[9]

Class A. Includes concentrations of factories in towns, of shopping and business centres in large cities and towns, and of docks and ship-building yards in congested areas.

Class B. Model factory estates, shopping and business centres in smaller cities and towns, old timbered property in medium-sized towns, and large seaside holiday resorts.

Class C. Built up areas not falling in Class A or B.

Class D. All other areas.

Given these risk categories one would expect higher spending authorities to have large industrial and commercial areas, and ports and shipyards. The league table for fire expenditure shows this to be the case, in general. Ten ports are in the top twenty-five, and only four are in the bottom twenty-five. Of the remaining fifteen high spenders, most are small industrial county boroughs – Bootle, Dewsbury, Wakefield, for example. The seaside resorts have higher than average expenditures, although they are only Class B risk authorities. Front-page pictures of blazing hotels are not good for the holiday business.

It is difficult to categorize the low spenders, since these cover a fairly wide range of cities, including some of the small industrial authorities, some ports, and some seaside resorts. Consequently a distribution of high risk and low risk fire areas is only part of the explanation.

Table 5.7 *Per Capita Fire Expenditure (£), by Fire Risk and Population Density, among English County Boroughs with Highest and Lowest Expenditures, 1972/3*

	High density		Low density	
High risk	1.643	(8)	1.385	(2)
Low risk	1.597	(3)	1.387	(9)

Note: The classification is approximate since fire risk figures in 1972/3 are estimated from those available for 1977/8.

The counties show a distinct but different pattern. In the first place, nine of the ten Welsh fire authorities appear in the top twenty, and in the second place, seven of the remaining high spenders have above average densities of more than one person per acre (their average is 1.38). In comparison with the latter, fourteen of the bottom twenty have below average densities (their average is 0.49 persons per acre). Low-density counties not only have fewer fire risks, but it is also more difficult and more expensive to provide them with even a fairly minimal protection. Sparsely populated counties tend to have a high proportion of part-time and volunteer firemen. For example, in 1972/3, the most sparsely populated county (Westmorland) employed full-time to part-time staff in the ratio of 1:6, but the most densely populated (Lancashire) had a ratio of 1:6:1. It should be noted that most of the high spending Welsh counties have a low density; so that density, as such, will not show up as a significant demographic correlation.

The Home Office's fire risk categories are only loosely related to expenditure among the counties, but a combination of high risk and high densities is likely to result in high expenditure (see Table 5.7).

Highways

The demographic approach explains (with a modest degree of success) the per capita highways expenditure of the county boroughs, but the league tables suggest ways of improving upon this. The metropolitan capitals are notably heavy spenders, as are the seaside resorts. Presumably the major capitals spend heavily because of their particularly high traffic densities, whereas the seaside resorts do so partly because of their heavy summer traffic, and partly to provide specially good roads in order to minimize summer congestion.

Cities spending the least on highways include many of the smaller, industrial boroughs, such as Smethwick, Bootle, East and West Ham, Preston, and Stoke. The suspicion that the small industrial cities spend relatively little is strengthened by the fact that the smaller residential and commercial cities such as Portsmouth, Reading, Worcester, and Canterbury spent average or above average amounts. A simple relationship between an industrial tax base and low highways expenditure, however, is disturbed by the seaside resorts at one extreme, and by the major capitals at the other.

The demographic approach works rather better in the counties, where spending was highest in the smaller, more rural, and more sparsely populated authorities. In fact, one indicator or another of these variables, plus high voting turn-out, explains 80 per cent of the variance in both 1960/1 and 1972/3. The league tables confirm this pattern, with Westmorland, Cumberland, Hereford, and · Devon consistently at the top, and West Yorkshire, Nottinghamshire, Staffordshire, Lancashire, and Surrey usually at the bottom. The tables also show a strong regional effect, with nine of the thirteen Welsh counties in the top thirteen spenders in both years.

Public Health

Like planning, public health accounts for only a small proportion of total local expenditure (little more than 2 per cent), and like planning it is firmly resistant to conventional explanation. An examination of the league tables reveals some regularities, although they are sometimes indistinct. The seaside resorts stand out for their high spending, for obvious reasons, as do the two wealthy suburban authorities of Wallasey and Croydon. The ports are also notable for having an average of £0.60 in 1960/1 compared with an average for the county boroughs of £0.44. At the other extreme, some of the poorer, industrial boroughs spent the least; of the twenty-five low spenders, fourteen are cities on the industrial periphery. What confuses the picture, however, is the fact that the highest spenders also include these sorts of cities, and it is not clear what distinguishes one group from the other. What is clear, however, is that public health spending is consistently associated with Labour strength, or an absence of Conservative strength, this being among the few significant variables in the regression equations.

Politics does not seem to matter as far as public health spending in the counties is concerned, where the smaller, more rural, and/or poorer seem to spend the most. Cornwall, Norfolk, Suffolk, and Lincolnshire all appear in the top fifteen, as do seven of the thirteen Welsh counties. The lowest spenders are largely, but not exclusively, the wealthier and/or more urban counties such as Cheshire, Oxfordshire, Kent, Essex, Sussex, and Surrey. There are quite a few exceptions, however, and a good deal of the variation remains unexplained.

Personal Health Services

One would expect personal health costs to be highest in the poorer, more urban, and more industrial authorities, and so it is in both the counties and the county boroughs, although the association is not strong. In the boroughs, indicators of poverty, poor housing, and an ageing population account for about 20 per cent of the variance. The affluent and commercial/residential cities, such as the seaside resorts and the county towns, make up the majority of the bottom twenty, and, conversely, the poor cities on the industrial periphery dominate the top twenty. The association between poverty and high spending is not complete, however, because boroughs like Tynemouth, Bootle, and Walsall, also appear in the bottom twenty. As with public health, it is not clear what distinguishes them from similar but high spending boroughs.

Among the counties, the Welsh authorities stand out, with eight appearing in the top fifteen. Many of the remaining high spenders are the more urbanized or industrial counties, such as Lancashire, Nottinghamshire, Essex, Durham, West Yorkshire, and Staffordshire. In contrast, a clear majority of low spenders are the most rural of the English counties (Suffolk, Rutland, Devon, East and North Yorkshire, Shropshire, and Lincolnshire). The exceptional high spending of the rural and sparsely populated Welsh counties obscures the tendency for their English equivalents to spend rather little.

Education

The results of an analysis of education expenditure depend on whether one takes per capita or per pupil figures. So far, expenditures have been analysed on a per capita basis, either because they are community-wide services (for example parks or libraries), or because there are no appropriate figures for the target population (for example those in need of public housing). But, in the case of education, the school-aged population is known, and the more interesting figure is what is spent on each pupil, rather than what is spent on education per capita of total population. It is worth noting that the greater the proportion of pupils in an authority, the higher its per capita education expenditure, but the lower its per pupil spending (see Table 5.8).   ·

Table 5.8 *Correlations between Percentage of Population of School Age, and Per Capita and Per Pupil Education Expenditure, Counties and County Boroughs, 1960/1 and 1972/3*

		County boroughs	County councils
Expenditure per capita	1960/1	0.69***	0.29*
	1972/3	0.74***	0.20
Expenditure per pupil	1960/1	−0.40***	−0.32*
	1972/3	−0.50***	−0.40*
(N)	1960/1	(77)	(61)
	1972/3	(76)	(56)

Generally speaking, authorities with a wealthy local tax base, and a small proportion of school-aged children, spend more on each pupil, particularly if they have a large proportion of Labour councillors. The latter is a strongly significant variable in both the county and the county borough regressions. Translated into the terms of actual cities, this means that the seaside resorts and the county towns, which are wealthy and have relatively few school children, have the highest per pupil figures, followed closely by a group of relatively wealthy and larger industrial cities such as Derby, Leicester, Coventry, and Nottingham. At the bottom of the table come the major capitals and their industrial satellites.

Among the counties, the Welsh authorities stand out for their exceptionally high spending, something noted in previous research.[10] Education costs are notoriously high in sparsely populated areas, and this might be thought to explain the Welsh figures, were it not for the fact that some of the sparsely populated English counties spend rather little — Devon, Cornwall, and Dorset, for example. Clearly the relationship between education spending and population sparsity in Welsh and English counties needs closer attention, and the topic will be taken up again in Chapter 8.

Children's, Welfare, and Social Services

The regression equations of the demographic approach have mixed success with spending on welfare and spending on children per child, but then little success when the two are amalgamated to form social services. This is to be expected since different types of city spend heavily on the two services, and this cancels out their different effects. Taking the children per child figures first, the high spenders were mainly major urban capitals and their industrial satellites. At the other extreme, the low spenders were primarily the more affluent seaside resorts and county towns.

This pattern is partly reversed for welfare spending, where the high spenders were the more affluent commercial and residential towns, plus a number of the poorest industrial boroughs. What confuses this simple pattern, however, is the appearance of some of the small industrial boroughs among the low spenders on welfare. And in addition there is a rather mixed collection of boroughs which spent little on both children and welfare.

However, something of value emerges from the league tables for they do show two fairly strong tendencies which contribute to an explanation.

(1) Expenditure on children's services is generally highest in the smallest and poorest industrial boroughs, which often have a large proportion of both children and bad housing and social conditions.

(2) Welfare spending is high in some of the industrial boroughs which have high levels of spending on children's services (Oldham, Bradford, Huddersfield, West Ham, Sunderland), but it is generally even higher in the seaside resorts and some of the county towns. Whereas poverty and a relatively large old population explains the former, the sheer weight of retired people, though many of them are well off, explains the latter.

The county figures are also mixed. Once again the Welsh counties stand out for their exceptionally high spending on welfare in the early years, and on social services in the later years. In addition, some of the south coast retirement counties spent a lot on welfare (East and West Sussex, and Dorset, but not Hampshire) and social services, as did some of the poorer counties such as Cornwall, Lancashire, Lincolnshire, and Durham. These counties have either a large proportion of old people, or low personal incomes.

Lastly, politics is of importance to a significant degree for the social services. In both the counties and the county boroughs, the percentage of Labour members on the council is significantly associated with high social services spending, and a political variable of one kind or another is included in three of the four regressions for spending on children and welfare. While it is the low-turn-out, Labour authorities which spent most on children, it is the high-turn-out and more affluent authorities which spent most on welfare.

Total Expenditure

Total spending, is, of course, heavily determined by the major spending services, which are education, housing, highways, police, and social services; and authorities spending more than the average on these will inevitably emerge at the top of the league table for total expenditure. These are likely to be those authorities which combine a relatively heavy need or demand for local services (a large working-class and school-aged population, poor housing and social conditions, and a large hinterland population making demands upon libraries, police, fire, and highways), a relatively good tax base of commerical and industrial property, and a disposition to tax and spend relatively heavily (a large Labour group on the council). The great majority of the top spenders in 1972/3 fit this profile: four are the major conurbation capitals of Manchester, Liverpool, Newcastle, and Birmingham, and fifteen are the smallest and poorest industrial boroughs.

At the other extreme are the predominantly commercial and residential cities which are Conservative controlled, and which have relatively little demand for, or inclination to spend on, many services. These include six of the seaside resorts, the middle-class suburbs of Solihull and Wallasey, and an assortment of county towns and commercial centres, including Plymouth, Worcester, Ipswich, Canterbury, and York. The pattern is not perfect, by any means, however, for the low spenders also include some small industrial boroughs (Dudley, Stockport, Wakefield, and Warley), just as some of the league leaders include the county towns of Exeter, Lincoln, Norwich, and Oxford.

Because the Welsh authorities are so regularly league leaders on a wide range of county services, it is no surprise that they also emerge at the very top of the table for total expenditure. The top six counties are Welsh, as are eight of the top ten.

Of the English counties in the top twenty, most are rural (Buckinghamshire, Hertfordshire, Gloucestershire, Herefordshire), while many of those at the bottom of the table were more urban and/or relatively industrial, but relatively wealthy – Essex, Surrey, West Yorkshire, Lancashire, Nottingham, Derbyshire, and Kent. There are enough exceptions to this general tendency, however, to suggest that further analysis is necessary, and it may well be that the exceptional nature of the Welsh figures has obscured general trends and tendencies among the English counties.

Conclusion

This chapter has worked its way through a great mass of data, although only a small fraction of the statistical material has been presented. It is possible to draw out some generalizations, however, and these will serve as a basis for more systematic analysis in the following chapters, the main purpose of this chapter being not to prove or disprove, but to search for leads which could guide future analysis. The most important of these are as follows:

(1) Some service expenditures such as those on police, libraries, and possibly highways, appear to be related to the position which a city has in the urban hierarchy of the county as a whole; high order or central place cities seem to spend relatively heavily on some services.

(2) Other services such as parks, public health, highways, police, and fire seem to be associated with city types. Ports stand out in one or two services, but mainly it is seaside resorts, county towns, industrial satellites, and the major conurbation capitals that appear to have their own special spending patterns.

(3) What might be termed geographical, spatial, or locational variables are also important influences on some service spending levels. Coastal cities generally spend little on sewerage, unless they are seaside resorts, whereas cities which are embedded in large urban agglomerations spend heavily on parks and refuse.

(4) Regional variations also appear, very markedly in the case of the Welsh counties, which regularly appear among the top ten or twenty in the league tables. Although the high spending of some Welsh counties may well be strongly affected by their characteristics of poverty, population sparsity, and strong Labour voting, there seems to be a strong regional effect operating on top of these. The strength of this regional variable has not, so far as we know, been identified before.

(5) Historical factors also play a part. The effect of wartime bomb damage was still clearly noticeable in planning expenditure in 1972/3.

(6) The evidence reinforces the view that politics matters, not generally as the major determinant of public policy, but often as a major determinant of expenditure on some of the most expensive local services. However, the whole question needs closer and more vigorous examination.

NOTES

1. In spite of these strictures about factor and cluster analysis, most statistical studies of cities and city types in Britain find a clear and homogenous group of seaside resorts: see C. A. Moser and W. Scott, *British Towns* (Edinburgh, Oliver and Boyd, 1961), p. 84; G. Armen, 'A classification of cities and city regions in England and Wales, 1966', *Regional Studies*, 6 (1972), 149–82; and P. L. Knox, 'Spatial variations in level of living in England and Wales in 1961', *Transactions of the Institute of British Geographers*, 62 (1974), 1–24. Long before all these studies, however, John and Ursula Hicks found that seaside resorts have their own special spending patterns, see J. R. and U. Hicks, *Standards of Local Expenditure: A Problem of the Inequality of Incomes* (Cambridge, Cambridge University Press, 1943).

2. The idiosyncratic nature of spending in some cities is underlined by the case of Burton-on-Trent where sewerage expenditure in 1972/3 was over three and a half times the county borough mean, and 63 per cent higher than the next highest city. Burton's figure is high because the city is not only inland, but also bears the costs of its beer industry, see Institute of Municipal Treasurers and Accountants, *Local Expenditure and Exchequer Grants* (London, IMTA, 1956), p. 84. This local peculiarity should not be allowed to obscure the overall national patterns, however.

3. For some evidence see the figures presented by the Greater London Council to the Layfield Committee, *Report of the Committee of Enquiry into Local Government Finance*, Appendix 1, Vol. 2, Evidence of Local Authority Association (London, HMSO, 1976), p. 303.

4. Figures for the number of air attacks and tons of high explosives dropped are given in T. H. O'Brien, *Civil Defence* (History of the Second World War, London, HMSO and Longmans, Green, 1955), p. 681.

5. Figures for the number of air attacks on provincial towns and cities are given in O'Brien, *Civil Defence*, p. 684.

6. For a further discussion of the problems of analysing police expenditure see Appendix 3.4.

7. On sparsity and police expenditure see IMTA, *Local Expenditure and Exchequer Grants*, p. 115.

8. The correlations between per capita police and fire expenditure in the counties and county boroughs are no higher than 0.36 and of not much substantial significance.

9. See *Fire Services Actual Statistics 1977/8* (London, Chartered Institute of Public Finance and Accountancy (CIPFA), 1978), p. 20.

10. D. Byrne, B. Williamson, and B. Fletcher, *The Poverty of Education* (London, Martin Robertson, 1975), p. 78.

6. CENTRAL PLACES AND URBAN SERVICE EXPENDITURES

Introduction

This chapter develops the suggestion, which emerged from the explorations of the previous chapter, that the service spending levels of cities, or to be more exact, the spending levels of cities both on some services and in total, appear to be related to the position that these cities occupy in the urban hierarchy of the country as a whole. High-ranking cities such as Birmingham and Manchester spend heavily in total, and on a particular range of services such as police, libraries, and highways. Conversely, low-ranking places such as Dewsbury and Tynemouth spend rather little. This chapter will, therefore, examine the relationship between the urban hierarchy and spending patterns in order to see how close the empirical associations between the two are, and also in order to develop a theory of the determinants of urban public policy. Though general in its scope, it should be pointed out at this early stage that the theory is not complete or comprehensive; it sets aside, for the time being, the other points which emerged from the previous chapter, and, in addition, since central place theory applies only to urban places, it also leaves the question of the counties for a later chapter. Nevertheless, central place theory does seem to offer an approach to the analysis and understanding of urban services which is both empirically satisfactory and theoretically appealing.

Central Place Theory and Public Services

At the heart of central place theory is the idea that urban places exist to provide services and facilities not only for their own populations but also for the populations of their hinterlands. Thus: 'one of the main functions of a town — or any service centre — is to supply the needs of the population around it.'[1] It is impossible for all towns and cities to provide the complete range of services and facilities required by their residents, for to do so each and every one would have to have an airport, a large public library, a range of specialized shops, an opera-house, an Olympic-sized swimming-pool, a university, and a wide assortment of other expensive amenities and facilities, as well as the daily necessities of urban life. Consequently, there is an urban division of labour in which the most important urban places, at the top of the hierarchy, cater for a wide range of specialist demands, as well as the needs of everyday life, while successively lower places in the hierarchy provide a narrower range of specialist facilities in addition to the requirements of everyday life. In general, the more important the central place, the larger its own population, and the population of its hinterland, and the more likely it is to have a population of sufficient size to be able to meet a wide variety of specialist demands. Conversely, the smaller the population of an urban place, the more limited its capacity to provide a wide range and variety of services, and the greater the proportion of its trade and commerce taken up by more routine requirements.

Central place theory thus conceives of the urban system as a nested hierarchy in which each city provides all the services and facilities of cities which are below it in the hierarchy, plus an additional range of more specialized services and facilities.[2] Cities can therefore be ranked from the low-order central places, such as market towns, which serve a rather small population with a narrow range of amenities, up to the very highest central places such as New York, London, Paris, and Tokyo, which provide the most specialized and costly services, in addition to all those provided by lower-order central places.

The main idea behind central place theory has been summarized by Carruthers in the following way:

This paper is concerned with the study of the relationships between 'town' and 'countryside' in England and Wales and in particular with those places on which these relationships centre. Such places are referred to here as 'service centres' because they act as the centres where shopping, entertainment, cultural, professional and similar services are sought by people from the surrounding areas. The centres extend over a complete range, varying in status from places of a very limited local significance to those whose influence is regional and, in the case of London, national. The less important a centre the greater its dependence upon other more important service centres. Ranged each according to status, the centres could be made to form an almost continuous list, but it is more convenient to think of them as being organised into the ranks or successive orders of a hierarchy or gradation, though the divisions proposed may not always be clear cut or well defined.[3]

Cities at the top of the urban hierarchy have a wide variety of interrelated characteristics. They are often large in terms of population and area.[4] They contain a wide range of shopping facilities, including many specialized wholesale and retail outlets.[5] They are centres for entertainment and leisure and therefore have theatres, museums, art galleries, libraries, cinemas, concert halls, restaurants, hotels, night-clubs, and sports facilities of all kinds.[6] They are the location for large numbers of lawyers, estate agents, stockbrokers and financial advisers, advertising agents, market researchers, and consultants on a great variety of professional and business matters.[7] They are also the location for the regional or national headquarters of organizations such as banks, insurance companies, chain stores, and trade unions, and also professional, business, and voluntary organizations.[8] They are often government centres, and the location for large central and local government departments.[9] Lastly, because they are centres of both business and pleasure, they attract large numbers of commuters and visitors, and, therefore, have large and extensive public transport systems and high traffic densities.[10]

Sociologists and economists have used central place theory, or variants of it, to explain the distribution and location of industry, commerce, and leisure facilities,[11] but, curiously, geographers have not used it in their attempts to explain local government spending, or the distribution of public services and facilities.[12] This is probably because central place theory was originally used to explain the location of economic activities in the private sector. However, centrality is also likely to affect public service provision and spending, and for the same general reason that it affects the private sector — the more important the central place the larger its population and the greater the range and variety of services it is able to provide. To be exact, centrality is likely to affect public services in two ways. First, urban authorities are likely to provide a range of specialized services in accordance with their city's importance as a central place. Cities which are low in the hierarchy are likely to have relatively small public libraries, museums, and art galleries, relatively small public recreational facilities, and relatively few specialized educational facilities for the gifted and the handicapped. High-order central places, by comparison, are more likely to have large and specialized municipal cultural centres, an extensive range of parks and recreational facilities, and a whole variety of specialized schools and educational institutions.[13] To this extent, it might be hypothesized that the higher the city ranks in the central place hierarchy the more likely it is to spend on the public services which form part of the city's function as a service centre.[14]

Second, the higher the city's position in the central place hierarchy, the greater the use made of its public services by those living outside it. Thus, high-order central places are likely to carry larger than average costs for roads and public transport, refuse collection, police, and public health services, because the need for these services is generated not only by the resident population, but also by the people who travel to it for business and pleasure purposes. On the topic of roads and transport, Berry and Garrison observe that: 'The higher the order of the centre, the greater the convergence of routes. The denser the distribution of purchasing power, the denser the transport network.'[15] And, of course, the larger the central place the greater the distances travelled by the population. Therefore, all other things being equal, the higher the rank of a city the more likely it is to spend on highways and public transport.[16]

The impact of centrality on highways and transport spending will be affected by how local political and administrative boundaries are drawn. If they are narowly drawn, in order to include little more than the central city, and to exclude a large proportion of its urban and suburban hinterland, as they so often are in the United States, then the effect of centrality is likely to be maximized.

If they are widely drawn, as they generally are in Britain, then the impact of centrality will be muted by virtue of the fact that much of the urban hinterland and its suburban periphery is incorporated with the central city in one large local government unit.

Central places are also likely to have a high density of restaurants, pubs, hotels, and other facilities, which are inspected or controlled by the public health authorities, and which generate the need for regular refuse collection and disposal. In addition, they are likely to be centres of crime (criminal services such as drug trafficking, fencing, prostitution, and gambling are no less a part of the central place complex than legitimate and legal activities), and the size of their commuting and visitor population is likely to introduce special and expensive problems of social control. Consequently, police costs are also likely to be related to the central place hierarchy. Once again, the size of the centrality effect will depend, in part, on the placing of local government boundaries.

Although this is speculative, there is some evidence to support the general thrust of the argument. In the USA, Kasarda has investigated the relationship between suburban population size and growth and the cost of central city public services (i.e. of major central places), and concludes that the former are strong influences on central city spending, particularly on expenditure on police, fire, highways, sanitation, recreation, and general administration.[17] And in Belgium, Aiken and Depré have found that ecological centrality (the sociological analogue of central place theory) has a strong and consistent influence on every category of expenditure, with only one small exception.[18] It remains to be shown, however, that centrality affects the spending of cities in England and Wales.

A Hierarchy of Expenditures?

The geographer W. I. Carruthers has ranked seventy-four major shopping centres of England and Wales in 1961 according to three aspects of their shopping patterns. First, he assigns points to each centre according to its type and amount of trade, with a slight weighting in favour of towns with an above average trade in non-food goods. Second, he estimates the theoretical net loss or gain of trade for each local authority area. In other words, he estimates the amount of trade which authorities gain from, or lose to their neighbours, with high-order central places gaining the most from their less important neighbours. And third, he assigns points for the provision of selected shopping facilities which are typically found in the strongest centres (shops for shoes, menswear, women's wear, furniture and furnishings, radio, electrical goods, bicycles, jewellery, and leather and sports goods).[19] These three scores are added together to produce a single figure which can be used to rank county boroughs according to their importance in the urban hierarchy (see Table 6.1), ranging from the highest, which is Manchester (London was not a county borough), to the lowest, which is Merthyr Tydfil.

Table 6.1 *County Boroughs in England and Wales, 1961, as Scored and Ranked by Carruthers according to their Shopping Patterns*

Group	City	Points score	Rank order
2B	Manchester	74	1
	Birmingham	72	2
	Liverpool	71	3
	Newcastle	70	4
	Leeds	69	5
2C	Nottingham	67	6
	Leicester	63	7
	Cardiff	62	8
	Sheffield	61	9
3A/3a	Wolverhampton	60	10
	Bristol	58	11
	Hull	58	11
	Blackpool	58	11
	Derby	58	11
	Bournemouth	58	11
	Bradford	57	16
	Coventry	57	16
	Southampton	57	16
	Doncaster	57	16
	Norwich	57	16
	Plymouth	56	21
	Reading	56	21
	York	56	21
	Brighton	56	21
	Swansea	55	25
	Preston	55	25
	Chester	55	25
	Gloucester	54	28
	Newport	54	28
	Northampton	54	28
	Exeter	53	31
	Sunderland	53	31
	Middlesborough	53	31
	Huddersfield	53	31
	Bolton	53	31
	Bath	53	31
	Southend	53	31
	Oxford	53	31
	Carlisle	52	39
	Worcester	52	39
	Barnsley	52	39
	Ipswich	52	39
	Wigan	52	39
3B/3b	Darlington	51	44
	Portsmouth	50	45
	Stoke	49	46
	Halifax	49	46
	Lincoln	49	46
	Walsall	49	46

Group	City	Points score	Rank order
	Wakefield	49	46
	Blackburn	48	51
	Warrington	48	51
	Canterbury	48	51
	Dudley	47	54
	Rotherham	46	55
	Stockport	45	56
	Gt. Yarmouth	45	56
	Birkenhead	44	58
	Burnley	44	58
3C/3c	Burton	42	60
	Grimsby	42	60
	Salford	42	60
	St. Helens	41	63
	East Ham	41	63
	Rochdale	41	63
	W. Hartlepool	41	63
	W. Bromwich	39	67
	Bury	38	68
	Hastings	38	68
	Dewsbury	36	70
	South Shields	35	71
	Newport	35	71
	Tynemouth	26	73
	Merthyr Tydfil	23	74

The points score for each county borough was then correlated with the per capita service expenditure figures, and the results are shown in Table 6.2. As in the previous chapter, results are given for two years, in order to minimize the chance of picking an unusual financial year, and in order to explore changes and stability in spending patterns over time. Three general points about the tables are worth making.

(1) The urban hierarchy seems to be at least as generally and strongly associated with urban service expenditures, and with total expenditure, as any of the variables considered in earlier chapters.

(2) The pattern of correlations is relatively stable over time, suggesting a consistent effect which is not peculiar to a particular year.

(3) The pattern makes theoretical sense in that it is largely consistent with the set of expectations discussed earlier in this chapter: the higher the position of a city in the urban hierarchy the more likely it is to spend on libraries, refuse, special education, and police. At the same time, the urban hierarchy does not appear to be strongly related to spending on education in general (as opposed to special education), sewerage, personal heath, welfare, or housing, and this is also consistent with the theory.

On the other hand, parks, public health, planning (in 1960/1), and total expenditure do not show significant correlations, as the theory suggests they should have, while, for reasons which are not clear, children and fire do.

Table 6.2 *Zero-order Pearsonian Correlations between Carruthers's Urban Hierarchy Measure and the Per Capita Service Expenditures of County Boroughs, 1960/1 and 1968/9*

	1960/1	1968/9
Special education	0.21*	0.28**
Libraries	0.49***	0.37***
Sewerage		
Refuse	0.25*	0.37***
Parks	0.20*	
Public health		0.23*
Personal health	0.20*	
Children per child	0.26*	
Welfare		
Housing		
Planning		0.30**
Highways		
Fire	−0.40***	−0.31**
Police	0.25*	0.49**
Total	0.25*	0.27*
(N)	(73)	(71)

These, however, are only bivariate results which tell us nothing of the net effects on expenditures of the urban hierarchy: the 'real' effect may be concealed by intervening variables, and equally the significant correlations reported so far may be removed after controlling for other variables. If, as the theory claims, position in the urban hierarchy is a very important feature of cities, then one would expect it to be associated with a whole cluster of urban characteristics. This is indeed the case, as Table 6.3 shows. The table reports the statistically significant, simple correlations between the urban hierarchy scores and the set of social, economic, and political variables which proved to be closely associated with expenditures. These variables therefore represent a short list of the most powerful social, economic, and political variables so far as county borough expenditures are concerned. In other words, to test the net effects of the urban hierarchy against these variables is to subject it to the most stringent and conservative test; if the urban hierarchy continues to be related to service spending while controlling for these variables, then there is good reason to believe that it does have explanatory power of its own.

Table 6.3 is not concerned with the general features of the urban hierarchy, but with those features which are also related to spending on urban services. It shows that higher-order cities typically have a high retail-trade turnover, a high density, a high rateable value per capita, and a small proportion of domestic property but a high proportion of offices, and also that they are generally large cities. None of this is at all surprising, given the general thrust of central place theory, but two particularly large correlations present problems of collinearity for regression analysis – those concerned with office property and city size – and these have been removed from the regressions which follow. The grounds for doing so are as follows. While it is clear why central places have a high proportion of office property, it is not clear why offices, as such, should generate a need for some forms of public expenditure. For example, to refer back to Table 6.2, there is no special reason why library expenditure should be associated with office property (unless it is hypothesized that office workers are particularly heavy users of libraries near their place of work in the central city, but not in the suburbs and small towns where they tend to live), although there is good reason why central places should spend relatively heavily on this central place service. In other words, on a priori, theoretical grounds we may expect library expenditure to be more a feature of central places than of concentrations of office property, even though central places and offices are closely linked by definition.

Table 6.3 *Zero-order Correlations between the Urban Hierarchy and a Selection of the Social, Economic, and Political Characteristics of County Boroughs, 1960/1 and 1968/9*

	1960/1	1968/9
Overcrowding		
Households without hot water		
Standardized mortality rate		
Manual workers		
Owner-occupiers		
Retail-trade turnover per capita	0.32**	0.32**
Density	0.42***	0.43***
Rateable value per capita	0.35***	0.41***
Domestic property (%)	−0.26**	−0.23*
Office property (%)	0.78***	0.72***
Industrial property (%)		
Old people (%)		
Population inflow	0.24*	0.24*
School population		
Log of population	0.74***	0.74***
Conservative seats, 1959 (%)		
Number years Labour control, 1955–9		
Number years Conservative control, 1955–9		
Turn-out	−0.21*	0.27*
Uncontested seats		

Population size is removed from the regressions on the same sort of grounds.[20] Repeated attempts have failed to uncover systematic or theoretically meaningful links between urban service costs and city size.[21] Economies and diseconomies of scale do appear to operate, but the shape of the cost curves varies enormously from one sub-service to another, and the population threshold at which economies are transformed into diseconomies, and vice versa, also varies enormously. Besides, there are a good many reasons why spending on urban services may tend to increase with city size, and economies and diseconomies of scale are only two of them.[22] Many of the others, such as population movement and specialized public services, are connected with the urban hierarchy rather than population size *per se*.

Consequently, it is argued, size is something of a surrogate for centrality, and the problems of collinearity which it raises can be solved, for the time being, by removing it from the list of independent variables. Future research should try to sort out the independent effects of size and centrality, although they are so closely related that this may be difficult to do. Not only is the full impact of size on costs and spending likely to depend on an interactive effect with centrality, but also the shape and proportions of the urban hierarchy are likely to depend partly upon the drawing of boundaries and the size of big city authorities. This makes the whole subject extremely complex, but centrality covers a much broader range of phenomena and offers far greater theoretical and explanatory potential than size.

Table 6.4 *Multiple Regression of Urban Hierarchy Measure on Service Expenditures of County Boroughs in England and Wales, 1960/1 and 1968/9*

Per capita expenditure	1960/1	1968/9
Special education	0.25*	
Libraries	0.38***	0.28*
Sewerage		
Refuse	0.36**	0.48***
Public health		
Local health		
Children per child	0.38**	
Welfare		
Housing		
Planning		
Highways	−0.24*	
Fire	−0.47*	−0.58***
Police	0.30**	0.26*
Total		

After this brief methodological diversion we can return to the regression analysis. Table 6.4 shows the statistically significant standardized regression coefficients (beta weights) between the urban hierarchy measure and service expenditures in 1960/1 and 1968/9. Five points should be made about this table.

(1) The results are generally good in the sense that there are a fairly large number of significant figures. In 1960/1 no other social, economic, or political variable was related to as many service expenditures as the urban hierarchy measure, even though the other variables were carefully chosen for their explanatory power. In 1968/9 the urban hierarchy measure is related to only four service expenditures, but even so only three other independent variables (domestic property, population density, and council housing) were related to more than this. In other words, the urban hierarchy measure proves itself to be among the most powerful explanatory variables so far as urban service expenditures are concerned.

(2) Having said this it should also be pointed out that the results in Table 6.4 are not outstandingly good. While the urban hierarchy variable does seem to be relatively powerful by comparison with the other social, economic, and political characteristics of cities, its overall explanatory power does not approach that of ecological centrality in Belgian cities as reported by Aiken and Depré. We will return to this theme a little later.

(3) The figures in Table 6.4 are generally consistent with the theory in that they show high-order central places to have high expenditures on libraries, refuse, special education, and police services, while sewerage, health, welfare, and housing do not, as predicted, have any relationship with city rank.

(4) Although the pattern is fairly consistent over the two years, the statistical fit is not as good in 1968/9. This may be partly because the urban hierarchy for both financial years is measured in terms of shopping activity in 1961, which may have changed to some extent by 1968/9.

(5) There are also some anomalies. Contrary to the theory, public health, planning, and total expenditure are not dependent upon city rank, and highways expenditure is only weakly and negatively related in 1960/1. Fire expenditure is strongly and negatively related to the urban hierarchy, while children's services expenditure is quite strongly related in 1960/1, although the theory does not predict this. In sum, while most of the figures fit the theory, not all do so.

Further examination of the regressions suggests possible explanations for some of the anomalies. Among the most powerful variables in the equations (see Table 6.5) are overcrowding, rateable value per capita, percentage domestic property, and retail trade turnover per capita, and all of these are fairly closely associated with centrality; the higher the rank of the city the more likely it is to have high densities, high rateable values, a small proportion of domestic

Table 6.5 *Multiple Regression of Urban Hierarchy Related Variables on Service Expenditures of County Boroughs in England and Wales, 1968/9*

Per capita expenditures	Overcrowding	Retail trade	Rateable value	Domestic property
Education				−0.28**
Libraries	0.31*	−0.49*		−0.71***
Sewerage	−0.33*			−0.45**
Refuse				
Public health			0.42**	
Personal health				
Children		−0.54**	0.32*	−0.48**
Welfare				−0.50**
Housing	0.29*			
Planning			0.27*	
Highways	0.37**			−0.64***
Fire				−0.50**
Police		−0.31*	0.37*	
Total	0.35**			−0.82***
Education per child				−0.33**
Children per child		−0.61**	0.49***	−0.43**

Notes:
1. This table reports standardized regression coefficients.
2. N = 73.
3. For reasons of space this table gives the results for only one year, but the figures for 1960/1 are much the same.

property, and high per capita retail sales (see Table 6.3). While city size and the proportion of office property were excluded from the regressions on the grounds that they were, (a) so closely related to the urban hierarchy as to produce severe problems of collinearity, and (b) largely surrogates for centrality, these other variables were included because they do not produce such severe collinearity problems. Nevertheless, they are all features of the urban hierarchy, and to this extent are associated with its explanatory power. Take, for example, the first figure in the first column of Table 6.5, that of 0.31 between overcrowding and library expenditure. There is no good reason to believe that people in over-crowded accommodation use libraries, museums, and art galleries to any great extent. On the contrary, these kinds of people in central cities are less likely to use these facilities than the residents of the spacious suburbs. On the other hand, there is an extremely strong and *negative* coefficient between library spending and domestic property, and yet it is precisely the people in residential areas who are likely to make the most use of libraries, museums, and art galleries. The most convincing explanation for the figures is that the higher the city ranks in the urban hierarchy, the more overcrowded it is, and also the more it spends on large libraries, museums, and art galleries, which are used not only by the residents of the city, but also by people who visit it from outside. In short, central places are densely populated but it is their centrality, not their density, which accounts for most of their high library spending.

Because of the statistical problems of multicollinearity, the regression results reported in Table 6.4 are likely to underestimate the full, direct influence of the urban hierarchy on service expenditures. The fact that centrality is an important feature of any urban place, and the fact that this feature, as one would expect, is strongly related to a number of other important features, means that some of the explanatory power of centrality is likely to be lost in the regressions, and consequently its full effects are not likely to be revealed in the regression coefficients.[23]

At the same time, centrality is not strongly associated with any of the political measures used in this study, as Table 6.3 shows. A city's position in the urban hierarchy is not strongly associated with the strength either of its parties or of its election turnout. Centrality is obviously independent of local politics, and this makes the task of establishing the importance of politics for local policies that much easier in later chapters.

Toward a General Theory

Combining the theory advanced in the earlier part of the chapter with the results produced in Tables 6.4 and 6.5, it is possible to go beyond a general statement about the probable relevance of the urban hierarchy to patterns of city expenditure, and construct a more detailed model which helps to explain this relevance. First, centrality, population size, and density are closely connected as Table 6.3 shows. Population size and density are also related to levels of expenditure to the extent that they generate diseconomies of scale. Thus:

Centrality $\longrightarrow$ large population size and high population density $\longrightarrow$ diseconomies of scale and density $\longrightarrow$ high service costs

Central places are also characterized by a high proportion of offices, shops, and other commercial property, and, as we have already seen, this type of property (as compared with domestic and industrial property) generally has a high rateable value. The importance of a city in the hierarchy will directly affect its tax base, because of the value of its commercial property, and also because of the wealth of its commercial and business population. These relationships may be expressed diagrammatically in the following way:

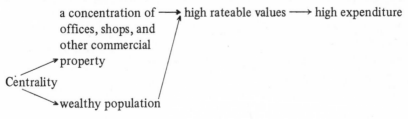

In addition, local government, no less than the private sector, provides various central place services, particularly libraries, museums, art galleries, some sports facilities, parks, botanic gardens, zoos, and special educational facilities. The need for parks and sports facilities is further increased by the fact that the open countryside is relatively inaccessible at the centre of large urban agglomerations, so the link between centrality and spreading may be specified as:

Centrality ⟶ high expenditure on public central place services, namely
— libraries, museums, art galleries
— sports facilities
— parks
— special education

Lastly, central places attract large numbers of commuters and visitors who use them for business and pleasure. The more important the central place, the heavier the demands placed upon some of its services, including police, planning, highways, and public transport.

Centrality ⟶ large population flows ⟶ high expenditure on
— police
— planning
— highways
— public transport

Combining this set of small diagrams into one produces Fig. 6.1, which, though large and complex, serves some useful functions. It specifies the relationships between a set of dependent and independent variables and thus helps to create theoretical coherence in a research area where there is, at present, little more than a collection of formless empirical findings. Moreover, it specifies a set of causal relationships between variables in a way which permits empirical tests, given adequate and appropriate data. To this extent, it also contains suggestions for future research. For example, to what extent are the higher per capita expenditures of large cities due to diseconomies of scale, and to what extent are they due to the heavy service burdens placed upon central places by their hinterlands? Or again, what exactly is the relationship between centrality, population wealth, tax base, and their resulting expenditure patterns? And last, there are practical implications for the way in which central government distributes its grants to local government. At the moment, central grants take no account of the needs generated by a city's place in the urban hierarchy. Perhaps. as in Germany, some allowances for the extra financial burdens of central place should be built into the grant distribution formula.

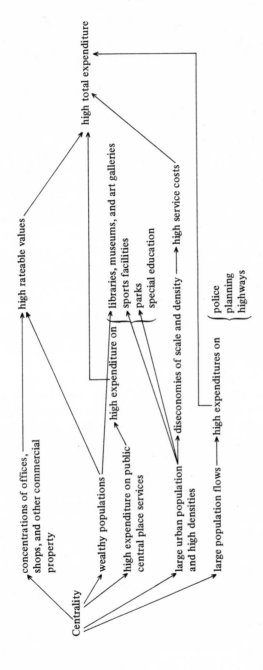

Fig. 6.1. A Causal Model Relating Centrality and Local Public Expenditure

Conclusions

The evidence in this chapter shows that central place theory, as developed by the geographers, or the theory of ecological centrality, as developed by the sociologists, can serve as a useful starting-point for an explanation of variations in city expenditures. The theory is relevant to public spending on two kinds of urban services: first, city governments will themselves produce central place services and facilities which, in Britain, are likely to include libraries, museums, art galleries, parks and sports facilities, and special educational services; second, the large number of people who visit central place cities for business and pleasure purposes are likely to use local services such as police, planning, highways, and public transport. Consequently, the higher a city's place in the urban hierarchy, the greater its per capita expenditures on these services are likely to be, and the higher its total per capita expenditure is likely to be.

However, centrality does not appear to be as powerful an influence on urban expenditures as in either the USA or Belgium. To some extent this may simply be due to the fact that the Belgian study of Aiken and Depré uses a more complex and precise measure of centrality. But, more importantly, it is also likely to be due to the fact that British local government is formed by large units which combine both central places and parts of their urban hinterlands, so that the costs and benefits of local government could be shared more equitably between the central cities and their suburbs. In other words, since central places are not segregated from their peripheral areas, as they are in the fragmented structure of urban government in the USA, the spending patterns of central places in Britain are not as clear and distinct as they might be.

Nevertheless, the degree of centrality clearly affects spending levels on a wide range of urban services, and to this extent the empirical results of this chapter add considerably to the statistical explanation of expenditure variations for local government generally. More importantly, central place theory adds to our understanding of the connection between spending variations and the characteristics of cities, cities conceived not as the sum of their individual parts, but as whole and indivisible entities which cannot be reduced to, or measured in terms of, aggregate census data. It is the holistic features of cities, deriving from their function as central places, which is important, and not any particular feature, or set of features, of their resident populations. However, we must be careful not to claim too much, for the urban hierarchy is not relevant to some services, and does not explain a good deal of the variation in the others. Consequently, the next chapter will turn to a different aspect of the national urban system which also influences urban policy and service spending.

NOTES

1. E. Jones, *Towns and Cities* (London, Oxford University Press, 1966), p. 87.
2. '... towns with more complex sets of activities will possess all the central activities of lower orders plus a group of central activities that will distinguish them from the central places of immediately lower orders.' K. S. O. Beavon, *Central Place Theory: A Reinterpretation* (London, Longman, 1977), p.6.
3. W. I. Carruthers, 'A Classification of service centres in England and Wales', *Geographical Journal*, 123 (1957), 371.
4. According to Carter, 'The importance but not the centrality of a town could be measured by its population.' H. Carter, *The Study of Urban Geography* (London, Edward Arnold, 3rd Edn., 1981), p. 77.
5. Volume of retail trade is the most frequent measure of centrality – see E. L. Ullman, 'A theory of location for cities', reprinted in W. H. Leahy, D. L. McKee, and R. D. Dean (eds.), *Urban Economics* (New York, The Free Press, 1970), p. 110.
6. The early work of Smailes uses the presence and number of cinemas as indicators. A. E. Smailes, 'The urban mesh of England and Wales', *Transactions of the Institute of British Geographers*, 87 (1946), and A. E. Smailes, 'The urban hierarchy of England and Wales', *Geography*, 29 (1944), 41–51.
7. One study of Finland shows a strong relationship between centrality and the presence of dentists, health clinics, veterinary surgeons, and hospitals – see Carter, *The Study of Urban Geography*, p. 82.
8. The location and distribution of business headquarters is given great importance by Pred, see A. Pred, *City-Systems in Advanced Economies* (London, Hutchinson, 1977), pp. 98–107.
9. According to Yeates the range of political influence of a city is a major determinant of its position in the urban hierarchy. M. Yeates, *North American Urban Patterns* (London, Edward Arnold, 1980), p. 11.
10. See B. J. L. Berry and W. L. Garrison, 'Recent developments of central place theory', in Leahy *et al.*, *Urban Economics*, pp. 117–28. For a summary of some of the empirical work on centrality and public and private transportation movements see Carter, *The Study of Urban Geography*, pp. 91–8.
11. Foremost among the sociologists is A. Hawley, *Human Ecology: A Theory of Community Structure* (New York, Ronald Press, 1950), and *Urban Society: An Ecological Approach* (New York, Ronald Press, 1971). For recent work by an economist see A. R. Watkins, *The Practice of Urban Economics* (Beverly Hills, California, Sage, 1980), pp. 85–114.
12. For example, the geographer R. J. Johnson borrows heavily from the political science and social administration literature in his discussion of variations in local government spending, but does not consider the possibilities of his own discipline; R. J. Johnson, *Political, Electoral and Spatial Systems* (Oxford, Clarendon Press, 1979), pp. 75–105.
13. The GLC's grant to the arts is as large, if not larger, than that of the Arts Council – see Evidence by the Greater London Council, *Report of the Committee of Inquiry into Local Government Finance*, Appendix 2 (London, HMSO, 1976), p. 278.
14. This chapter assumes the existence of an urban hierarchy, no matter how indistinct. It does not try, as central place theory does, to explain the

number, size, and distribution of urban centres, and it does not deny that central place theory has many problems in its attempts to explain the shapes and dimensions of national urban systems — see, for example, D. Harvey, *Explanation in Geography* (London, Edward Arnold, 1973), p. 138; B. Ayeni, *Concepts and Techniques in Urban Analysis* (London, Croom Helm, 1979), p. 111; and Carter, *The Study of Urban Geography*, pp. 101–41.

15. Berry and Garrison, 'Recent developments of central place theory', p. 124.

16. The length of the journey to work in Greater London, for example, is twice the national average. Traffic density within the GLC is ten times greater than the national average, and off-peak traffic levels are fifty times greater. For the details see Evidence by the Greater London Council, *Report of the Committee of Inquiry*, Appendix 2, p. 277.

17. J. D. Kasarda, 'The impact of the suburban population growth on central city service functions', *American Journal of Sociology*, 77 (1972), 1121 and 1123.

18. M. Aiken and R. Depré, 'The urban system, politics, and policy in Belgian cities', in K. Newton (ed.), *Urban Political Economy* (London, Frances Pinter, 1981), pp. 85–116.

19. W. I. Carruthers, 'Major shopping centres in England and Wales, 1961', *Regional Studies*, 1 (1967), pp. 65–9.

20. On the relationship between the urban hierarchy and population size see J. B. Parr *et al.*, 'City-size models and the economic base: a recent controversy', *Journal of Regional Science*, 15 (1975), 1–8, and R. L. Davies, 'Variable relationships in central place and retail potential models', *Regional Studies*, 4 (1970), 49–61.

21. On the evidence for economies and diseconomies of scale in British local government see K. Newton, 'Comparative community performance', *Current Sociology*, 26 (1976), 75–6. American work, which yields much the same absence of any generalized relationship between size and service spending, is summarized in W. F. Fox, J. M. Stam, W. M. Godsey, and S. D. Brown, *Economies of Size in Local Government: An Annotated Bibliography* (Washington, DC, United States Department of Agriculture, Rural Development Research Report No. 9, 1979).

22. Details of the argument are spelled out in K. Newton, *et al.*, *Balancing The Books: The Financial Problems of Local Government in Western Europe* (London, Sage Publications, 1980), pp. 161–83.

23. Aiken and Depré avoid the problems of multicollinearity because they use factor analysis on the independent variables describing the social and economic characteristics of Belgian cities — Aiken and Depré, 'The urban system, politics, and policy in Belgian cities'.

7. CITY TYPES

Introduction

The previous chapter concluded that although a city's general rank in the urban hierarchy has a clear effect on its spending on some services, this is not the end of the story by any means. A re-examination of Table 6.1 will show that quite a few cities with a similar position in the hierarchy vary in their spending. For example, Blackpool and Derby have the same rank, but Blackpool is a seaside resort which spends comparatively large amounts on parks, highways, public health, and refuse, whereas Derby is a more industrial city which spends less than average on these services. Blackpool, it may be argued, must maintain its attraction as a holiday and tourist centre, but Derby has less need to do this.

Many other comparisons of a similar kind might be drawn from Table 6.1: for example Exeter and Sunderland, Bolton and Bath, Lincoln and Walsall, Warrington and Canterbury, Bury and Hastings. In each case the pair have the same hierarchical ranking, but, at the same time, they are very different types of city, with different economic functions, different population types, and different sorts of location and environment. The seaside resorts have a marked family resemblance which distinguishes them from the major capitals, which, in turn, are different from county towns and industrial towns, and so on. This chapter will develop the theme that different types of city have different sets of service expenditures, and that to understand the nature and location of each city type is to understand and explain its spending patterns. As in the previous chapter the work will be confined to the county boroughs.

There is, of course, a large literature on city types in the UK, starting with Moser and Scott's pioneering *British Towns*, and progressing through studies with more elaborate statistical methods and more comprehensive empirical data. An initial attempt to use this work, however, proved rather unsatisfactory. Two main factors explain this. *First*, most of the studies produce rather incongruous results in which different types of cities are mixed in the same category. Moser and Scott, for example, group Bristol and Worcester together, although the former is a large commercial and industrial port, and the latter a relatively small county town. At the same time, some of the remaining county towns are grouped with a different set of cities, while ports similar to Bristol are collected together in a third category. This category, incidentally, is labelled 'Including many of the large ports, as well as two Black Country towns', and although this is itself a rather strange mixture, the problem is magnified by the fact that the category does not include all the large ports, while most of the other Black Country towns are to be found in two further categories.[1]

There are many such anomalies in the city-types literature: in one case Birmingham and Dewsbury are grouped together, as are Bristol and Lincoln, Wakefield and Norwich;[2] in another, Worcester and Southampton are placed cheek by jowl;[3] and in a third, Birmingham and Copeland (Cumbria) are found to have much in common, as are Darlington and Edinburgh.[4] These are not isolated cases, but part of a more general set of problems,[5] problems which make it difficult to use the existing city-types literature for the purpose of understanding and explaining service expenditure patterns.

Second, even the best study of city types in England and Wales (that by Garbis Armen),[6] one which avoids the problem of anomalous groupings, produced rather disappointing results. The county boroughs were grouped according to Armen's classification, and the average expenditure on each major service computed and compared with figures for other groups of cities. The aim in this work, as in all the city-types literature, is to produce a set of groups each with a clear and distinctive pattern of service expenditures. In the language of cluster analysis, the aim is to minimize within-group variance, and to maximize between-group variance. The results with the Armen classifications were generally poor because the patterns were not at all clear and distinct. It was, therefore, decided to devise a new set of categories which would serve our purpose to better effect.

To be convincing and useful the typology must stand up to some exacting specifications: it must comply with two logical criteria, follow one strict rule of procedure, and achieve two statistical goals. These specifications are as follows:

(1) In order to avoid the incongruities of the Moser and Scott kind of classification, all cities of a given social and economic type must be grouped together, and should not be distributed between two or more categories. Manchester, as a major conurbation capital, must be grouped with other major conurbation capitals, such as Liverpool and Birmingham. In other words each group must be inclusive.

(2) Each category should be internally consistent, in that it must include one type of city, and no others. A category of seaside resorts and spas should include only those kinds of places, and nothing else.

(3) The typology must be based entirely upon the social and economic characteristics and functions of cities, and should not, in the first place, have any regard for service expenditures. This is because expenditures are to be explained in terms of social and economic functions, so it is important that cities are first classified according to these functions. Having devised a typology of this kind, the service expenditures for each type can be computed and compared with those for other types.

(4) The differences in service spending between groups should, so far as possible, be maximized.

(5) The differences within groups should, so far as possible, be minimized.

Unfortunately, the real world cannot be treated in such a cut-and-dried fashion as these five ground rules demand. The county boroughs, as political units created by a political process, did not always follow the most obvious economic contours of the urban system, and consequently any economic classification is likely to leave some loose ends. For example, some cities without county borough status were larger than others with, and one or two authorities were incorporated into a wider conurbation so that it is difficult to define a self-contained role for them. At the same time, and quite apart from these sorts of difficulties, no single way of classifying cities according to their economic function is the most obvious, since some cities had more than one major economic role. Does Liverpool belong in a category of large ports, along with Newcastle and Bristol, or is it best matched with major conurbation capitals such as Birmingham? Is Bath, as a spa, to be classified with the seaside resorts, or is it more like the inland county towns? These, however, are empirical questions. Underlying the whole exercise is the need to devise a set of categories which meets the logical criteria set out above, which will stand up as a classificatory exercise in its own right, which is based upon the social and economic features and functions of cities, but which will, at the same time, throw explanatory light upon the service spending levels of city types.

The three main criteria which we used to classify cities in this study were derived from the preliminary work reported in Chapter 5.

(1) *Centrality and city size*. So far as possible, the aim was to group large and important central places together, and to avoid grouping them with small and low-ranking cities. Manchester does not belong with Merthyr Tydfil, but Merthyr, Newport, and South Shields may well go together.

(2) *Urban or rural environments*. A distinction was made between cities which are constituent parts of large urban agglomerations, and free-standing places which are surrounded mainly by rural areas.

(3) *Industrial or commercial/residential cities*. The economic role or base of a city is useful in distinguishing small, free-standing industrial places, such as Barrow-in-Furness, from small, free-standing residential and commercial places, such as Exeter. It also serves to distinguish between small industrial cities which are part of a large urban area (St. Helens or Wigan), and small suburban authorities (such as Solihull or Wallasey).

In addition, some key indicators of social and economic conditions were computed: percentage overcrowding and percentage working class, percentage domestic property, population size, percentage old population, and net daily population inflow/outflow, were all used as indicators of poor social conditions, land use and rateable value, city size, age structure, and daily population movement, respectively. These measures were chosen because each one was quite strongly related to a range of other useful social indicators, while not being particularly strongly related to each other. These indicators are intended to give a general picture of the main features of each city type, but they are not a set of definitive characteristics. Using the five general criteria for constructing a typology, together with the three criteria for city classification and the indicators, a set of nine city types was devised, as follows:

(1) Metropolitan Capitals,
(2) Secondary Capitals,
(3) Industrial Satellites,
(4) Suburban Authorities,
(5) Large Free-standing, Commercial, and Industrial Cities,
(6) Small, Free-standing Industrial Cities,
(7) County Towns,
(8) Administrative and Commercial Centres,
(9) Seaside Resorts.

This typology not only meets most (it must be said, not all) of the conditions already discussed, but it also produces a set of relatively sharply defined service expenditure patterns for each group of cities. Finally, as the typology unfolds itself, it will become clear that it is not simply a statistical artifact, but a way of understanding and explaining urban outputs. The bulk of what follows in this chapter will describe and analyse each of the city types in turn.

(1) *Metropolitan Capitals*

This group of five cities consists of Manchester, Birmingham, Liverpool, Newcastle, and Leeds, which were at the very top of the urban hierarchy in England and Wales, excluding London. As Table 7.1 shows, they had a large population, some fairly serious social and housing problems, a fairly small proportion of domestic property, and a large net daily inflow of people to work, as well as a relatively small old population but a relatively large school-aged one. They were also embedded at the heart of the nation's largest urban agglomerations. As a grouping of cities they clearly have much in common, and are readily distinguishable from the great majority of other county boroughs as the largest and most important cities in the nation's largest and most important industrial and commercial agglomerations.

The metropolitan capitals also have a unique profile of service spending (see Table 7.2). They spent a great deal on most of the indivisible services, and on some of the divisible ones, and in both cases the reasons are not difficult to find. Libraries, museums, and art galleries, as we have seen in the previous chapter, are central place services, and, accordingly, the five cities spent considerably more than the national average. Similar considerations help to account for

Table 7.1 Indicators of the Social and Economic Characteristics of City Types, 1972

	Overcrowded %	Working class %	Domestic property %	Population size (1000)	Old population %	Net population inflow %	(n)
Metropolitan capitals	5.4	64.6	38.8	576	16.6	32.5	(5)
Secondary capitals	5.6	67.5	43.6	219	15.8	14.1	(6)
Industrial satellites	4.5	68.9	45.8	116	15.5	6.5	(19)
Suburbs	1.2	46.9	61.2	102	15.3	48.0	(2)
Large free-standing industrial cities	3.5	67.8	39.8	323	15.5	18.5	(7)
Small free-standing industrial cities	2.9	67.3	42.2	100	16.3	17.9	(18)
County towns	2.2	59.1	42.8	87	17.1	33.2	(10)
Administrative centres	2.5	54.9	46.9	204	17.5	15.6	(7)
Seaside resorts	1.7	48.9	57.2	113	27.0	1.8	(9)
County borough average	3.4	62.9	45.2	169	17.4	10.0	(83)

Table 7.2 *Service Expenditures of City Types, 1972/3*

Per capita expenditures (£)	Metropolitan capitals	Secondary capitals	Industrial satellites	Suburbs	Large industrial	Small industrial	County towns	Administrative centres	Seaside resorts	CB average
Education	50.28	49.49	49.27	50.24	52.51	50.77	47.14	48.34	39.64	48.59
Libraries	2.42	1.68	1.42	1.33	1.96	1.62	2.01	1.60	1.55	1.66
Refuse	3.62	2.75	2.63	2.28	2.52	2.38	2.71	2.08	2.31	2.50
Parks	1.68	1.62	1.58	1.62	1.96	1.77	1.50	1.68	2.24	1.80
Public health	2.27	1.87	1.95	1.62	2.02	2.04	1.64	1.62	1.73	1.89
Local health	3.08	2.70	3.04	2.47	3.02	2.85	3.11	2.81	2.95	2.94
Social services	8.13	7.38	6.90	5.37	7.31	6.81	6.75	6.80	6.81	6.95
Housing	8.53	6.45	7.00	1.32	6.94	5.64	4.29	3.76	3.71	5.61
Planning	2.52	0.92	1.05	0.36	1.51	1.18	1.34	2.06	0.97	1.29
Highways	8.03	7.00	6.40	5.55	5.76	6.40	6.45	6.54	6.72	6.53
Fire	2.27	1.85	2.19	1.90	1.83	2.19	1.99	1.97	1.91	2.06
Police	10.86	7.78	7.40	6.45	7.72	7.25	7.48	7.88	8.16	7.74
Total	113.97	98.57	96.71	88.60	100.57	97.85	94.44	91.96	85.86	96.41
Education per pupil	266.40	276.93	260.18	270.12	278.61	268.56	282.72	29.73	278.60	272.20
(n)	(5)	(6)	(12)	(2)	(7)	(18)	(10)	(7)	(9)	(83)

spending on police, public health, and highways. At the same time, these cities need their parks because they are surrounded by densely populated urban areas, a fact which also helps to account for high refuse expenditure. Moreover, as old and major urban centres with old housing stocks, large working-class and young populations, and inner-city slums, they have a range of social problems which call for relatively high spending on some of the divisible services, particularly housing, local health, services for children, and education per capita (but not per pupil).

Perhaps the most notable single feature of the conurbation capitals is their high spending on a wide range of services. Of the thirteen major services, they spent less than average in 1960/1 on only sewerage (two are coastal cities), welfare (a small retired population), planning, and fire services. On all other items they spent heavily. The temptation to ascribe this to diseconomies of scale, or to the profligate and grand ideas of their city councils, must be resisted. It is clear that their spending was derived from the pressures and demands created by their physical environment and location, by their role in the national system of cities, and by the demographic and housing characteristics of their populations. Although their commercial and industrial tax base gave them high rateable values, their financial resources also had to stretch to meet a range of specially heavy demands.

Although for reasons of space, Tables 7.1 and 7.2 present figures for only the last year of the study, the same figures were computed for the metropolitan capitals for the first year (1960/1) to see if there were any shifts or changes over the period. In fact, with only a few minor exceptions, the metropolitan capitals show little variation, and the same is overwhelmingly true of all the other city types discussed in this chapter. In other words, the typology is not a transitory phenomenon, but a stable and persistent one.

(2) *Secondary Capitals*

The six secondary capitals are Bolton, Bradford, Coventry, Huddersfield, Salford, and Wolverhampton. These were large and important cities in their own right, and they were all situated in large conurbations, but they did not have the pre-eminence in the national urban system of the metropolitan capitals, and in some ways lived in their shadow. Like the metropolitan capitals, they had strong commercial and industrial economies and a good tax base, though they also had most of the acute social and housing problems characteristic of large cities in the UK, together with a relatively large school-aged population which was expensive to educate. As a group of cities they fitted in between the metropolitan capitals and the county borough average, with, perhaps, more in common with the capitals than most other cities. In a simpler typology the two groups might well be collapsed, but in this one they are seen as two sub-types of the same general category of large and important conurbation cities.

The spending levels of the secondary capitals, as one might expect from this description, were between the metropolitan capitals and the county borough average. Their spending on indivisible services — most notably libraries, refuse, highways, and police — was high, but not quite as high as that of the metropolitan capitals. Their library spending, for example, was high, but they did not need to provide the elaborate facilities of the capitals which were quite close by, and, indeed, they may well feed off these facilities, saving money in the process.

At the same time, the secondary capitals were large, industrial cities with social problems that were generally worse than average, and worse than those of the metropolitan capitals (Table 7.2). They had large working-class populations, a relatively high proportion of children, and low rateable values. Consequently, they spent heavily on a range of social and redistributive services, including education (per pupil and per capita), local health, children, welfare, and housing. They did not have the same intense pressure on space as the metropolitan capitals and consequently they did not have to spend quite as much on housing, but for this service expenditure they are still well above the national average.

In some respects, therefore, the secondary capitals were pale reflections of the metropolitan capitals, and spent accordingly, but in others, concerned primarily with social problems, they outranked the major capitals, and spent more than them. In other words, they usually spent less on the indivisible but more on the divisible services, and ended up spending a total figure which is well above average, but below the unusually high figures achieved by Birmingham, Manchester, and the like.

(3) Industrial Satellites

This is the largest single category of the typology, and consisted of twenty-one county boroughs in 1960/1, and nineteen in 1972/3. The group was composed of the decaying, old, industrial towns which mostly ring the capitals of the largest urban agglomerations — in alphabetical order the members of the group were Barnsley, Birkenhead, Blackburn, Bootle, Bury, Dewsbury, Dudley, East Ham, Gateshead, Halifax, Hartlepool, Oldham, Smethwick, South Shields, Stockport, Sunderland, Tynemouth, Walsall, Warrington, West Bromwich, West Ham, and Wigan. These towns had in common their heavy industry, their large working-class populations, their high proportion of school children, their low rateable values, and their areas of acute deprivation. Many of them were the Rugby League towns of the north, but some were Black Country towns of the West Midlands, or towns in the docklands of the East End of London. They were the price paid for the industrial revolution. They were, in short, a distinctive grouping of the smallest and poorest industrial cities, for the most part embedded in large industrial conurbations.

As one would expect, the industrial satellites spent relatively heavily on education (per capita, but not per pupil), children (per capita, but not per child), local health, and housing. But they compensated for this by spending little on libraries, parks, planning, highways, and police. Their low ranking in the urban hierarchy, and the fact that many are situated on the periphery of metropolitan regions help to explain these figures.

Overall, the industrial satellites are the poorest and the neediest of any of the nine types, and they therefore tended to spend heavily on social and redistributive services. On the other hand, they had a poor tax base, which prevented them from raising large amounts in local revenues, and, therefore, they were heavily dependent upon central-government grants. The pressure they experienced to spend on the expensive services of education, health, social services, and housing probably restrained their ability to spend on other services. Nevertheless, their total figure was up to, or higher than, the average.

It is worth noting that the three types discussed so far can be ranked fairly neatly in terms of their indivisible services, with the metropolitan capitals having the highest, and the industrial satellites the lowest spending on libraries, refuse, parks, highways, and police. Public health deviated only very marginally from this pattern, although planning and fire were not consistent with the general run of figures. Fire spending may be high in the industrial satellites because of the Class A fire risks of factories in congested areas. In general, however, Table 7.3 suggests a consistent and predictable pattern of spending on indivisible services on the part of these three types of conurbation authorities.

Table 7.3 *Per Capita Spending (£) by Conurbation Authorities on Indivisible Services, 1960/1*

	Metropolitan capitals	Secondary capitals	Industrial satellites
Libraries	0.67	0.52	0.43
Refuse	1.05	0.82	0.77
Parks	0.92	0.83	0.81
Public health	0.50	0.40	0.41
Planning	0.13	0.17	0.14
Highways	2.55	2.24	2.07
Police	2.80	2.23	2.08
Fire	0.61	0.53	0.70
Subtotal	9.23	7.74	7.41
(n)	(5)	(6)	(21)

(4) *Suburban Authorities*

The dormitory suburbs are the last of the conurbation authorities. This is a distinctive type of urban place but very few of them ever gained full county borough status in England and Wales. However, their importance in the political economy of metropolitan regions of the United States and of some other countries, gives them a degree of theoretical interest in a British study.[7] In England and Wales, only Croydon and Wallasey can be regarded as suburban county boroughs in 1960/1. Croydon then became a London borough in 1965, but Solihull was given county borough status in 1964. Thus there are only two cases, for each year examined here, and it is difficult to generalize from so small a number. Nevertheless, the suburbs stood out, as one would expect, for their pervasive middle-class affluence, for their lack of social problems, for their high proportion of domestic property and their relative lack of industry, and for their daily flow of population to the big city during the day, and back again at night. Like the three other city types discussed so far, therefore, the suburbs were integral parts of metropolitan regions, but unlike them they were primarily middle class and residential, and had few of the social problems of their industrial and commercial neighbours.

It goes almost without saying that they spent little on social and ameliorative services such as personal health, children, welfare, and housing. Of all the city types discussed in the chapter, the suburbs had the least need for these provisions. They also spent little on libraries (perhaps they rely upon the metropolitan and secondary capitals), on parks in 1972/3 (most houses had gardens, or cars to get out into the countryside which was not far away), on planning (the new and spacious suburbs need little), on refuse (no expensive industrial waste, and open space not too far away), and perhaps, surprisingly, they spent little on highways, police, and fire. The absence of high fire-risk industrial plant may explain fire, and a relatively low placing in the urban hierarchy may help to explain low police and highways spending.

Education was their only costly major service, partly because they had relatively large school populations, and partly because each child had an average to high amount spent on it. Even this does not reflect the real cost of education in Solihull, where, it has been suggested, rather large amounts were raised directly from parents.[8] The overall picture, however, was one of affluence coupled with a need to spend little on most services, so that total spending was well below the average.

(5) Large, Free-standing, Commercial, and Industrial Cities

In 1960/1 the six large, free-standing cities were Hull, Leicester, Nottingham, Southampton, Sheffield, and Stoke. Later Teesside was created, to bring the number up to seven. In social and economic terms, they were like the metropolitan and secondary capitals, in that they were large cities with a relatively prosperous industrial and commercial economy, a large working class, and a relatively large young population. For the most part they ranked just below the metropolitan capitals in the urban hierarchy, and like them they served as major service centres for the regions surrounding them. They also had a relatively wealthy local tax base of industrial and commercial property. But they differed from metropolitan capitals in one important respect; they were the capitals of predominantly small-town and rural regions, not continuously built-up urban ones. So, they were rather like the metropolitan and secondary capitals in terms of their importance as urban centres, and in terms of their social and economic characteristics, but they were situated in predominantly rural, not urban areas, and this gave them a different complexion.

Their spending on indivisible services (libraries, refuse, parks, public health), was higher than the national average, but not up to the high levels of the metropolitan capitals, partly because they were not such important central places, and partly because nearby open country reduced both the need for parks and the cost of refuse. They also had a smaller daily inflow of commuters, and so their highways and police spending was lower than the major urban centres. It is interesting to compare their library spending with that of the secondary capitals, for although the two types had much in common, the secondary capitals can feed off their larger and more important neighbours, whereas the large, free-standing cities provide services both for their own and their hinterland populations. Hence, they spent more on libraries than the secondary capitals, but less than the metropolitan capitals.

Because they were large cities with urban problems, they also spent more heavily than the average county borough on social and redistributive services such as education, local health, children, welfare, social services (in 1972/3), and housing. Nevertheless, they tended not to reach the high spending levels of the metropolitan capitals on these services, mainly because they did not have such acute inner-city problems, particularly the special pressures on housing and urban space. This may well have had the effect of releasing some funds which were taken up by high per capita and per pupil spending on education. Thus, like the metropolitan capitals, they had relatively large school-aged populations, but unlike them, they did not have urgent pressures to spend on a wide range of services, and so could afford something extra on the education budget.

(6) Small, Free-standing Industrial Cities

The small, free-standing industrial cities were very much like the industrial satellites in that both were small, industrial, working class, and poor, and had relatively young populations. But the two types are distinguishable in two important respects: the satellites were component parts of metropolitan regions, and they had net population outflow; whereas the small, free-standing cities had a predominantly rural environment, and a net population inflow, indicating that they served as urban centres for small and usually agricultural surrounding regions. The small, free-standing industrial cities were, therefore, the direct equivalents of the cities of the industrial periphery, but situated in a rural rather than an urban environment, and serving as small centres for their areas, rather than being merely small attachments to large and important urban places. The group consisted of Barrow-in-Furness, Burnley, Burton, Darlington, Derby, Doncaster, Grimsby, Luton, Merthyr Tydfil, Newport, Northampton, Preston, Rochdale, Rotherham, St. Helens, Swansea, Wakefield, and Warrington.

Because they were low in the urban hierarchy and because they were also free-standing with rather small hinterland populations, this group of cities usually spent well-below-average amounts on the indivisible services, particularly libraries, refuse, parks, planning, highways, and police. Like the industrial satellites they spent rather more than average on fire and public health, because of the demands of their industry. However, the small, free-standing industrial cities usually spent rather more than the industrial satellites on the indivisible services, because by comparison with the satellites, they were small service centres for a limited surrounding area.

Although they have large working-class populations and pockets of severe multiple deprivation, the small, free-standing industrial cities usually spent relatively little on their social services. They spent either average or below average amounts on local health, children, welfare, social services (in 1972/3), and housing. The reasons for this are not all clear, but perhaps two things contribute towards an explanation. First, they are mainly poor cities and may have had difficulty in raising local revenues, and second, the high service standards set by the metropolitan authorities may have taken some time to diffuse to them.

(7) County Towns

The last three city types differ from the others discussed so far in that they are predominantly residential and commercial, relatively small, and non-industrial authorities. In some way, therefore, they are three variations, or sub-types, of a more general category, but they each differ enough to merit separate discussion.

The county towns, as their name implies, were the old administrative centres of the counties established well before the industrial revolution, but they might also be called market or cathedral towns. They are Canterbury, Chester, Exeter, Gloucester, Ipswich, Lincoln, Norwich, Oxford, Worcester, and York. In population size, these places were comparable with the small, free-standing industrial cities, and like them they were embedded in predominantly rural areas. But here the comparison ends. The county towns were higher in the urban hierarchy, were wealthy, with a large amount of commercial and fairly expensive residential property, and they had relatively small working-class and young populations. The county towns, therefore, had their own special image as historic places which have served as commercial and administrative centres for many centuries, and which, in the period under study, were relatively small, middle-class, prosperous, commercial, and residential places, serving a mainly rural and agricultural hinterland.

The county towns were in the fortunate position of not having to spend a great deal on many services. Their scale and rural surroundings meant that refuse was cheap to dispose of, and that parks were, to some extent, unnecessary. Their wealthy and relatively old populations called for comparatively low expenditure on children, local health, and housing, and the fact that they were small and quiet cities meant that the police was not an expensive service, either. On the other hand they did have a greater than average need for welfare services for the old, and their role as fairly important centres for regional services placed demands upon their libraries and roads. A desire to maintain their historic and attractive environment may account for above average spending on planning. Their middle-class populations also demanded high educational standards, so that although they had average to low school-aged populations, they usually spent above average on each pupil. But for this last service, they would probably have spent below average in total, though the final figure was about the national average.

(8) *Administrative and Commercial Centres*

This is the most mixed category of the typology, consisting of Bath, Bristol, Cardiff, Carlisle, Plymouth, Portsmouth, and Reading. These cities had in common their free-standing situation, a relatively high proportion of affluent middle-class residents, and a local economy which mixed a certain amount of industrial with a rather large amount of commercial activity. In some ways they were quite like the large free-standing industrial cities, although they were smaller, wealthier, and less industrial, but in other respects they were akin to the county towns, although they were larger, and had greater extremes of social conditions – both a larger middle class, and more housing problems and old people.

The spending patterns of administrative centres were also like the county towns. Like them they had a low figure for many services, both divisible and indivisible. They spent less than the national county borough average on refuse, parks, public health, fire, education per capita, health, social services, and housing, and spent about average, or little more than average, on libraries, highways, and police. Their low spending was attributable to a combination of their free-standing location, a relatively low position in the urban hierarchy, a relative absence of industry with a high fire risk and high refuse costs, and an affluent population with lower than average demands for housing, health, and social services. In fact, the administrative centres even spent less on most services, and in total, than the county towns, although their figures for planning and education per pupil are higher. Planning is explained by the fact that the group happens to contain Plymouth, Portsmouth, and Bristol, which all suffered heavy wartime bomb damge, and their higher than average spending on each pupil was based upon an affluent middle class, a good local tax base, and relatively few school-aged children.

(9) Seaside Resorts

The eight seaside resorts in 1960/1 were Bournemouth, Brighton, Eastbourne, Hastings, Southend, Southport, Blackpool, and Great Yarmouth, to which Torbay was added, as a new authority, by 1972/3. Some other county boroughs (Swansea, for example) had resort facilities, but unlike those listed above, were not primarily geared to the holiday trade.[9] Bath, as a spa, also had some of the characteristics and functions of a resort, but was not, of course, on the sea, and did not fully conform to the characteristics of the group. In some ways the resorts were similar to county towns in that both were relatively small, free-standing, commercial, and residential, and had affluent middle-class populations. The resorts were particularly wealthy, however, and they were also notable for their large proportion of retired people. Most particularly, they were seaside resorts which were heavily dependent upon the holiday and tourist trade (the conference trade out of season), and which did their utmost to attract as much of this business as possible. In this respect they competed with one another.

Seaside resorts had a special range of service requirements. In order to maintain themselves as holiday resorts they had to be clean and tidy, well lit, and hygienic; their parks and gardens had to be large and attractive; their roads wide and well-surfaced and capable of carrying heavy holiday traffic without congestion; refuse had to be disposed of quickly, and public health services maintained to the highest standards; fire services had to be good, and public safety well organ-ized. Consequently, the seaside resorts spent well-above-average amounts on refuse, parks, public health, highways, fire, and police. They also spent more than most cities on welfare services for the old, as might be expected given their age distribution. When it comes to education spending, they were at opposite extremes of the two measures. They had small school populations so spent the least of all the city types on a per capita basis, but their middle-class parents demanded high educational standards, and so they spent most heavily on each pupil. On all other services the seaside resorts had little need for expensive provision, and they spent little on children (per capita and per child), local health, housing, and planning. Overall, their spending was low, in spite of the fact that they were heavily committed to some of the more minor services.

Conclusions

All the county boroughs have been classified, without exception, but a price has to be paid for being comprehensive: the fact that all authorities are covered by the typology means that one of the types (no more) consists of a rather mixed bunch, and perhaps is as much a residual as a true category. The cities classified as administrative centres are not wholly disparate by any means, but they differ on common-sense grounds. Bristol was a different kind of city to Carlisle, which, in turn, differed from Plymouth. There is also a certain amount of variation within the industrial satellites as a group, and it may be possible to further subdivide them. And there are also difficulties in fitting in some cities which are marginal to two or more categories. Bristol seems to be one of a kind, although it was fairly close to commercial centres. Bath was part county town, but it has some of the characteristics of a seaside resort. Carlisle was part county town, but it was more like the commercial centres. Coventry shared some of the features of free-standing industrial cities, but was close enough to Birmingham to be more like a secondary capital.

A frank recognition of these problems ought not to obscure the fact that the typology is comprehensive, and that it meets the twin criteria of consistency and exhaustiveness discussed at the start of the chapter. It also has the merit of being a typology based upon the social and economic functions of cities, which also throws light upon their service spending patterns in a way that central place theory does not. We will conclude the chapter by summarizing its contribution to the study of urban outputs and service provision.

First, and most obviously, the evidence in this chapter shows that spending is influenced by the particular economic base and function of a city, as well as its position in the urban hierarchy. While all cities are similar in that they provide economic services to their surrounding areas (to a greater or lesser extent), their economic roles may also differ; the cities might be industrial or commercial centres, or residential areas, or holiday and tourist centres, and so on. Their role in the national economy influences their service spending, just as their rank in the national system of cities does. For example, Blackpool and Reading have the same rank in the urban hierarchy, but the former is a seaside resort and spends relatively heavily on the services necessary to the holiday and tourist industry, while Reading has less need to do this. Their service spending levels are similar, up to a point, because of their importance as central places, but their spending levels also differ according to their particular local economies.

The point can be illustrated by comparing cities of a similar rank but different economic functions (Table 7.4). In general, the higher the rank of the city, the more it spent on highways, but within each level of the urban hierarchy, the seaside resorts spent the most. Consequently, knowing both a city's rank in the hierarchy and its economic role will tell us more about its spending levels, than knowing just one of these. Or to put the same point in more statistical terms, some of the variance left unexplained by the urban hierarchy can be accounted for by economic role.

Table 7.4 *Per Capita Highways Expenditure (£) of a Selection of County Boroughs with Similar Rank in the Urban Hierarchy but Different Economic Roles*

City	Rank	Highways spending
Blackpool	11	2.89
Reading	11	2.64
Brighton	21	2.45
Plymouth	21	2.35
Southend	31	2.36
Sunderland	31	2.17
Hastings	68	2.19
West Bromwich	67	1.63

Note: Urban hierarchy rank is taken from Table 6.1.

Further evidence from this chapter enables us to refine this statement a little more. It has already been established that the budgetary patterns of any given city are strongly influenced by the size of its hinterland population, but the evidence of this chapter also shows that other characteristics, of the surrounding areas and local authorities, will be influential. Conurbation cities, especially those embedded in continuously built-up areas, have different service expenditure profiles from free-standing cities, and within any conurbation, one city's spending may well be affected by another's. For example, the conurbation capitals put the most money into libraries, museums, and art galleries, and the secondary capitals spend so much less, given their importance as major urban centres, that it seems they must live off nearby conurbation capitals to some extent. The industrial satellites and the suburbs seem to rely on large neighbouring authorities even more, since they spend least of all nine types. In constrast, the large, free-standing industrial cities spend marginally more than the secondary capitals, because they cannot live off the conurbation capitals. Similarly, the small, free-standing industrial cities spend more than the industrial satellites, for the same reason. In short, what a city spends on its public services will depend partly upon whether it is part of a larger metropolitan complex or not, and if it is, also on the role it plays within that complex – capital, secondary capital, industrial satellite, suburb.

At the most general level, this means that spending on services is influenced by three features of urban authorities.

(1) Their role and importance as central places, as discussed in the previous chapter.

(2) Their main economic role, besides that of provider of central place services. This chapter has picked out four dimensions of particular

importance — the industrial, the commercial, the residential, and a fourth rather special one, that concerning the holiday and tourist economy.

(3) The urban/rural nature of the surrounding area. Two cities with approximately the same rank in the urban hierarchy, and approximately the same economic role, will tend to differ if one is embedded in an urban, and the other in a rural environment. The distinction between metropolitan capitals and secondary capitals, on the one hand, and large free-standing industrial cities, on the other, is based upon the importance of this distinction, as is the distinction between those cities on the industrial periphery and small free-standing industrial cities.

Another general conclusion to emerge is that just as the spending of any given authority may be influenced by spending in neighbouring authorities, so also spending on one service in a given authority may be related to spending on other services. The links seem to be of two kinds. First, a high proportion of people in one section of the population requiring one particular service, usually means a low proportion of people in other sections of the population requiring a different service. Young and old people are an obvious case in point, and since they usually vary inversely, high spending on children usually goes with low spending on old people. The seaside resorts, which had the largest retired populations, spent the least (per capita) on children and education in 1960/1. Second, the conditions which tend to result in high costs for one service, quite often produce high costs for another. For example, low spending on parks by free-standing cities often goes with low refuse costs, because of the proximity of open space, and, conversely, authorities in urban agglomerations tend to spend relatively heavily on both parks and refuse. There is also some indication that industrial areas tend to be a high fire risk, and that they generate industrial waste which can be expensive to dispose of.

Ultimately, the amount spent on any one service is linked to other services because of the fact of scarce resources — if, relative to the income available, more is spent on A, then there is less for service B. This feature of the budget is compounded by the fact that the poorest cities often have the greatest need to spend heavily on some of the most expensive services — education, housing, social services, local health. Perhaps the best example is that of the industrial satellites which, with their relatively poor and youthful populations, spend average to high per capita amounts on education, housing, children, and local health services. Their industrial nature also tends to generate high refuse and fire costs. These considerations, plus their poor local tax base (and notwithstanding their high grant levels), leaves them little extra to spare for education, and consequently their per pupil spending is the lowest of all nine city types. It is also notable that the budgets of the metropolitan capitals are strained to their limits (in spite of an ample local tax base) by pressures to spend on a wide variety of services – roads, police, parks, libraries, housing, refuse, public health, planning. This leaves them with no extras for education, and they spend less than average on each of their pupils. The large free-standing cities, with their sparsely populated hinterlands, have less need/demand to spend on many of their services, so they not only spend less in total, but also more on each pupil. A combination of a relatively wealthy population and few demands to spend heavily on expensive services other than education, enables county towns, administrative centres, suburbs, and seaside resorts to spend less in total than the national average, but more on each pupil.

In other words, spending on any one service cannot be understood in isolation from spending on others, and it is useful to view local services as a single package tied together, loosely in some cases, more tightly in others. The strings tying the package together are: (a) the nature of the local authority's population, which may place heavy demands on one service, or group of services, and concomitantly lighter demands on others, (b) the nature of the local authority's internal and external environment, which may generate costs, either high or low, for a set of different services (parks and refuse, fire and refuse), and (c) the limits of scarce resources which mean that more money on A means less on B.

Thus, studying the budget of any one authority or group of authorities leads, on the one hand, outwards and upwards to neighbouring authorities and to the form and structure of the national urban system, and, on the other hand, inwards and downwards, to a consideration of particular service costs and the ways in which one service, or group of them, is likely to affect other services.

And finally, the evidence again underlines the need to treat cities as holistic entities, rather than to try to understand them as the sum of their individual parts.[10] Perhaps the best example is the contrast between county towns and seaside resorts. Both city types were similar in terms of their population, in that they were generally wealthy, middle class, commercial and residential, and controlled by Conservative councils. Yet this similarity contrasts with a difference in spending patterns due to the fact that county types had a different economic base and function, and a different role in the system of cities, compared with seaside resorts. The spending profiles of the two types were determined not by the age, class, or educational structure of their resident populations, but by the economic role they performed as units in the national urban system and its economy.

NOTES

1. C. A. Moser and W. Scott, *British Towns* (Edinburgh, Oliver and Boyd, 1961), pp. 84–6. For an interesting earlier attempt to group local authorities

according to their spending patterns see J. R. and U. K. Hicks, *Standards of Local Expenditure: a Problem of the Inequality of Incomes* (Cambridge, Cambridge University Press, 1943).

2. H. F. Andrews, 'A cluster analysis of British towns', *Urban Studies*, 8 (1971), 271–84.

3. J. H. Johnson, J. Salt, and P. A. Wood, *Housing and the Migration of Labour in England and Wales* (Farnborough, Hants, Saxon House, 1974), p. 63.

4. R. Webber and J. Craig, 'Which local authorities are alike', *Population Trends*, Autumn (1976), 14.

5. For an excellent commentary on why the methods and assumptions of much of the city classification literature produce results which are sometimes rather odd see R. R. Alford, 'Critical evaluation of the principles of city classification', in B. J. L. Berry, *City Classification Handbook* (New York, John Wiley, 1974), pp. 331–58.

6. G. Armen, 'A classification of cities and city regions in England and Wales, 1966', *Regional Studies*, 6 (1974), 149–82.

7. For an account of the social, political, and economic importance of suburbs in the typical American metropolitan system see R. C. Wood, *Suburbia* (Boston, Houghton Mifflin, 1958); B. T. Downes (ed.), *Cities and Suburbs* (Belmont, California, Wadsworth, 1971); A. Downs, *Opening up the Suburbs* (New Haven, Yale University Press, 1973); and more recently M. Schneider and J. R. Logan, 'Fiscal implications of class segregation', *Urban Affairs Quarterly*, 17 (1981), 23–36.

8. D. Byrne, B. Williamson, and B. Fletcher, *The Poverty of Education* (London, Martin Robertson, 1975), p. 89.

9. The majority of studies which cluster British cities group the seaside resorts together, sometimes with other places, but often in a category of their own — see, for example, Moser and Scott, *British Towns*, p. 84; Armen, 'A classification of cities and city regions', 166; Webber and Craig, 'Which local authorities are alike', 14; Hicks and Hicks, *Standards of Local Expenditure*; P. L. Knox, 'Spatial variations in the level of living in England and Wales in 1961', *Transactions of the Institute of British Geographers*, 62 (1974), 18.

10. This corresponds to what Peterson terms the unitary model of local authorities, which assumes that each system has its own set of interests, and consequently its own set of policies, in contrast to the bargaining model, which assumes that local policies are best understood in terms of competition between the local factions, groups, and agencies within each authority. The unitary model treats local authorities as holistic entities, whereas the bargaining model more readily lends itself to an analysis of the struggle between different groups and strata within the population, and hence leads to the use of the demographic approach in output studies. See P. Peterson, 'A unitary model of local taxation and expenditure policies in the United States', *British Journal of Political Science*, 9 (1979), 281–314.

8. THE COUNTIES AND THE WELSH EFFECT

Introduction

This chapter turns from the county boroughs to consider the rather neglected counties of England and Wales. The first section examines the very special spending patterns of the thirteen Welsh counties which cannot be wholly explained in terms of the usual explanatory variables, such as population sparsity or age structure, grant levels, or political patterns. These sorts of variables do go part of the way towards understanding the high service spending levels of the Welsh counties, but they are not the whole of the story by any means, and there seems to be an additional Welsh effect which must be attributed to more intangible regional or cultural influences.

Drawing on the lessons of the first section of the chapter, the next section considers English counties separately and delineates four county types, each of which has its own special set of social, economic, political, and spending characteristics. In other words, the section complements the work of the city-types chapter, and uses its strict criteria in order to devise a satisfactory typology of counties, and so reveals the relationships between different features of the local political systems and the public policies they develop.

The Welsh Effect

County councils have not attracted much research interest. Apart from a few general books on county government, there are few studies which deal with county finances and services, compared with the many which consider county boroughs and urban authorities.[1] The counties deserve more attention, if only because more than half the nation's population lives in them, a proportion which is increasing with the trends of suburbanization and counter-urbanization.[2] Moreover, counties were responsible for 37 per cent of total local revenue expenditure in England and Wales in 1972/3 (county boroughs spent 27 per cent), and nearly 25 per cent of capital expenditure (county boroughs spent 28 per cent).[3] In addition, the inclusion of counties in this study gives it a much wider range of variation in local conditions, and, therefore, enables us to draw more broadly based generalizations about the relationship between social, economic, and political circumstances, and local policies and service expenditures.

The different service responsibilities of counties and county boroughs, however, means that the two are best analysed separately. The circumstances of the counties were also different from those of the boroughs, and require a slightly different approach. For example, as Chapter 2 shows, there was a clear difference between the counties and the county boroughs so far as the relationship between grants and expenditure was concerned, suggesting either that the two types of authorities were different in their financial operations, or that there were major differences within the types which give rise to different financial profiles. Hence, the counties are analysed separately from the boroughs and have this chapter to themselves.

In general, conventional output studies have had no more success with the counties than with the county boroughs. The Tiebout hypothesis can be applied only to large metropolitan areas with many local government units, and has little or no relevance to large geographical units such as the counties. The demographic approach has mixed results, explaining some services such as education, highways, and health quite well, but others, such as children, planning, police, and fire rather poorly (see Table 3.2). But even these 'good' results (good in the sense of strong regression coefficients) are sometimes misleading, as we shall see a little later in this chapter. Nor does factor or cluster analysis offer anything promising, since it proves impossible to extract factors which are either general or explanatory, or to cluster authorities in a way which makes sense of their spending variations.

Fortunately, the league tables discussed in Chapter 5 offer some useful leads and clues, most notably the finding that the thirteen Welsh counties stood out for their consistently high spending. Exactly how high and consistent is shown in Table 8.1, which reveals that the Welsh authorities not only exceeded the English in every one of the nine services, but did so by a considerable margin in some cases. In education, for example, Merioneth, Radnor, Montgomery, and Brecon filled the first four places in the county league tables for per pupil spending in 1972/3. We also find Cardigan, Monmouth, and Pembroke in the top ten, and eleven of the Welsh counties were in the top twenty. None were in the bottom twenty. The picture was much the same for health and social services. In picking out the unusual and high spending figures of the Welsh counties on education we are simply confirming what is already a well-attested phenomenon in the literature,[4] but one which has not been adequately explained.

Welsh counties were big spenders across the whole range of services, not just the social and educational ones. Highways have little in common with education, for example, and yet eight of the Welsh authorities were in the top ten, eleven in the top thirteen. Similar sorts of figures can be produced for police, planning, libraries, and fire; and, since spending on every individual service is high, so also is the total.

Though remarkable, these figures do not prove that there is anything unique about Wales. The Welsh pattern may simply be an extension of more general trends in both England and Wales whereby counties with, say, low population

Table 8.1 *Average Per Capita Service Expenditures (£) of Welsh Counties compared with English Counties, 1972/3*

	Welsh counties (n = 13)	English counties (n = 45)	Welsh spending as a percentage of English
Education (per capita)	58.03	49.58	117.0
Education (per pupil)	314.83	283.60	110.0
Health services	5.06	3.34	151.5
Social services	5.84	4.80	121.7
Highways	14.25	6.87	207.4
Fire	1.87	1.57	119.1
Police	7.72	6.72	114.9
Libraries	1.38	1.19	116.0
Planning	1.24	0.85	145.9
Total	101.99	78.11	130.6

densities, low incomes, and a mining and agricultural economy, tend to spend heavily. In other words, Welsh counties may well conform to the general county pattern, but in a rather stronger form because they have stronger features. Yet this seems not to be the case, or at least, not wholly the case. There seems to be something about the Welsh figures which cannot be wholly understood or explained in terms of tendencies common to all counties − there seems to be a *Welsh effect*, which is not found in English counties, not even in the English counties which are most like the Welsh. We will try to show the strength and significance of this Welsh effect by looking closely at: (1) education spending in sparsely populated counties, and (2) the relationship between spending, local election turnout, and uncontested seats. Education and sparsity are chosen because of their special social and financial importance, while turnout and uncontested seats are selected for their relevance to the next chapter, which considers the importance of political factors in determining public policy.

Population Sparsity and Per Pupil Education Spending

It has been common knowledge for two decades or more that population sparsity contributes to high education costs, partly because of the costs of transporting children from outlying areas, and partly because small primary classes and schools are expensive.[5] Because of this, a large number of rural schools have been closed in order to achieve the economies of scale of larger units. This was often carried through in the teeth of campaigns to save village schools. At the same time, population sparsity was found to be such an important determinant of high local government costs that a sparsity factor was built into the regression formula of the rate support grant, and this determined the distribution of hundreds, if not thousands, of millions of pounds. In spite of all this, our evidence suggests that population sparsity has little, if anything, to do with spending on education (or indeed, any other service, other than highways). Rather, the Welsh counties that happen to be thinly populated spend heavily on education, but it is mainly a Welsh effect and not a sparsity effect which causes this.

Table 8.2 *Simple Correlations between Population Density (Population Per Acre) and Per Pupil Education Spending in English, Welsh, and All Counties, 1972/3*

All counties (n = 58)	English counties (n = 45)	Welsh counties (n = 13)
−0.27*	0.10	−0.75**

First, as Table 8.2 shows, there is a significant negative correlation between population density and per pupil spending in all counties, but when the Welsh and English authorities are separated, it becomes clear that the figure is as insignificant for the English authorities as it is highly significant for the Welsh ones.

Next, when English and Welsh counties are matched for sparsity, it is evident that the former almost invariably spent much less than the latter (Table 8.3). A *t* test shows that while the population sparsities of the two sets of authorities in this table are not significantly different, the spending figures are significantly different at 5 per cent, using a one-tailed test.

Table 8.3 *Per Pupil Education Spending in English and Welsh Counties matched for Population Sparsity, 1972/3*

Welsh counties	Population per acre	Per pupil (£)	English counties	Population per acre	Per pupil (£)
Cardigan	0.12	345	Westmorland	0.14	290
Pembroke	0.25	289	North Yorkshire	0.25	280
Carmarthen	0.28	314	Devon	0.29	281
Anglesey	0.34	295	Norfolk	0.35	287
Caernarvon	0.34	304	Lincs.–Kesteven	0.35	282
Denbigh	0.44	302	Cornwall	0.44	273
Monmouth	1.05	296	Bedfordshire	1.06	285
Flint	1.10	267	Derbyshire	1.08	290
Glamorgan	1.62	278	Kent	1.52	283
Average	0.62	300		0.61	283

However, four of the Welsh counties were so thinly populated that they could not be matched with English counterparts, and, moreover, these four spent heavily on education, even by Welsh standards. This group of statistical outliers

— the four were Radnor, Merioneth, Montgomery, and Brecon — appears as a distinct group on the scattergrams, and the four counties are largely, though not entirely, responsible for the statistical association between sparsity and spending in all Welsh and English counties, as the figures in Table 8.4 indicate.

Table 8.4 *Simple Correlations between Population Sparsity and Education Spending in selected English and Welsh counties, 1972/3*

	Education expenditure		(n)
	Per capita	Per pupil	
All counties	0.16	−0.27*	(58)
All counties, less the four most sparsely populated in Wales	0.06	−0.08	(54)
All Welsh counties	−0.56*	−0.75**	(13)
Welsh counties, less the four most sparsely populated	−0.26	−0.68*	(9)
English counties	0.22	0.10	

When the four outliers are removed, the correlations between sparsity and education spending drop to insignificance, and, equally, when the same authorities are removed from the Welsh calculations the correlations also drop, though the correlation is still high for per pupil spending. This suggests that the sparsity effect is strong mainly in Wales, that it shows no signs of importance in England, and that even in Wales it is magnified by a handful of extreme cases. In other words, the relationship between population sparsity and high education spending is largely spurious. This is also the case with the relationship beween voting turnout and spending levels, which we will now consider.

Election Turnout, Uncontested Seats, and Service Spending

Voting turnout is considered in this section of the chapter for two reasons. First, examining the relationship between turnout and spending levels (or rather, the absence of any causal relationship) helps to underline the importance of the Welsh effect. Second, if a powerful case is to be made out in the following chapter for the importance of politics as a determinant of local policies and spending patterns, then care must be taken to pick out genuinely important political variables, and not spurious ones like voting turnout.

Many studies have used election turnout as a political indicator, and many of them have found a statistical association between turnout and service spending,[6] but turnout seems to have been used, in some cases, because it is an easy figure to obtain, not because of its general or theoretical interest. Why should turnout have anything to do with local outputs? What is the link between a high or a low poll, and, say, spending on planning? It may be that high turnout authorities tend to be competitive ones which change party control, a fact which induces caution in the majority party, but in this case it is the competitive nature of the council, and not turnout, which explains spending. Or it may be that working-class authorities have a low turnout and a particular pattern of spending, in which case class needs more careful investigation. However, until a plausible story can be told that links turnout and spending, it seems reasonable to suspect that any correlation between the two is spurious, a statistical artefact which tells us little about causal relationships.

Table 8.5 *Simple Correlations between Local Election Turnout (1970) and Per Capita Service Expenditures (1972/3) in all Counties, in English Counties, and in Welsh Counties*

	All counties (n = 58)	English counties (n = 45)	Welsh counties (n = 13)
Highways	0.82***	0.25	0.89***
Health	0.81***	0.05	0.83***
Education (per capita)	0.71***	0.21	0.77**
Education (per pupil)	0.71***	0.19	0.88***
Police	0.58***	0.06	0.62*
Planning	0.57***	0.18	0.48
Social services	0.49***	0.26	0.18
Libraries	0.43***	0.05	0.51
Fire	0.37**	0.19	0.11
Total	0.85***	0.26	0.88***

This study also finds strong correlations between turnout and service spending, particularly in the counties where the figures are particularly substantial (Table 8.5), and hold up in regression analysis. However, the figures also show that the Welsh authorities often have a high turnout (57 per cent in 1970, compared with the English figure of 33 per cent), and that a few of them combine particularly high voting percentages with particularly high spending. As before, this raises the possibility that it is not turnout which is important, but a coincidence of the two in Welsh counties. This suspicion is confirmed by the figures. Table 8.5 compares the simple correlations between turnout and total service spending for all counties, all English counties, and all Welsh counties. The statistical significance of the figures for all counties is eliminated in every single case by taking the Welsh counties out of the calculations. Equally, in seven out of ten cases the strength of the Welsh correlation is increased when the Welsh counties are taken separately. There is, in other words, no general relationship between turnout and spending, except in Wales. And as it happens, the same four counties which stand out for their population sparsity and education spending, also stand out for their high turnout (Table 8.6). It seems, therefore, that turnout has about as much to do with service expenditures as population sparsity: that is to say, little or nothing.

Table 8.6 *Spending, Sparsity, Turnout, and Uncontested Seats in Four Welsh Counties compared with Welsh and English Counties*

	Total spending	Rank	Population density	Rank	Uncontested seats, 1970	Rank	Turnout 1970	Rank
Radnor	134	1	0.06	1	97	1	75.6	1
Merioneth	129	2	0.08	2=	81	2	74.7	3
Montgomery	128	3	0.08	2=	80	3=	74.6	4
Brecon	108	5	0.11	3	80	3=	63.7	5
Welsh counties (n = 13)	102		0.45		69.5		56.76	
English counties (n = 45)	78		0.88		54.1		33.07	

Note: The ranking is for all counties (English and Welsh).

While on this general topic, it would be as well to clear up a closely related question concerning strong correlations between the proportion of uncontested seats and service spending. Like voting turnout, the proportion of uncontested seats appeared strongly significant in many of our preliminary tables, and like turnout it was difficult to imagine what could account for this, other than statistical spuriousness. A further look at the figures shows, as one might expect, a close relationship between population sparsity, high voting turnout, and a high proportion of uncontested seats.[7] The most rural authorities had few contests, but a high turnout in the few elections which were held. The Welsh authorities, being sparsely populated, were also notable for their few contests, and for their high turnout in places where there were elections. Four counties were notable in this respect (see Table 8.6), and as one would expect, they are also the same four which spent a lot. It is these four which explain a great deal of the statistical strength of correlations between spending, on the one hand, and sparsity, turnout, and uncontested seats, on the other.

The special nature of the Welsh counties means that the patterns of correlations between service spending and county characteristics vary considerably between England and Wales. Some correlations which are highly significant for all counties are insignificant for England, others which are insignificant for all counties are significant for either England or Wales. For reasons of space it is only possible to illustrate this point with a few figures for per pupil spending (Table 8.7), but it should be noted that similar shifts in the strength of the correlations occur for most county services in most years.

THE COUNTIES AND THE WELSH EFFECT

Table 8.7 *Changing Correlations between Per Pupil Education Spending (1972/3), and a Selection of Social, Economic, and Political Variables, for All Counties compared with English and Welsh Counties*

	All counties (n = 58)	English counties (n = 45)	Welsh counties (n = 13)
Low household density	0.49***	0.19	0.70**
No hot-water tap	0.50***	−0.04	0.74**
% Rateable value offices	0.08	0.55***	−0.23
% RV industry	−0.36**	−0.14	−0.75**
% Old population	0.37**	0.22	0.57*
Log population	−0.59***	−0.20	−0.80**
% School population	−0.12	−0.32*	−0.50
% Lower middle class	−0.40**	0.08	−0.73**
% Small self-employed	0.70***	0.16	0.88**
% Agricultural workers	0.60***	0.11	0.85***
% Working class	−0.36**	−0.42**	−0.74**
Turnout	0.71***	0.19	0.87**

Two other lines of exploration, though inconclusive in themselves, add circumstantial evidence to the claim for a Welsh effect. First, the Welsh county boroughs also spent slightly more than average (Table 8.8), though it must be said that the figures should be treated with caution since the differences were not large and there were only four Welsh county boroughs. Second, the Welsh border counties spent considerably more than their immediate neighbours in England, and yet the Welsh counties were not much more sparsely populated than the English, which, in their turn were rather more sparsely populated than the English average. In other words, crossing the border did not radically change the nature of the physical and social environment, but it did change spending levels quite markedly. It is also notable that the Welsh border counties had appreciably more uncontested seats and high turnouts (Table 8.9).

Table 8.8 *Total Per Capita Expenditure (£) in Welsh County Boroughs compared with All County Boroughs, 1960/1 and 1972/3*

	Total expenditure 1960/1	1972/3
Cardiff	29	98
Swansea	35	123
Newport	31	99
Merthyr Tydfil	30	96
Welsh average	31.25	104
CB average	29.71	96.41

Table 8.9 *Total Per Capita Expenditure (£) in Welsh and English Border Counties, 1972/3*

	Sparsity	Turnout	% Uncontested (1970)	Total per capita
Welsh border counties[a]	0.35	59.4	76.6	109.6
English border counties[b]	0.80	33.8	58.0	82.0
All Welsh counties	0.45	56.8	69.5	102.0
All English counties	0.88	33.1	54.1	78.0

Notes: [a] Monmouth, Brecon, Radnor, Montgomery, and Denbigh.
[b] Gloucester, Hereford, Salop, and Cheshire.

We are back, therefore, to the conclusion that some sort of Welsh effect was operating which could not be reduced entirely to the sorts of things which can be encompassed by a large computer file, variables such as population sparsity or class composition, or grant levels, or voting levels. The Welsh effect was not entirely dissociated from these sorts of influences, but, at the same time, there seemed to be other things over and on top of them which can best be summarized, however inadequate these terms may be as hard explanatory variables, under the headings of political culture, historical patterns, regional variation, and religious and educational influences.

We can speculate briefly about the possible causes of this special Welsh spending pattern. It might be, for example, that the special status of Wales in central government, first with a Minister of Welsh Affairs (created 1951), then with a Minister of State (1957), and finally with a Secretary of State for Wales (1964), may have given Welsh authorities an extra leverage over central government which helped to channel extra grants in their own direction. It is certainly true that the Welsh authorities received a disproportionate share of the total grant to local authorities in England and Wales, for with about five and a half per cent of the population they had between 6.6 and 7.5 per cent of the grant (Table 8.10). In per capita terms, Welsh grants were a third to a fifth higher than English ones. It is also noticeable, however, that the gap between the two countries was closing between 1960 and 1972, so that whatever advantage, if any, may have accrued from having a special status in central government, does not seem to have been sustained throughout the 1960s. And more to the point, spending in Welsh counties was higher even than one might expect from their grant levels, in each of the four observation years from 1960/1 to 1972/3. In addition, Welsh spending levels were considerably higher than those for the English agricultural counties which the Welsh counties resembled most closely in social, economic, and political terms, and which were treated in a closely similar way in terms of the various grant distribution formulae of the period. Grant levels seem to explain part, but certainly not the whole of the high spending levels in Wales.

Table 8.10 *Welsh and English Authorities Compared*

	Welsh population as % of Welsh and English population	Welsh grants as % of English and Welsh grants	Welsh grants (per capita) as % of English grants (per capita)	Total per capita expenditure in Welsh counties as % of total per capita spending in English counties	Total per capita expenditure in Welsh counties as % of total per capita expenditure in English agricultural counties
1960/1	5.7	7.5	130.4	137.0	130.9
1964/5	5.7	7.5	134.4	135.3	130.0
1968/9	5.6	7.1	129.9	128.5	126.4
1972/3	5.6	6.6	120.1	130.6	128.8

To summarize briefly the findings so far: Welsh counties spent considerably more on all their services than English ones, but this had little, if anything, to do with population sparsity, local election turnout, or uncontested seats; Welsh counties spent considerably more on education than English counties, even when the two are matched carefully for population sparsity; the significance of the correlations between service spending, on the one hand, and sparsity, turnout, and uncontested seats, on the other, is usually greatly reduced or eliminated altogether when the Welsh counties are removed from the calculations; further to this, a small group of Welsh authorities which are far above the average on all these variables act as statistical outliers which distort the overall relationships in all counties. The high level of central government grants helps to explain some of the differences between Welsh and English counties, but, on the other hand, Welsh spending was higher even than one would expect from their grants, and so also was spending in Welsh counties compared with that in the English agricultural counties which most closely match them in social, economic, and political terms. It is difficult to escape the conclusion that there was a Welsh effect operating independently of all these considerations, and which must be put down to the influence of other, perhaps regional, cultural, historical, educational, or religious, factors.

A set of figures summarizing the social, economic, and political differences between Welsh and English counties is given in Table 8.11. They show that the Welsh authorities were small, agricultural, sparsely populated, poor with low rateable values and poor housing conditions, and with a large majority of Independent (politically) councillors, but few contested seats. In most of these respects they resembled the most sparsely populated and agricultural of the English counties, although the Welsh authorities were, if anything, rather poorer and more sparsely populated.

In spite of their similarities with the English agricultural counties, the thirteen Welsh authorities financed their public services on an altogther different scale. Whereas the English agricultural counties spent heavily on three services, the Welsh authorities spent even more heavily on these three, and on all other services as well. In 1972/3, no group of English counties came anywhere near the Welsh spending levels for any given service, or for the total of all services together. Although the gap between English and Welsh authorities was closing during the period 1960/1 to 1972/3 − the Welsh counties were spending 137 per cent of the English figure in 1960/1, but 130 per cent by 1972/3 − there was still a large gap between the two even in the later years. The second part of the chapter will turn from the Welsh counties to the English ones, and will consider the spending patterns of different types of counties in much the same way as the previous chapter examined the spending levels of city types.

As in the chapter on city types, all the figures reported in Tables 8.11 and 8.12

Table 8.11 *The Social, Economic, and Political Characteristics of County Types, 1972*

	Welsh counties	English counties				
		Industrial	Commuter	South coast	Agricultural	Average
Household density	1.8	2.2	1.8	1.3	1.5	1.6
No hot tap (%)	10.4	6.1	4.1	4.7	7.3	6.1
Population density (per acre)	0.5	1.3	1.5	1.1	0.4	0.9
RV per capita (£)	33.8	37.0	51.2	50.3	37.7	41.9
Offices (%)	7.7	8.7	20.3	14.5	10.7	12.8
Population (000)	162.0	1040.0	763.0	731.0	285.0	556.0
School age (%)	18.5	18.4	18.0	16.0	17.3	17.5
Agricultural workers	14.5	3.1	3.1	5.0	11.6	7.4
Middle class (%)	27.2	30.3	39.0	37.6	30.9	33.3
Conservative (%)	6.4	44.4	72.2	79.4	23.9	44.1
Labour (%)	23.2	40.4	14.9	5.2	12.4	16.3
Independent (%)	65.5	12.6	10.6	16.6	61.7	37.4
(N)	(13)	(7)	(9)	(5)	(21)	(45)

Table 8.12 Per Capita Service Expenditures (£) of County Types, 1972/3

	Welsh counties	English counties				
		Industrial	Commuter	South coast	Agricultural	Average
Health	5.06	3.19	3.26	3.21	3.48	3.34
Social services	5.84	5.42	4.64	5.06	4.63	4.80
Highways	14.25	5.56	5.94	6.13	7.99	6.87
Fire	1.87	1.72	1.67	1.64	1.52	1.57
Police	7.72	6.74	6.41	7.01	6.86	6.72
Libraries	1.38	1.21	1.22	1.25	1.13	1.19
Planning	1.24	0.86	0.80	0.87	0.84	0.85
Education (per capita)	58.02	49.59	52.74	46.02	49.54	49.57
Education (per pupil)	314.83	265.80	290.35	288.58	285.84	283.66
Total	101.99	77.21	77.84	75.76	79.19	78.11
(N)	(13)	(7)	(9)	(5)	(21)	(45)

were computed for the first year of the study, but for reasons of space are not presented here. And, as in the previous chapter, it was found that the figures vary only a little, relative to each county type, from one year to the next. This suggests that the county typology, like that for the county boroughs, is fairly stable over time, and that the results reported in the tables are not the product of an unusual set of circumstances which happened to come together for the financial year 1972/3.

County Types

Counties do not lend themselves to as clear-cut a typology as do county boroughs. The latter were smaller, in terms of both geographical and population size, and their social and economic features were usually more sharply defined. Counties, in contrast, were larger and more heterogeneous, and most had a mixture of economic functions — agricultural, industrial, commercial, and residential — within their boundaries. For example, Warrington, as an industrial city, contrasted strongly with Exeter, while Gloucestershire, though primarily agricultural, contained some quite large urban pockets, as well as some manufacturing and commercial areas. In this respect it overlapped with a county such as Lancashire which had more manufacturing and commercial activity than most, but which was also partly agricultural. The fact that the counties were all more economically mixed than the cities, makes it more difficult to group them according to their economic functions, and means that any county categories are likely to be fuzzy at the edges.

Moreover, cities, seen as service centres for their own and their hinterland populations, exist as social and economic entities, whereas counties are more arbitrary units created by more purely administrative needs. This is not a matter of just some local authority boundaries being arbitrary, for all of them (with the possible exception of coastlines) are arbitrary in the sense that they cut across social and economic patterns to some extent. Rather, it is a matter of cities being 'natural' entities with social and economic functions of their own, and spheres of influence which can be marked out, no matter how roughly. On the other hand, the lines dividing one county from another were more usually for organizational convenience, and justified mainly by history and tradition. For example, Norwich and Ipswich were separate urban centres, and distinguishable as such, but no such division can be drawn between the tracts of land called Norfolk and Suffolk. The division of this part of East Anglia into two, irrespective of where the boundary was placed, was a matter of administrative convenience, rather than a matter of social and economic logic. It no doubt made more sense to follow the lines cut by the River Waveney and the Little Ouse, rather than to draw a straight line on a map from Lowestoft to Cambridge, but it is the need for a boundary rather than its exact position which is at the heart of the matter. The arbitrary nature of many of the boundaries between counties means that any classification of these authorities is itself likely to be arbitrary up to a point.

Similarly, the counties did not form a national hierarchy as the cities did, so the central place approach developed for the cities in Chapter 6 is entirely inappropriate to the counties. Nor was there a division of labour between the counties, as there was between the cities, or a system of counties comparable in any important way with the national system of cities. The counties need their own approach, but it must be frankly recognized that their size, their heterogeneity, and, to some extent, the greater arbitrariness of their boundaries make it impossible to deal with them with the same degree of theoretical neatness or empirical precision as the cities.

Nevertheless the relative success of the city typology led us to try the same sort of exercise on the counties, while recognizing that the county types were bound, by the very nature of the authorities, to overlap quite considerably, thereby leaving the edges of the categories blurred. Their associated spending patterns, if these ever emerged, were likely to be considerably less distinct than those of the cities. Thus the exercise is a tentative and hesitant one. However, it did prove possible to discern a rough and ready typology of counties, and this does help toward an understanding of the variations in their service expenditures. We do not wish to claim too much for the work, and recognize that it is not as satisfactory as the analysis of the county boroughs, but in spite of this, some general tendencies and patterns do show through. To pick these out may help new developments in an area which, as Stanyer has pointed out, has been neglected in the past.[8]

The ground rules and procedure for marking out a county typology were the same as those for the county boroughs. Each category is exhaustive of all counties of that kind, so that, for example, all counties with more than the average percentage of agricultural workers are included in the same group, and all of those with more than the average percentage of working-class residents are placed in the industrial type. At the same time, each category is internally consistent and homogeneous, so that, for example, the category including agricultural counties includes no other kinds of county. In short, all counties of Type A are included in the same category, and that category includes only counties of Type A. To this extent the typology is logically and empirically consistent.

The procedure used social, economic, and political indicators in order to contruct a typology of counties which would stand up in its own right quite apart from service spending levels. To this end a set of eleven variables were used as indicators of social and economic conditions, taxable capacity, economic base, population age, size and density, social class, and political colour. Once the typology was constructed on the basis of these data, it was then applied to spending levels to see if there was a correspondence which would help us to understand variations in outputs. Because the Welsh authorities have already been discussed at some length, this part of the work will deal only with the English counties, which are grouped as follows:

(1) Industrial counties,
(2) Commuter counties,
(3) South-coast retirement counties,
(4) Agricultural counties.

As already emphasized these categories are not as clear-cut and distinct as those in the city typology. Since each county tends to cover a range of different population types and economic functions, the categories tend to run into each other at the edges. For example, Northumberland was part industrial, working class, and Labour, but also part rural, agricultural, and Conservative. Warwickshire, Worcestershire, Cambridgeshire, and Bedfordshire were revealed by the social indicators as being a mixture of agricultural and commuter types. Besides this lack of sharp definition, three of the counties (5 per cent of the total) did not fit into any category. The Isle of Wight, the only island authority, was in a group of its own, though it most closely resembled the south-coast retirement counties. Oxfordshire did not resemble any type at all closely, and nor did neighbouring Wiltshire. Both of them had unusual spending patterns to match their unusual social, economic, and political features.

Some of the differences in the per capita spending of the counties are also quite small when compared with the differences between the city types. Nevertheless, small per capita differences can amount to substantial sums in absolute terms. The average county council had a population of 467,436 in 1971, so that a difference of only £0.01 in per capita spending amounted to £4,674 on the total service bill of the average county. Most of the differences reported in this chapter are considerably larger than this. For example, to take Table 8.1 (simply because it happens to be the first in the chapter), this shows a difference of £8.45 in per capita spending on education between Welsh and English counties. This represented £3,949,834 on the education bill of the average county. The smallest variation reported in Table 8.1 is that between Welsh and English library spending, where the gap was only £0.19, but this amounted to £88,812 on the average library total — enough to stock and run a small library. In other words, although the county types do not differ as much as the cities in their spending, the importance of the differences which do exist should not be underestimated.

With these important caveats in mind we can proceed to the county typology.

(1) *Industrial Counties*

This rather small group of authorities located in the Midlands and the North were the poorest and most industrial of the counties. They were Derbyshire, Durham, Nottinghamshire, Northamptonshire, Leicestershire, Lancashire, and West Yorkshire. The group as a whole had a considerably higher than average proportion of working class residents by English county standards, and most of the social and economic conditions associated with this – poor quality and overcrowded housing, low rateable values, and only a small proportion of the most highly rated commercial property and shops, a large school-aged population, and a large proportion of industrial property. These counties were also by far the largest and the most densely populated of the county types, having an average population of over one million and greater densities per household and per acre than the average.

The population density and the working-class nature of these counties were accompanied, as one would expect, by strong Labour councils. In fact, they were the only counties of the time which were both organized along strong party lines and had comfortable Labour majorities. They had two or three times the average percentage of Labour councillors, and more than the average number of Conservatives, but far fewer Independents. In many ways, therefore, the working-class and industrial counties were comparable to some of the industrial county boroughs, especially those which were situated in rural or semi-urban surroundings, such as the free-standing industrial cities. Among the counties, however, the seven industrial ones stand as forming a rather small but fairly distinctive category (see Table 8.11).

By overall county standards, the spending of the industrial counties was also distinctive. Because of their working-class populations and their poor tax base they spent less than average both in total and on a range of services – most notably health, roads, and education per pupil. They were about average on the services whose costs tend to be high in urban places, such as police, libraries, and planning, and above average on only two services, fire and social services. The first of the latter is explained in terms of the high fire risks of industry and dense populations, and the second by the social and economic problems of the industrial counties. In 1971/2, Northamptonshire, Lancashire, and Durham were at the top of the league table for social services spending.

Education spending is interesting in its own right, and because it follows the general pattern noted for the cities in the previous chapter. Because industrial counties had a high proportion of school-aged children (the highest of all the county types), their per capita education spending was comparatively high, but, in contrast, their per pupil spending was relatively low. Northamptonshire, Lancashire, Nottinghamshire, and West Yorkshire were all at the tail-end of the league table for counties in 1971/2, spending around £250 per pupil, compared with the league leaders' figures of £310-20. Or to put the same figures a different way, had the industrial counties spent the average on each of their pupils, each of their total education bills would have been £3,404,898 greater. Had Northamptonshire spent as much on each pupil as Surrey, its education bill would have been £15,876,771 larger. At the same time, the extra per capita spending caused by the high proportion of school children, combined with a poor local tax base, left little over for extra spending on other services (see Table 8.12).

(2) Commuter Counties

After the industrial counties of the Midlands and the North, the next most urbanized counties were found in the Midlands and the South, but instead of containing working-class manufacturing and mining towns, they included middle-class suburbs and commuter villages which lie just beyond the perimeter of major metropolitan centres. They supplied the metropolitan capitals with many of their professional and managerial workers, and they consisted in 1971 of the affluent home counties of Hertfordshire, Buckinghamshire, Berkshire, Surrey, and Essex, plus their Midland and Northern equivalents, Staffordshire, Warwickshire, and Cheshire. Bedfordshire was also included in this group, as was Middlesex before it became incorporated into the GLC. Like the industrial counties, the commuter counties were large in population size (an average of 760,000 in 1971), densely populated, and also like the industrial counties they had well-developed party systems, with large Conservative majorities, large Labour minorities, and a small and declining number of Independents. After this the similarities end. The commuter counties were wealthy and middle class, with good housing conditions, high rateable values, and a good local tax base of commercial property and shops. There is some overlap between the commuter counties and some of the agricultural counties with suburban developments, but otherwise the commuter counties form quite a cohesive category, by county standards, representing the more affluent, middle class, and Conservative of the urban and suburban areas.

As in the wealthiest and most middle-class county boroughs, spending was low in total, and average to low on health, social services, roads, police, fire, and planning. The only notable exception to this low funding of public services was education, where both per capita and per pupil spending were high. The commuter counties had a high proportion of school-aged children (presumably the young managers and professionals moving out of the cities and into the suburbs and the surrounding villages), and could well afford to devote ample resources to their education. They had the highest per capita and per pupil figures of all the English county types. Surrey and Hertfordshire were the league leaders in 1971/2, closely followed by Buckinghamshire and Cheshire. Surrey spent £42.40 (15 per cent) more than the county average on each of its school-children in 1971/2. Had it not spent above the average, its total education bill would have been close to six million pounds less.

(3) South-coast Retirement Counties

In many ways the South-coast retirement counties constitute a sub-group of the commuter counties, since the two are closely aligned in many different ways. But the South-coast retirement authorities do differ to an extent which sets them apart. The group consists of Dorset, Hampshire, Kent, and East and West Sussex. The Isle of Wight is loosely attached to the group, but, as the only island county in England it is set apart from the sub-group to some extent. The group had all the characteristics of the commuter counties – prosperity and all its accompanying features in the form of a large middle class, good housing, high rateable values, little industry, and strongly Conservative councils – but in addition its members had the special needs of tourist economies, plus a relatively high proportion of retired people.

Consequently, though total spending was low (the lowest of all the county types), that on a special range of old people's and resort services was relatively high, and appreciably higher than in the commuter counties. This pattern shows itself in social services, roads, police, fire, and planning. It is notable that the South-coast counties had the highest highways figure after the agricultural counties, which, as we shall see, were unusual for their own special reasons.

With fewer than the average number of schoolchildren, per capita education costs were low, but per pupil spending was high. On the whole, however, the spending patterns of the commuter and South-coast counties were similar, and it was only the special economic needs and the special population structure which made the seaside counties a slight variation on the theme.

(4) Agricultural Counties

The largest group of counties contains those which are closest to the typical picture of an English county – agricultural, rural, and sparsely populated. The group consisted of the agricultural periphery, Northumberland, Westmorland, Cumberland, Cornwall, Norfolk, Lincolnshire, and Suffolk, and East and North Yorkshire, plus what might be termed the agricultural heartland of England, Somerset, Devon, Gloucester, Salop, Hereford, Rutland, Huntingdonshire, Cambridgeshire, and Worcestershire. All these counties are marked by a large proportion of agricultural workers and small farmers. By and large, housing and social conditions were not good, and rateable values were rather low, with little commercial or industrial property. Populations were also small and thinly distributed. The local political systems were dominated by Independents, and had only small minorities of Labour and Conservative councillors. Overall, these counties stood out as the most agricultural, the most sparsely populated, and the poorest, and as having the least well-developed local party systems among the English counties.

This configuration was associated with its own special pattern of public service provision and spending. Total spending was very high, with Cumberland, Westmorland, Rutland, and Northumberland at the very top of the league table. But this high spending was the result of only three services — health, roads, and police. On all other headings the agricultural counties spent average or less than average amounts. Health spending was high because outlying villages and farms, often with poor housing conditions and limited local medical facilities, required extra health visitors who had to travel long distances, and extra medical services and provisions. Roads were particularly expensive because of the high mileage of roads per capita, and also because of all the natural hazards to rural roads, from mountain snow to fenland subsidence. Police costs were rather high because of the extra expense of maintaining a police presence in outlying areas. One might say the same about fire costs (which were average to low), except that whereas a farmer might be expected to handle his own small fires, he cannot act as his local arm of the law.

We have already dwelt upon education and sparsity at some length in this chapter, but it is worth observing that agricultural counties had slightly less than the average proportion of schoolchildren, and slightly less than average per capita spending to match. On the other hand, they spent more than average on each pupil, suggesting either that population sparsity (or some other influence of this kind) caused high education costs, or else that their local education authorities chose to devote more than average resources to their children. Sparsity does not seem to be the cause of high costs, since the more densely populated commuter counties, which had a higher proportion of schoolchildren, outspent the agricultural counties on both a per capita and a per pupil basis. While it is true that Cumberland and Hereford were sparsely populated and spent well above the average on each of their pupils, so also did Surrey, Hertford-shire, and East Sussex, and they were much more densely populated. Once again, the evidence suggests that it was not population sparsity which caused high education spending. Yet the main feature of the agricultural counties is not their high education spending, but their low spending on most other services.

Summary and Conclusions

This chapter started off with the puzzling finding that there seemed to be no general relationships between social, economic, and political conditions in the counties and their spending on particular local services. Investigation of this puzzle showed that the Welsh authorities often stood out as a group on their own, separated from the general trends of the other counties. Closer examination suggested that the Welsh counties were indeed *sui generis* and that their local policies of heavy spending on all county services could not be explained entirely by their demographic, environmental, and political characteristics. Over and above considerations of this kind, which can be captured more or less accurately by variables on an extensive data file, there seems to be a Welsh effect, the nature and origin of which is more elusive, but which, nevertheless, seems to have a strong impact.

Two conclusions flow from this finding. The first, mainly of theoretical interest, underlines the significance of somewhat intangible cultural, religious, and historical variables in the determination of public policy, at least in the case of the thirteen Welsh counties. At the very least there were influences operating in Wales which could not be detected in any set of English counties, even among the English counties which most closely matched the Welsh ones. There was, in other words, a Welsh effect which was special and unique to the principality, and which could not be reduced entirely to such things as class, politics, grants, sparsity, or the agricultural basis of the local economy.

The second conclusion is of more practical importance and concerns the misleading nature of regression analysis as a basis for the distribution of central government grants. Regression analysis has, of course, been used extensively in both academic and governmental circles as a means of discovering the causes and correlates of local spending levels in Britain, and more particularly for the determination of the needs element of the rate support grant before it gave way to the block grant system. In the case of English and Welsh counties its results were misleading since it assumed that the same set of relationships holding in England would be repeated in Wales, and vice versa. This assumption, though politically neutral between the two countries, weighted the grant distribution formulae in favour of English counties which had the same objective features (population sparsity, etc.) as the high spending Welsh counties, but which did not spend at the same high level. In other words, the Welsh counties, being at the extremes of the county distribution, are likely to have weighed disproportionately in the regression formula for the rate support grant, and, consequently, they and their most sparsely populated and agricultural equivalents in England are likely to have benefited in the resulting distribution of grant.

For the same sorts of reasons, the finding that schools tend to be expensive in the most sparsely populated counties is largely based upon the fact that Welsh counties are the most sparsely populated in England and Wales, and spent the most heavily on education. However, sparsely populated English counties spent no more than some of the most densely populated, and, therefore, the connection between sparsity and education costs appears to be an artefact of the Welsh effect, rather than the result of any underlying causal connection between the two.

The uncovering of a Welsh effect suggests that counties in England and Wales should be treated separately, and the second section of the chapter has done so by devising a fourfold typology of English counties and distinguishing them from the Welsh, which form a fifth type. The five county types are:

(1) *The industrial counties*. This group consists of a small number of counties in the North and the Midlands which were mainly industrial, working class, and Labour. They spent rather little on most services, but about average on those services which tend to be costly in urban places, such as police, libraries, planning, and fire. They also spent heavily on social services because of the nature of their populations.

(2) *The commuter counties*. Though urban (and suburban) like the industrial counties, these were the middle-class areas which surround the main metropolitan centres and provide them with their professional and managerial workers. They spent below, or no more than average on most services, with the major and notable exception of education, where per pupil and per capita spending were unusually high.

(3) *The South-coast retirement counties*. The South-coast retirement counties formed a sub-type of the commuter category, and shared its general pattern of lower than average spending on most services, except those which were necessary for the holiday trade (roads, police, fire, and planning) and for the retired population (social services). Like the wealthy, middle-class commuter counties, the South-coast counties spent relatively heavily on the education of their children.

(4) *The agricultural counties*. These agricultural, rural, and sparsely populated counties had the least well-developed local party systems, and had, in general, rather poor populations and low rateable values. They spent rather little on the majority of county services, with the major exception of roads and police (where rural costs are high), and education. Their high education spending seems attributable not to their population sparsity, so much as a wish to educate their children well. This, in turn, may be connected either with their high proportion of Independent councillors (also found in Wales), or with the fact that such councils tend to give Chief Education Officers a great deal of autonomous power in the system.

(5) *The Welsh counties*. The Welsh counties form their own distinct group, not in social, economic, and political terms, where they resemble the English agricultural counties, but in terms of their spending which is high on every local service.

The material presented in this chapter demonstrates a relationship between the social and economic features of county governments, and their spending of public money on services. Some of these are features of resident populations (age structure, density, and so on), but others are characteristics of the whole local authority (for example, whether it sustains a holiday trade). However, we should end as we began the county-types section, on a cautionary note. The county data do demonstrate the existence of a rough and ready typology, and this does help towards an understanding of variations in public spending, but we must be careful not to exaggerate the clarity of the differences between types, and it must be recognized that the approach does not offer an all-powerful explanation of spending differences. It may be that the classification can be improved, or that its explanatory power can be augmented by some other approach, but that must wait for future work on county outputs.

NOTES

1. The term county, or county council, refers to administrative counties throughout this work. Studies of county services and expenditure include D. Byrne, B. Williamson, and B. Fletcher, *The Poverty of Education* (London, Martin Robertson, 1977); D. S. Lees *et al.*, *Local Expenditure and Exchequer Grants* (London, IMTA, 1956); B. Davies, 'Local authority size: Some associations with standards of performance of services for deprived children and old people', *Public Administration*, 47 (1969), 225–48; D. E. Ashford, 'The effects of central finance on the British system of local government', *British Journal of Political Science*, 4 (1974), 305–22; B. Davies, A. J. Barton, and I. S. McMillan, 'Variations in the provision of local authority health and welfare services for the elderly: A comparison between counties and county boroughs', *Social and Economic Administration*, 5 (1971), 100–24; D. E. Ashford, 'Resources, spending and party politics in British local government', *Administration and Society*, 7 (1975), 286–311; D. N. King, 'Why do local authority rate poundages differ?', *Public Administration*, 51 (1975), 165–73; D. J. Storey, 'Statistical analysis of education expenditure in county councils', *Local Government Studies*, 1 (1975), 39–57; B. Davies, 'Welfare departments and territorial justice; Some implications for the reform of local government', *Social and Economic Administration*, 3 (1969), 235–52; D. E. Ashford, R. Berne, and R. Schramm, 'The expenditure-financing decision in British local government', *Policy and Politics*, 5 (1976), 5–24; and T. Karran, ' "Borough politics" and "County Government": Administrative Styles in the Old Structure', *Policy and Politics*, 10 (1982).
2. Karran, ' "Borough politics" and "County Government" ', 1–2.
3. Department of the Environment and the Welsh Office, *Local Government Financial Statistics, England and Wales, 1972/3* (London, HMSO, 1974), pp. 14 and 22.
4. The high education spending of Welsh counties has been noted many times in the past — see, for example, J. Pratt *et al.*, *Your Local Education* (Harmondsworth, Middx., Penguin Books, 1973), p. 219; Byrne, Williamson, and Fletcher, *The Poverty of Education*, pp. 78–9; and C. Howick and H. Hassani, 'Education spending: primary', *CES Review*, 5 (1979), 48.

5. On the link between population sparsity and education costs see, *inter alia*, Lees *et al.*, *Local Expenditure*, pp. 116–24; B. Moore and J. Rhodes, 'The relative needs of local authorities: The "Standard Expenditure" approach as an alternative to regression analysis in determining the needs element of the rate support grant', Report of the Committee of Inquiry into Local Government Finance (Layfield Committee), Appendix 7, *Government Grants to Local Authorities: Evidence and Commissioned Work* (London, HMSO, 1976), pp. 106–14; and Storey, 'Statistical analysis of education expenditure in county councils', 39–57.

6. For a useful summary of the voting turnout results in output studies see R. C. Fried, 'Comparative urban performance', in F. L. Greenstein and N. W. Polsby (eds.), *The Handbook of Political Science*, Volume 6 (Reading, Mass., Addison-Wesley, 1975), pp. 305–81.

7. The correlations between sparsity, turnout, uncontested seats, and total spending in all counties are as follows:

	Turnout 1970	Uncontested seats 1970	Sparsity
Total spending 1972/3	0.85***	0.41**	−0.43***
Sparsity	−0.39***	−0.75***	
Uncontested seats 1970	0.34**		
(n = 58)			

For a discussion of the relationship between voting turnout and uncontested seats see L. J. Sharpe, *A Metropolis Votes* (London, London School of Economics, Greater London Paper, No. 8), p. 6.

8. J. Stanyer, *County Government in England and Wales* (London, Routledge and Kegan Paul, 1967), p. 1.

9. DO PARTIES MATTER?

Introduction

We now come to one of the central questions of our book: what effect do the political characteristics of local authorities have on the services they provide? In Chapters 5, 6, 7, and 8 we saw that there is very persuasive evidence to suggest that an important determinant for some local service expenditures is, first, the place of the local authority within a national socio-economic system. This is especially so for the cities — the county boroughs — where there emerged something akin to a division of labour within what may be regarded as a national system of cities. Some cities and towns have evolved a relatively specialized role within this national system, most notably seaside resorts. Secondly, some cities also perform a central service role in relation to their hinterlands. Finally, in Chapter 8 we saw that among the counties there is very strong evidence of what seems to be a cultural factor influencing service outputs. That is to say, in the Welsh counties the level of expenditure on a wide range of services has tended to be much higher than that for the English counties.

All three characteristics — centrality, urban specialization and location, and an assortment of cultural factors — were revealed as being better predictors of local expenditure than the demographic characteristics that most other output studies run against expenditure. However, as we suggested in Chapter 1, there is a fourth cluster of factors that seem likely to affect local expenditure. These are the political characteristics of the local authority, and this chapter will be devoted to analysing the relationship between these and expenditure patterns in the cities and counties, in the light of the discussion in Chapter 1. Before so doing, however, it is necessary to take stock of the results of previous research on the influence of politics on local government outputs in this country.

Previous Findings

In their work on the financial behaviour of English county boroughs, Oliver and Stanyer conclude that 'there is no evidence that political attitudes have any effect on current expenditure or on-rate receipts'.[1] However, as King has pointed out, they may have underestimated the importance of the relationship they discover between Labour strength and per capita expenditure, even though the relationship is not statistically significant. King argues that, in so far as central government grants are supposed to equalize the financial resources of local authorities, any positive relationship between Labour strength and per capita expenditure may represent a tendency for Labour areas to spend more.[2] This argument is strengthened by the finding that central government grants do not, in fact, equalize financial resources; the purchasing power of a given tax rate in areas such as Merthyr, Burton-on-Trent, and Rotherham being considerably lower than that in Brighton, Westminster, or Kensington, even after central government grants are taken into account.[3] Since Labour authorities are generally poor, and their purchasing power seems to be relatively low, any indication that Labour authorities have a higher per capita expenditure suggests that they have a relatively greater determination to spend on public services.

Alt's figures for the 1958–68 period show that the usual relationship between rate levels and Labour strength was temporarily disturbed by the 1963 revaluation, the situation returning to its normal state of affairs after one or two years.[4] Since Oliver and Stanyer chose the financial year 1964–5 for their study their figures are almost certainly strongly affected by the effects of revaluation. In this respect, Boaden's study of 1965–6 and Davies's study of 1965–7 may prove more reliable guides.[5] Also, as both Alt, and Oliver and Stanyer, argue, total revenue expenditure figures may conceal party variations in expenditure on particular services. There are certainly good grounds for this claim since Alt himself, together with Boaden and Davies, does find significant differences in the service spending patterns of Labour and Conservative councils. Even if the disaggregation argument has no validity, Oliver and Stanyer's findings have to be set against those of Alt, Boaden, Davies, Danziger,[6] Ashford, Ashford et al.,[7] and Foster et al.,[8] which do find differences associated with party control.

The other British study which finds no evidence of significant political effect on expenditure patterns is that of Nicholson and Topham.[9] It must be emphasized, however, that this deals with capital and not revenue expenditure. This is an important distinction because capital expenditure is more dependent on central government control and therefore may be less susceptible to party. Moreover, in order to overcome the problem of the 'lumpiness' of capital expenditure Nicholson and Topham averaged out their expenditure figures over a ten-year period. This adjustment will have rendered their figures much less sensitive to any revealing variations that are related to changes in party control.

Size of Labour majority is the favoured variable used in British studies for measuring party effect, yet it is doubtful whether this is very helpful since Labour parties with a small plurality may be in just as secure a position for pushing through policies as those with 90 per cent of the seats. The Labour party, almost invariably, will take full control of the council with the barest majority, and in the technical sense sometimes even without a majority.[10] All that can be said with any confidence is that a very small majority may be more constraining than a comfortable one. One possible way of refining the scale problem is to use either the logarithm of the Labour majority, or perhaps, more simply, whether the Labour party is or is not in control, if that information is available. What is almost certainly more important than size of majority is the length of the Labour party's tenure in office. Most major policy changes take time, and only when sufficient time has elapsed can we therefore expect any change to reveal itself. Conversely, the effects of the party previously in a majority may live on for some time thus obscuring the party effect at any given point in time.

The general hypothesis that is usually tested in relation to the party effect, as we noted in Chapter 1, is that Left-controlled councils will spend more than anti-Left controlled councils. But it must be emphasized that, whatever the broad accuracy of the high-spending socialist hypothesis for aggregate expenditure, this is somewhat crude, since we may presume that a Left party's tendency to spend more is unlikely to operate across the board for all services. Indeed, some studies for other countries have suggested that such discrimination between services does take place.[11] It seems likely, for example, that Labour will tend to spend more on those services that are overtly, or are thought to be,[12] redistributive and socially ameliorative. Such services include primary and secondary education, housing and welfare, personal health and children's services. By the same token we may expect Labour to spend less on non-ameliorative services such as highways and police.

The association of Left control with high aggregate expenditure may be misleading on other grounds. As we saw in Chapters 5 and 6, where high levels of expenditure are seen as being essential to maintaining the overall prosperity of the town — in a seaside resort or tourist centre for example — councils may be enthusiastic spenders whatever their party colour. Conservative parties as parties, broadly speaking, representing the interests of local capital holders, may be more enthusiastic big spenders than Labour.

Also, as we noted in Chapter 1, some ideological differences between Right and Left when expressed in policy change may not have very big, or even any, expenditure effects. A good example of such relatively non-financial ideological policy change is the area of planning where a Labour majority could make substantial changes through the exercise of their discretionary powers over development control. Similarly, the creation of comprehensive schools, possibly one of the most contentious local party political issues in the post-war period in this country, was achieved in some cases with minimal expenditure increases by reallocating buildings and staff. In Chapter 1, we also noted that incoming Left parties may seek not so much to spend more, since raising the revenue will take time, as to seek policies that can be implemented quickly and which have a high visibility. For some services the Labour party, like most Left parties, may seek to reduce expenditure. All of these possibilities render questionable the assumption that the Left party effect can be measured simply by the increase in total expenditure. This possibility is illustrated in Table 9.1 which sets out in very broad terms the expenditure consequences for the major services of policy

Table 9.1 *Expenditure Effects of New Policies in a County Borough controlled by Labour for the First Time*

New policy		Net expenditure effect
Education		
(i)	Abolition of corporal punishment in schools	Nil
(ii)	Abolition of scholarships taken up by the city in semi-private grammar schools	Negative
(iii)	Larger expansion of polytechnic than opponents would have contemplated	Positive
Housing		
(iv)	Expansion of municipalization of private housing	Positive
(v)	Expansion of public house-building programme	Positive
Planning		
(vi)	Abolition of any increase in planning permission for office space	Nil
(vii)	Relocation of non-conforming industrial plants	Positive
Transportation		
(viii)	Subsidized bus fares for old people	Positive
(ix)	Park-and-ride schemes	Positive
(x)	Intensified traffic management schemes	Positive
(xi)	Municipally run multi-storey car-park	Negative
(xii)	Abolition of urban relief-road	Negative
(xiii)	Pedestrianization of central streets	Positive
(xiv)	Increased parking charges	Negative
Recreation and Leisure		
(xv)	New swimming-pool	Positive

Note: Although the summary illustrates the extent to which left-wing policies have either nil or negative expenditure effects on some services, it is clear that the conventional assumption that Left policies tend to have positive expenditure effects appears, at first glance, to be confirmed. Out of a total of fifteen major policy changes nine had positive net effects. However, when the actual amounts are totted up the overall effect is clearly negative since policy (xii) — the decision not to build a projected urban motorway — saved the city £45m. spread over ten years. Even the big spending projects such as the park-and-ride schemes, the expansion of the house-building programme, and the swimming-pool did not in total approach this figure.

change introduced by the Labour party after it had won a majority for the first time ever on an English city council in the mid-1970s. It was not possible to put precise monetary values on each of the fifteen new policies introduced by the party in its first two years in office. The majority of them had positive expenditure effects, as is conventionally assumed. However, the net long-term result in expenditure terms was undoubtedly negative. This was because of the considerable saving made by cancelling the urban relief-road. The cancellation is possibly a transient feature of the city's politics at the time, but Table 9.1 provides a graphic example of the dangers of looking only at total expenditure as a measure of party effect.

In Chapter 1 we also discussed the question of party *system* effect. We noted that American research had assumed that the more competitive the party system the more the party in power was likely to spend, as it competed with its opponent for the marginal voter, who, it was argued, was a higher consumer of public services. Where there was little or no competition, parties in power could rest on their laurels. We questioned this hypothesis for Britain; parties here are less like transmission belts of majority wishes, they are more inclined to apply party ideology when in the saddle, and will only modify it when forced to do so by close competition from a party rival. Thus parties would tend to spend either considerably more or considerably less when in a monopoly situation, depending on which party had the monopoly. Somewhat surprisingly, the party system effect has rarely been examined in British output research, one way or the other, despite the possibility that it could have an important influence on expenditure patterns.

Summarizing this brief survey of previous research on the effect of political variables on outputs in British local government, we may say that although the results may appear to be mixed, most of the research results which suggest that political variables had no effect on expenditure can be more or less explained. There seems, in short, to be evidence that party does matter in Britain.

The Results Analysed: Party Control

In this section of the chapter we examine how far our analysis reveals that politics does in fact matter. In this analysis we have attempted to follow most of the conclusions of the preceding discussion about the deficiencies of previous research on political determinants. We will indicate at each stage in the analysis how we have done this, but five aspects of the discussion in Chapter 1 are of special importance, and therefore need to be restated. The first is that some of the political variables we employ are time series (notably length of party control), and so constitute a more realistic measure of political control than that found in cross-sectional studies. Secondly, not only is expenditure examined in total, but it is also disaggregated to main service heads, thus making it possible to see to what extent parties discriminate between different services. Thirdly, since the whole analysis is spread over time, with service expenditures examined at either three or four points over a thirteen-year period, the possibility of aberrant relationships emerging is minimized. Fourthly, and perhaps most important of all, in recognition of the fact that policy change takes time and parties are often in competition with each other, we have paid a great deal of attention to the party system effect. Finally, both the urban and the rural authorities have been examined, thus ensuring a wider range of party systems to be examined than would have been possible if only urban authorities were covered.

The analysis presented in this chapter is for the current or revenue expenditure in the financial years 1960/1, 1968/9, and 1972/3, and covers fourteen per capita service expenditures, two per pupil/child expenditures, and total expenditure. Six independent political variables that lend themselves relatively easily to regression analysis were chosen from a much larger list, which is given in Section 2.3 of the Appendices. These were:

Turnout,
Percentage of uncontested seats,
Percentage of Conservative seats,
Percentage of Labour seats,
Years of Conservative control,
Years of Labour control.

Taking the county boroughs first, Table 9.2 sets out the significant simple correlations between the six political variables and the seventeen service expenditures. As is usual in such correlations, the outcome is decidedly patchy and both *turnout* and *uncontested seats* emerge as predictors of service expenditures. In Chapter 1 it was argued that Conservative (i.e. party of the Right) control and duration of Conservative control may be better party variables than Left control. This was because, so it was argued, maintaining the status quo is easier than changing it, so that the possibility of party ideology being translated into policy is that much more likely. However, in the analysis set out in Table 9.2 the two Labour-control variables reveal themselves to be the best predictors. It was also argued in Chapter 1 and earlier in this chapter that total expenditure may be an inadequate indicator of the party effect since it took no account of the fact that party ideology might discriminate between services. Thus it is likely that Left parties will favour high expenditure on redistributive services but not on, say, police. As we saw in Table 9.1, for example, where highway building becomes a party political issue the Labour party may be a lower spender overall than the Conservatives. However, whatever the accuracy of the differential service expenditure thesis, this kind of situation did not apply among county boroughs during the period 1960/73, for *total* expenditure is unmistakably susceptible to which party is in power, and the Labour party clearly spends more.

Contrary to the earliest output research, and thus to Fried's conclusions quoted in Chapter 1, but in line with other research on British local government, party colour reveals itself as being relatively strongly associated with expenditure variation. This is especially so for the redistributive (or what are conventionally assumed to be redistributive) and socially ameliorative services. Interestingly, too, Table 9.2 suggests that party does have an impact on highway expenditure, and the general pattern of policy preference suggested in Table 9.1 is confirmed, for it is clear that Labour control exerted a clear negative effect. As might be expected the two services most affected by party colour are education and

Table 9.2 Zero-order Correlation Coefficients between selected Political Variables and Service Expenditures, County Boroughs, 1960/1, 1968/9, and 1972/3

Expenditure per capita	Year	Turnout	Uncontested	Conservative % of seats 1959	Labour % of seats 1959	Years Conservative control 1955–9	Years Labour control 1955–9
Education	a			−0.39***	0.51***	−0.58***	0.43***
	b			−0.28**	0.35***	−0.48***	0.49***
	c			−0.34**	0.36***	−0.26*	
Libraries	a						
	b						
	c						
Sewerage	a						
	b		0.23*	0.24*			
	c						
Refuse	a						
	b	−0.41**					
	c						
Parks/baths	a						
	b						
	c						
Public health	a				0.23*		
	b				0.34**		
	c						
Local health	a					−0.28*	0.28*
	b						
	c						
Children	a				0.31**	−0.34**	0.26*
	b	−0.22*			0.22*		
	c						

Welfare	a		0.23*				
	b						
	c						
Housing	a	-0.22*		-0.49***	0.61***	-0.51***	0.59***
	b	-0.24*		-0.45***	0.59***	-0.43***	0.58***
	c			-0.36***	0.38***	-0.32**	0.29**
Planning	a			—			
	b						
	c						
Highways	a	0.37***		0.24*	-0.43***		-0.31**
	b			-0.26*	0.23*		
	c						
Fire	a						
	b						
	c						
Police	a			0.23*			
	b						
	c						
Children (per child)	a						
	b						
	c						
Education (per child)	a						
	b						
	c						
Total expenditure	a			-0.34**	0.50***	-0.41***	0.38***
	b			-0.31**	0.39***	-0.37***	0.42***
	c			-0.31**	0.34**	-0.23*	0.23*

Note: a = 1960/1
b = 1968/9
c = 1972/3.

Table 9.3 *Multiple Regression of selected Political Characteristics on Service Expenditures, County Boroughs, 1960/1, 1968/9, and 1972/3*

Expenditure per capita	Year	Turnout	Labour % of seats 1959	Years Conservative control 1955-9	Years Labour control 1955-9
Education	a	0.22*	0.36*		
	b	0.27*		-0.26*	
	c				
Libraries	a		0.36*		
	b	0.27*			
	c				
Sewerage	a				
	b	-0.24*			
	c				
Refuse	a	-0.46***	-0.49*		
	b		0.33*		
	c				
Parks/bath	a				0.66**
	b				
	c				
Public health	a				-0.37*
	b		0.81***		
	c				
Local health	a				
	b				
	c				
Children	a				
	b				
	c				

Service	Year	(1)	(2)	(3)	(4)
Welfare	a				0.24*
	b	0.37**			
	c	0.41***			
Housing	a				
	b				
	c		−0.32***		
Planning	a				
	b				0.41***
	c				
Highways	a				
	b		0.30*		0.35***
	c	−0.32**			
Fire	a				
	b				
	c				
Police	a				
	b				
	c				
Children (per child)	a			0.51**	
	b		−0.32*	−0.27*	
	c				
Education (per pupil)	a				
	b	−0.34*			
	c				
Total expenditure	a			0.55**	
	b				
	c				

Notes: 1. a = 1960/1
       b = 1968/9
       c = 1972/3.
2. The table shows only the statistically significant standardized coefficients (beta coefficients).

housing, which are not only the biggest spending services, but also the two over which the most party dogfighting has occurred in the post-war period.

We now turn to Table 9.3. This also covers the county boroughs, but unlike Table 9.2, the figures it reports allow for the effects of socio-economic variables. Table 9.3 shows the standardized regression coefficients (beta coefficients) which are significant at the 5 per cent level, and these were produced in the following way:

(1) A matrix showing all correlations between social, economic, and political variables was drawn up from which the thirty most powerful independent variables were selected.

(2) Another matrix concerning these thirty independent variables was drawn up and inspected for variables which were strongly associated. Where two variables indicating the same or complementary characteristics were strongly correlated (0.70 or more), the one with the strongest association with expenditures was chosen for inclusion in the regression. For example, where two social-class variables were strongly correlated with each other and with expenditure patterns, then the one with the strongest relationship with expenditure was selected.

(3) In the same way, the weakest political variables were weeded out, either because they had weak or insignificant correlations with most expenditure variables, or because they were less strongly correlated with another political variable which measured essentially the same or complementary characteristics. The political variables dropped from the analysis were: percentage of uncontested seats, percentage of Liberal seats, percentage of Independent seats, percentage of other seats, years of Independent control 1955–9, years of Conservative and Independent control, 1955–9, and years with no party in control, 1955–9.

(4) In this way the strength of the most powerful political variables was compared with that of the most powerful social and economic variables, this being the most conservative and stringent test for the strength of the political variables. The social and economic variables included in the regressions were: overcrowding, housing quality, mortality rates, manual workers, proportion of council tenants, retail turnover per capita, population density, rateable values, domestic rateable values, offices and industry as a percentage of rateable value, retired population, inflow of population into the local authority for work, school-aged population, and population size. These variables in turn were chosen for their strong association with a range of expenditure variables from a list of fifty-five social and economic indicators. In other words, there is good reason to believe that a range of the most powerful social and economic indicators was entered into the regressions.

The first feature of Table 9.3 to be noted is that turnout appears to emerge as being the strongest of the political variables; however, as we saw in Chapter 8, this is almost certainly a spurious relationship. Of much greater significance is, again, the fact that the Left party effect emerges clearly and decidedly more strongly than the Right party effect. The expenditures most strongly associated with political variables are education (per pupil and per capita, but especially the latter), public health, libraries, parks and baths, welfare, housing, and highways. Total expenditure appears, again, as being related to the Left party effect. As in Table 9.2, this list includes some of the redistributive and socially ameliorative services but it does not include them all. There is no correlation with child care and local health, for example. Moreover, the list includes services that are not usually associated with welfare, such as libraries, and parks and baths. As in Table 9.2, highways emerge as having a negative relationship with Labour control.

Summarizing then the results as set out in Table 9.3, we may say that political variables do appear to have a significant effect on a fairly wide range of service expenditures and especially the big spending, highly politicized, and redistributive services. Nevertheless, these political variables, although at least as powerful as a whole battery of social and economic variables, do not add up to a very convincing case for politics being an important determinant of local policy, even when the effect of these variables is taken into account in the multiple regression analysis.[13]

We now come to the examination of county expenditure. The first analysis is set out in Table 9.4. Apart from a slightly different range of functions and a similarly adjusted range of political variables — the years of party control being excluded because they were unobtainable — the table is essentially the same as Table 9.2. That is to say, it shows the simple correlations between the most powerful political variables and service expenditures in the counties. All expenditures are per capita except the two shown for education per pupil and children's services per child. Table 9.4 reveals that in the counties the political variables have a stronger relationship with service expenditures than in the county boroughs, and, in this sense, it amply justifies the inclusion of the counties in the analysis.

The political variable with the strongest association with expenditure is turnout; the association is even stronger than for the county boroughs. But as we have already noted, this association is a spurious one which, as we demonstrated in Chapter 8, is largely an artefact of the Welsh effect.

Another feature of Table 9.4 is that it shows that in the counties both the percentage of Conservative seats, and the percentage of Conservative and Independent seats, are more strongly associated with service expenditure than is the percentage of Labour seats, and they are associated for all the significant correlations in the expected direction, i.e. negative.

We now come to the second analysis of the counties, and this is set out in

Table 9.4 *Zero-order Correlation Coefficients between selected Political Variables and Service Expenditures, Counties, 1960/1, 1968/9, and 1972/3*

Expenditure per capita	Year	Turnout	Uncontested seats	Conservative % of seats	Labour % of seats	Conservative and Independent % of seats	Independent % of seats
Education: milk and meals	a	0.57***	0.33**	−0.31*			0.39**
	b†						
	c						
Education: other	a	0.74***	0.26*	−0.30*		−0.26*	0.26*
	b†						
	c						
Total education	a	0.76***	0.29*	−0.32*		−0.26*	0.29*
	b						
	c						
Education (per pupil)	a	0.64***	0.29*	−0.28*	−0.26*		0.39**
	b						
	c						
Local health	a	0.49***				−0.38**	
	b						
	c						
Public health	a	0.45***	0.36**	−0.32*	−0.39**		0.43**
	b†						
	c						
Welfare	a	0.48***	0.35**				
	b†						
	c						
Children	a				0.26*		
	b†						
	c						

Children (per child)	a						
	b†						0.64***
	c						
Highways	a	0.73***	0.55***	−0.45***	−0.49***		
	b						
	c						
Fire	a	0.31*				−0.25*	
	b						
	c						
Police	a						
	b						
	c						
Libraries	a		−0.44***		0.31*		
	b						
	c						
Total expenditure	a	0.82***	0.54***	−0.48***	−0.27*	−0.26*	0.56***
	b						
	c						

Notes: † Only 61 counties analysed.
1. a = 1960/1
   b = 1968/9
   c = 1972/3.
2. Turnout is defined as the percentage of the electorate voting in contested areas.

Table 9.5 *Multiple Regression of selected Political Characteristics on Service Expenditures, Counties, England and Wales, 1960/1, 1968/9, and 1972/3*

Expenditure per capita	Year	Turnout	Labour % of seats	Other Independent % of seats
Education: milk and meals	a	0.55**		
	b			
	c			
Education: other	a	0.20*	0.37***	−0.21*
	b			
	c			
Total education	a		0.46***	
	b			−0.53***
	c	0.47***	0.19*	
Education (per pupil)	a		0.61***	
	b			−0.50**
	c	0.46**	0.42**	
Local health	a		0.56**	
	b	0.37*		
	c			
Public health	a	0.37*		
	b			
	c			
Welfare	a	0.54**		
	b		0.35*	
	c			
Children	a			
	b			
	c			
Children (per child)	a			
	b			
	c			
Highways	a			
	b			
	c	0.35**		
Fire	a		0.52*	
	b			
	c			
Police	a			
	b		0.49**	
	c		1.03*	
Libraries	a		0.53+*	
	b			−0.58**
	c			−1.55*

Expenditure per capita	Year	Turnout	Labour % of seats	Other Independent % of seats
	a		0.19*	
Total	b		0.27**	
expenditure	c		0.62*	

Notes: 1. a = 1960/1
  b = 1968/9
  c = 1972/3.
2. The table includes only the statistically significant regression coefficients (beta coefficients).

Table 9.5. The table is derived in precisely the same way as Table 9.3, with a necessary reduction in the number of political variables, similar to that in Table 9.4. That is to say, Table 9.5 reports the results of regressions which include the most powerful social, economic, and political variables, thus providing the most stringent test of the significance of the political variables. As in Table 9.3 the political variables are revealed to be significantly associated with some of the service expenditures. The percentage of Labour seats has a particularly significant, and sometimes very strong, positive relationship with spending on education, health, fire, and libraries, and again on total expenditure. The association with total expenditure, however, is much less strong than for some of the other expenditure items. As in the earlier tables not all the services that are strongly associated with Labour control can be defined as socially ameliorative or redistributive, and it must remain something of a puzzle why Labour control should be so strongly associated with high expenditure on the library and fire services. Again, turnout appears to have had a strong association with some services. But, as we have already noted, this is almost certainly misleading and is the consequence of the Welsh effect discussed in Chapter 8.

To summarize very briefly the findings as set out in Tables 9.2 to 9.5: some of the suggestions for improving output studies made in Chapter 1 do not appear to be as potentially fruitful as was expected. Notable among such is the apparent failure of Right dominance to be a better predictor of expenditure variation than Left dominance. Equally, total expenditure does appear to be quite strongly affected by party colour despite some persuasive reasons for assuming otherwise. Finally, politics matters more in the counties, but this is likely to be because they have a wider range of political characteristics than the county borough.

It may be claimed, however, that these unexpected results are overriden by the general, but weak, confirmation of one of the central claims of the earlier discussion, namely that there is an association between the political variables and expenditure as compared with the socio-economic variables. In particular, the Left-dominance variables have a significant but not especially strong association with some of the redistributive and socially ameliorative services.

The Left Party Effect

The remainder of this chapter will be devoted to exploring the Left party effect in more detail and also the party system effect. We begin with the Left party effect, and in Table 9.6 there is a summary of total per capita expenditures for the four financial years for the county boroughs and the counties. The authorities are divided into five categories according to party strength on the council, ranging from Conservative-monopoly authorities to Labour-monopoly councils. Again it will be seen that total expenditure does seem to be affected by the Left party effect and in a quite striking manner.

Table 9.6 *Total Per Capita Expenditure (£) and Party Control: Counties and County Boroughs, 1960/1 and 1972/3*

	1960/1(n)	1964/5(n)	1968/9(n)	1972/3(n)
County boroughs				
Conservative monopoly	26.09(1)	37.24(1)	54.76(3)	100.83(3)
Conservative dominant	28.29(7)	39.20(2)	57.40(20)	89.60(20)
Two-party	29.52(12)	40.48(17)	60.43(17)	95.40(24)
Labour dominant	30.22(31)	42.38(27)	59.86(12)	97.23(10)
Labour monopoly	31.16(13)	43.76(7)	64.99(4)	111.44(2)
County councils				
Conservative monopoly	n/a (0)	27.71(2)	44.22(3)	74.24(4)
Conservative dominant	n/a (0)	29.73(1)	49.30(8)	76.59(11)
Two-party	24.31(4)	35.81(5)	45.58(1)	90.30(1)
Labour dominant	24.41(2)	35.95(2)	53.24(2)	91.12(2)
Labour monopoly	27.26(3)	37.13(2)	55.29(1)	89.96(1)

Note: Monopoly: Party takes 80 per cent or more of seats,
Dominant: Party takes 60–70 per cent of seats,
Two-party: Neither party takes more than 59 per cent of seats.

Only for four of the thirty-eight observations – Labour-dominant county boroughs (1968/9) and Conservative-monopoly county boroughs (1972/3), two-party counties (1968/9), and Labour-monopoly counties (1972/3) – is the positive relationship between degree of Labour control and per capita total expenditure broken. All the other thirty-four statistics form a perfect pattern of Labour high spending and Conservative low spending. Table 9.6 also shows that the assumption in the literature discussed in Chapter 1 that the party competition would always lead to higher expenditures on services is not borne out. In both the county boroughs and the counties, the authorities with the more competitive two-party system occupy the median position.

Tables 9.7, 9.8, and 9.9 explore the Left party effect in relation to per capita spending on a selected group of services. These services have been chosen because they are politically sensitive, either being favoured by Labour because

Table 9.7 *Per Capita Spending (£) on selected Services in County Boroughs, 1960/1 and 1972/3, and Party Control*

	Conservative monopoly and dominant	Multi- and two-party systems	Labour monopoly and dominant
Children and Welfare			
1960/1	1.141	1.186	1.697
Social services			
1972/3	6.859	7.019	7.220
Public health			
1960/1	0.423	0.425	0.454
1972/3	1.739	1.941	1.964
Personal health			
1960/1	1.335	1.406	1.456
1972/3	2.882	2.937	3.006
Highways			
1960/1	2.571	2.333	2.164
1972/3	6.479	6.589	6.460
Police			
1960/1	2.503	2.271	2.210
1972/3	7.948	7.727	7.459
(N)			
1960/1	(8)	(30)	(44)
1972/3	(23)	(44)	(12)

Note: For an explanation of the categories for each column see Table 9.6.

they are seen as being ameliorative and redistributive, or by the Conservatives because they are not seen as such. Two financial years are covered, 1960/1 and 1972/3. In Table 9.7 the degree of party control has been reduced to three categories for reasons of convenience and space. Three features of Table 9.7 are important. The first is that for the four redistributive and ameliorative services – children and welfare, social services, public health, and personal health – there is again the direct positive relationship between the degree of Left control and per capita expenditure for all 12 observations except one – public health for 1972/3 in Conservative majority councils. The second feature of Table 9.7 we must note is that for highways and police the relationship is exactly the reverse of that for the redistributive services. That is to say, the weaker the Labour party on the council, the more is spent per capita on highways and police. The third feature of Table 9.7 to be noted is that, as in Table 9.6, party competition does not lead to higher expenditure than does party monopoly, even for those services where it might be expected that the parties might bid up in order to attract votes.

Table 9.8 Education and Housing Expenditures (£) in 1960/1 and 1972/3, and Party Control in County Boroughs

	Education per capita		Education per pupil		Housing per capita		(N)	
	1960/1	1972/3	1960/1	1972/3	1960/1	1972/3	1960/1	1972/3
Conservative monopoly	12.1	45.6	105.6	293.1	0.50	4.9	(1)	(3)
Conservative dominant	13.5	46.2	99.3	278.3	1.2	3.6	(7)	(20)
Multi-party	14.9	48.7	98.4	273.7	1.4	6.0	(18)	(22)
Two-party	15.5	50.2	95.8	263.1	1.8	6.3	(12)	(24)
Labour dominant	15.8	48.5	95.6	269.5	2.1	6.6	(31)	(10)
Labour monopoly	15.9	53.0	96.3	282.2	2.3	9.0	(13)	(2)

The six services examined in Table 9.7 are all major services but they are not as politically important as housing and education. These two services were therefore subjected to a more extensive analysis and the results are set out in Table 9.8. Once again, expenditure per capita rises directly with each increase in Labour predominance. Once again, there is almost perfect symmetry except for education per pupil, where there is almost a complete reversal of the relationship between degree of Labour control and expenditure: the greater the degree of Conservative control the less is spent per capita, but the more is spent per pupil. This result is unlikely to refute the Left party effect, however, since it arises because Labour authorities have a higher proportion of children of school age in their populations as compared with Conservative authorities. So, although Labour-controlled authorities make a bigger effort than Conservatives in education, that effort has to be spread over more pupils. Conversely, the higher per pupil expenditures of Conservative authorities is likely to mean either that they waste money on education as compared with Labour authorities, or that they spend more in order to give their pupils a better education. Again it must be

Table 9.9 *Per Capita Spending (£) on selected Services in Counties, 1960/1 and 1972/3, and Party Control*

	Conservative monopoly and dominant	Multi- and Two-party systems	Labour monopoly and dominant
Children and welfare 1960/1		0.89	1.0
Social services 1972/3	4.92	4.85	5.98
Public health and local health 1960/1		1.61	1.69
Health services 1972/3	3.27	3.43	3.87
Highways 1960/1		2.77	2.05
1972/3	6.16	7.03	5.70
Police 1960/1		1.96	1.87
1972/3	6.54	7.03	5.70
Education (per capita) 1960/1		16.30	17.26
1972/3	49.47	51.08	55.71
Education (per pupil) 1960/1		105.72	104.00
1972/3	200.17	202.11	195.07

noted that, as in the two preceding tables, party competition only seems to increase expenditure when compared with strongly Conservative councils. We will return to the possible impact of party interaction on expenditure patterns in a moment.

We now come to the analysis of per capita expenditure for counties. The same two observation years are examined as for the county boroughs. The results are set out in Table 9.9, but before discussing them it is important to emphasize that during the period covered the counties were much less politicized than the county boroughs. Indeed the majority of county councils during the period were dominated by Independents. This means, of course, that the party effect is much less likely to reveal itself than in the county boroughs where Independent control was a rarity. In some cases a category that was analysed for the county boroughs cannot be analysed for the counties because it does not exist. This is the case for the Conservative monopoly and dominant groups for 1960/1. Bearing this characteristic of the county data in mind, Table 9.9 shows that the Left party effect is still strongly evident. Again, there is the same reversal of the 'normal' relationship between party and expenditure level for per pupil expenditure on education as there was for the county boroughs, probably for similar reasons.

Pervasive Left Effect

The data presented so far show a clear pattern, but any remaining doubts about whether there is a Left party effect for service expenditures as well as total expenditure should be dispelled by Tables 9.10 and 9.11. They confirm, in short, that Labour spends more on the redistributive and ameliorative services, whereas the Conservatives tend to spend more on the non-redistributive services. Both tables compare party spending for all four financial years by expressing Labour spending as a percentage of Conservative expenditure. Thus a figure of more than 100 shows higher Labour spending, and a figure of 99 or less shows lower Labour spending than the Conservatives. Table 9.10 examines the spending patterns in the county boroughs, and it will be seen that the figures for the socially ameliorative services for each of the four financial years are almost all in excess of 100. The major exception, as before, is education per pupil. The most striking difference in party spending inclinations concerns housing, where Labour expenditure is more than twice as high as Conservative for two of the observation years, and over 80 per cent higher in the remaining two. For no other service is there this magnitude of difference. The next biggest difference concerns education, but the difference never exceeds 13 per cent.

Table 9.11 compares spending patterns in the counties for the same period. Again there is an unmistakably consistent pattern with a big difference occurring for education (in the absence of housing), but education per pupil again showing

Table 9.10 *Per Capita Labour Service Expenditures as a Percentage of Conservative Service Expenditures in Authorities controlled continuously by either Labour or Conservative, 1960/1 to 1972/3, County Boroughs*

	1960/1	1964/5	1968/9	1972/3
Housing	181	206	213	181
Public health	97	110	113	128
Refuse	105	105	110	123
Education	114	116	115	118
Fire	101	109	104	117
Sewerage	118	128	98	113
Total	108	111	111	113
Highways	91	90	104	103
Social services				100
Libraries	97	102	104	99
Police	95	92	94	96
Parks	95	92		96
Personal health	114	118	106	95
Education (per pupil)	97	91	92	94
Children (per child)	104	93	82	
Planning	79	70	93	82
(n) Conservative	(16)	(6)	(6)	(5)
(n) Labour	(44)	(44)	(18)	(13)

Note: The figure for 1960/1 is based on party control 1955/9, for 1964/5 on 1955/63, for 1968/9 on 1955/68, and for 1972/3 on 1955/72.

Table 9.11 *Per Capita Labour Service Expenditures as a Percentage of Conservative Service Expenditures in Authorities controlled continuously by either Labour or Conservative, 1960/1 to 1972/3, Counties*

	1960/1	1964/5	1968/9	1972/3
Education	112	120	119	123
Planning	158	165	147	121
Police	90	94	107	121
Total	112	116	116	119
Local health			117	114
Fire	100	110	107	113
Education (per pupil)	99	70	99	103
Social services				102
Libraries	116	94	90	99
Highways	92	84	83	91
(n) Conservative	(5)	(3)	(3)	(3)
(n) Labour	(6)	(4)	(3)	(3)

Note: The figure for 1960/1 is based on party control 1955/8, for 1964/5 on 1955/64, for 1968/9 on 1955/67, and for 1972/3 on 1955/70.

a higher Conservative expenditure. What is perhaps most surprising about Table 9.11 is that Labour consistently spends more on planning than the Conservatives, and planning is well ahead of any other service in terms of the difference in party spending priorities. There seems to be no obvious explanation for the difference.

In our earlier discussion we suggested that one reason why the full impact of party may be obscured is because some policies take a long time to mature and existing policies are sometimes hard to change quickly. Thus the policies of party X 'live on' during party Y's early years of office. In Tables 9.12 and 9.13 this hypothesis is examined by comparing total expenditure per capita in those authorities where there had been alternating power over the period 1960 to 1973, with that in those authorities where one party was in power throughout the period. The expectation is that in the former groups the party effect will be less marked than in the latter. That is to say, the per capita spending of the mixed control group should be less than that of Labour-monopoly authorities, but more than that of Conservative-monopoly authorities.

Table 9.12 *Total Per Capita Expenditure (£) in County Boroughs which change Party Control compared with continuously Labour and continuously Conservative Authorities, 1960/1 to 1972/3*

	1960/1(n)	1964/5(n)	1968/9(n)	1972/3(n)
Continuously Labour	30.49 (44)→42.60 (42)→61.43 (18)→102.21(13)			
Mixed control				
			Conservative 61.11 (15)→Labour 107.08(2)	
				Conservative 94.80(11)
			Conservative 58.12 (3)→	Conservative 91.80 (3)
		Labour 40.67 (3)		
Continuously Conservative	28.13 (16)→38.22 (6)→55.44 (6)→90.68 (5)			

Notes: 1. No other permutations of mixed Labour/Conservative control are present in the period.
2. Party control for the 1960/1 budget refers to the period 1955–9, for the 1964/5 budget to 1960–3, for the 1968 budget to 1963–7, and for the 1972/3 budget to 1967–71.

Table 9.12 compares the total per capita expenditures of those borough authorities which stay in the same party hands, with the total expenditures of those which change control. To make full sense of the figures, therefore, the table should be read across, in order to show changes over time, and, at the same time, it should also be read up and down, in order to compare the spending of authorities which change hands with those which do not. The first row of the table shows the average total per capita expenditure of authorities which stayed under Labour control throughout the period 1955-71. Similarly, the last row shows the comparable figure for continuously Conservative authorities. A comparison of the two shows that continuously Labour authorities not only spend more, but also increase their differences with Conservative authorities over time.

In between the first and last rows of Table 9.12 are the authorities which changed party control. Of the forty-two authorities which were Labour controlled from 1955-63, fifteen switched to the Conservatives by 1967-8, and the budgets which they set for the following financial year (1968-9) fell slightly (when compared with the continuously Labour authorities) to a per capita expenditure of £61.11. Of the fifteen authorities, eleven remained under Conservative control, and their average expenditure fell again, relative to continuously Labour authorities, to £94.80 in 1972-3. Another two authorities, however, switched back to Labour control, and their total per capita expenditure rose, relative to those authorities which had stayed Conservative, to £107.08.

Similarly, of the sixteen authorities under Conservative control from 1955-9, three had switched to Labour by 1963-4, and in the financial year 1964-5 their spending rose relative to authorities which stayed Conservative. All these three authorities then switched back to Conservative control, and their spending started to fall back to the continuously Conservative figures – sinking to £91.80 by 1972-3.

In sum, the figures in Table 9.12 show that authorities which stay under Labour control increase their spending more than authorities under continuous Conservative control. Authorities which switch to the Conservatives cut their spending in relative terms, but do so slowly. Conservative authorities which switch to Labour control increase their spending, and do so quite rapidly. There is, in other words, a clear party control effect on spending, and the Labour high spending effect is stronger after a change of control than the Conservative low spending effect.

In Table 9.13 a similar analysis is made for the counties. Unfortunately, because of the lower politicization, only one authority changed party control over the period. Although there were other cases where either Conservative or Labour ceased to be the biggest party, the presence of Independents confuses the issue. The county picture is further complicated by the fact that we have to assume that party control in an election year persists throughout the three-year period, or until the budget year, which ever came first. Lastly, there were two elections between the budget years 1964/5 and 1968/9, and this accounts for the two columns of data between these budget years.

Table 9.13 *Total Per Capita Expenditure (£) in Counties which change Party Control compared with continuously Labour and continuously Conservative Authorities, 1960/1 to 1972/3*

Party control	1960/1 (n)	1964/5 (n)	1968/9 (n)	1972/3 (n)
Continuously Labour	23.34 (10)→37.58	(6)→53.93	(3)——→90.74	(3)
Mixed			↘Conservative 51.15 (1)——→83.89	Conservative (1)
Continuously Conservative	23.35 (5)→31.64	(3)—→46.53	(3)——→76.01	(3)

Notes: 1. No other permutations or examples of mixed party control were present in the period.
　　　 2. Party control for the 1960/1 budget was established in the 1958 elections, for 1964/5 in 1961, for 1968/9 in 1964 and 1967, and for 1972/3 in 1970.

For the one authority that did change hands, Table 9.13 does support the conclusion drawn from Table 9.12, that alternating power does modify party expenditure patterns. It also confirms a more general point, which bears repeating, about the need to look at expenditure over time, and taken together the two tables do suggest that the period needs to be a long one. Table 9.12 suggests that it may take at least eight years for the Conservative party to get total expenditure to a level cognizant with party attitudes.

Before we move on from Tables 9.12 and 9.13 it should be noted that both put the question 'Does politics matter?' to the acid test. By examining the expenditure patterns of the set of authorities which change hands and comparing them with another group which do not change hands, we are holding social and economic variables constant. Although numbers are inevitably small towards the end of the period, the two tables suffer from none of the problems of covariance of socio-economic and political variables which beset correlation and regression analysis. And since party control changes, but the socio-economic characteristics of the authorities change only slowly, it follows that changes in expenditure must be the result of changing political circumstances.

Party System Effects

Tables 9.14 and 9.15 explore the party system effect more systematically by showing the spending differences of authorities with different types of party system. They reinforce the conclusion noted earlier that the more competitive the party systems the more similar the expenditure patterns of authorities, irrespective of party control. In other words, multi- and two-party systems are most alike in their spending patterns. Conversely, the larger the majority the party enjoys the greater party ideology shows itself in quantitative terms. Thus if we look at Table 9.14, which covers the county boroughs and compares each successive row of figures for the different party systems, it is evident that

Table 9.14 *Differences between Total Per Capita Expenditures (£) of County Boroughs under different Party Systems, 1960/1 to 1972/3*

	1960/1 (n)		1964/5 (n)		1968/9 (n)		1972/3 (n)	
Difference between multi-party and two-party systems	0.66	(30)	0.02	(44)	0.63	(42)	0.27	(46)
Difference between two-party and one-party dominant systems	0.34	(50)	1.68	(46)	2.11	(49)	6.26	(54)
Difference between Labour and Conservative dominant systems	1.93	(38)	3.18	(30)	2.46	(32)	7.63	(30)
Difference between Labour and Conservative monopoly systems	5.07	(14)	6.52	(5)	10.23	(7)	10.61	(15)

there is an increase in the degree of difference with each increase in one-party dominance. A similar though less marked relationship between the competitiveness of the party system and expenditure is evident in Table 9.15, which covers the counties. For 1960/1 it was not possible to make a comparison since there were no Conservative-monopoly counties in that year.

Table 9.15 *Difference between Total Per Capita Expenditures (£) of Counties under different Party Systems, 1960/1 to 1972/3*

	1960/1 (n)		1964/5 (n)		1968/9 (n)		1972/3 (n)	
Difference between multi-party and two-party systems	0.41	(29)	0.12	(24)	3.90	(23)	10.7	(21)
Difference between two-party and one-party dominant systems	0.10	(6)	1.34	(3)	4.56	(10)	11.48	(14)
Difference between Labour and Conservative dominant systems	n/a		6.22	(3)	3.94	(11)	14.53	(13)
Difference between Labour and Conservative monopoly systems	n/a		9.42	(4)	11.07	(4)	15.72	(5)

Note: There are no Conservative monopoly or dominant systems in 1960/1.

Both tables underline yet again the fact that the type of party system seems to have an unmistakable effect on expenditure. However, it must be noted that this relationship could be an illusion because the differences in expenditure could merely reflect socio-economic differences in the population. Thus, Labour-controlled councils tend to have a higher proportion of working-class citizens who need, and are eligible for, more redistributive services. There may be, in other words, no party system effect but merely a demographic effect. While accepting that variations in the demographic structure do produce some of the variation

Table 9.16 *Difference between Average Total Per Capita Expenditure (£) in all County Boroughs and Average Total Per Capita Expenditure in County Boroughs with different Types of Party System, 1960/1 to 1972/3*

	1960/1 (n)	1964/5 (n)	1968/9 (n)	1972/3 (n)
Non-party systems	−3.7 (1)	−2.43 (1)	−4.32 (2)	−0.41 (2)
Party-monopoly systems	± 1.65 (14)	± 2.69 (8)	± 5.20 (7)	± 8.67 (7)
Party-dominant systems	± 0.68 (38)	± 1.79 (29)	± 1.40 (33)	± 4.81 (30)
Two-party systems	−0.19 (12)	−0.78 (17)	+1.12 (17)	+1.99 (24)
Multi-party systems	−0.55 (18)	−0.80 (27)	−0.49 (25)	+1.72 (22)

in expenditure revealed in Tables 9.14 and 9.15, both the symmetry in the two tables of the gradation in difference, and, above all, the extent of the difference as between party competitive councils and one-party councils suggest very strongly that there is some degree of party autonomy being exercised. That is to say, contrary to some assumptions in output studies that we discussed in Chapter 1, the parties are not mere transmission belts of majority interests or needs, but they have views of their own as to what policies they wish to pursue, and they only modify these views if forced to do so becaue they have a close competitor. In a word, parties with small majorities may tend to be cautious irrespective of party colour.

Table 9.17 *Differences between Average Total Expenditure Per Capita (£) in all Counties, and Average Total Per Capita Expenditure in Counties with different Types of Party System, 1960/1 to 1972/3*

	1960/1 (n)	1964/5 (n)	1968/9 (n)	1972/3 (n)
Non-party systems	+2.37 (27)	+3.01 (26)	+4.19 (21)	+8.47 (19)
Monopoly and dominant systems	± 1.24 (5)	± 4.27 (7)	± 3.42 (14)	± 7.46 (18)
Two-and multi-party systems	−2.10 (29)	−2.01 (24)	± 2.34 (23)	± 4.00 (21)

This tendency is explored further in the final three tables. Table 9.16 and 9.17 record the extent to which total expenditures in authorities with different party systems deviate from the average for all authorities. Table 9.16 covers the county boroughs and shows that, broadly speaking, the more competitive the party system, the more the level of total spending moves towards the median for all county boroughs, irrespective of the party in control. Table 9.17 covers the same ground for the counties except that the numbers are reduced. Like Table 9.16 it shows a regression to the mean as party competition increases, and further strengthens the evidence that when parties only possess narrow majorities they are less inclined to pursue their ideological aims, at least as far as overall expenditure is concerned.

Table 9.18 *Percentage Increases in Total Per Capita Expenditure with different Types of Party System: All Authorities*

	1960/1–1964/5	(n)	1964/5–1968/9	(n)	1968/9–1972/3	(n)
County boroughs						
Multi-and two-party systems	38.91	(22)	42.54	(20)	61.27	(26)
Dominant systems	42.53	(22)	42.49	(9)	60.67	(18)
Monopoly systems	39.85	(7)	46.00	(4)	61.89	(3)
County councils						
Multi-and two-party systems	40.52	(21)	40.67	(13)	59.85	(15)
Dominant systems	31.55	(1)	n/a	(0)	63.20	(7)
Monopoly systems	38.27	(2)	57.45	(2)	63.86	(3)

Note: Since percentage increase is measured over a four-year period, councils are also grouped according to their party system for the four years up to and including the budget year.

In Table 9.18 the caution-inducing effect of competition is further underlined. This table compares the rate of increase in total per capita expenditure between budget years of different party systems. As will be seen, there is an unmistakable trend in both county boroughs and counties for the increase to be greater with increasing one-party dominance. This trend is not quite so marked for the counties, where the numbers for the dominant and monopoly councils are fairly small in any case. But, overall, Table 9.18 further confirms that, first, the party system effect is important in influencing expenditure. Secondly, that parties in close competition with each other appear to follow the Downsian model in the sense that they compete for the median voter by pursuing median expenditure policies. We will return to these extremely important findings when we draw together our general conclusions in the next chapter. Suffice it to say at this point that party and party systems have been revealed as being critical determinants of local expenditure.

NOTES

1. F. R. Oliver and J. Stanyer, 'Some Aspects of the Financial Behaviour of County Boroughs', *Public Administration*, 47 (1963), 183.
2. D. N. King, 'Why Do Local Authorities Rate Poundages Differ', *Public Administration*, 51:3 (1973).
3. See J. LeGrand, 'Fiscal Equity and Central Government Grants to Local Authorities', *The Economic Journal*, 85 (1975), 546; L. Boyle, *Equalisation and the Future of Local Government Finance* (Edinburgh, Oliver and Boyd,

1966), p. 124; and G. Taylor, 'North and South: The Education Split', *New Society*, 4 March 1971.

4. J. Alt, 'Some Social and Political Correlates of County Borough Expenditures', *British Journal of Political Science*, 1 (1971), 54–5.

5. N. Boaden, *Urban Policy-making* (Cambridge, Cambridge University Press, 1971), and B. P. Davies, *et al.*, *Variations in Services for the Aged* (London, Bell, 1971).

6. J. N. Danziger, *Making Budgets Public Resource Allocation* (Beverly Hills, Sage, 1978).

7. D. E. Ashford, 'Resources, Spending and Party Politics in British Local Government', *Administration and Society*, 7 (1975), and D. E. Ashford, R. Berne and R. Schramm, 'The Expenditure-Financing Decision in British Local Government', *Policy and Politics*, 5 (1976).

8. C. D. Foster, R. A. Jackman, and M. Perlman, *Local Government Finance in a Unitary State* (London, Allen & Unwin, 1980) Ch. 5. See also Boyle, *Equalisation and the Future of Local Government Finance*; C. Howick and H. Hassani, 'Education Spending: Primary', *CES Review*, 5 (1979); C. Howick and H. Hassani, 'Education Spending: Secondary', *CES Review*, 8 (1980); K. Hoggart, 'Political Parties and Local Authority Capital Investment in English Cities, 1966–1971', Department of Geography, King's College London, Mimeo; and T. J. Karran, '"Borough Politics" and "County Government"': Administrative Styles in the Old Structure', *Policy and Politics*, 10 (1982).

9. R. J. Nicholson and N. Topham, 'The Determinants of Investment in Housing by Local Authorities: An Econometric Approach', *Journal of the Royal Statistical Society*, Series A, 134, No. 3 (1971); Nicholson and Topham, 'Investment Decisions and the Size of Local Authorities', *Policy and Politics*, 1 (1972); Nicholson and Topham, 'Urban Road Provision in England and Wales', *Policy and Politics*, 4 (1975).

10. G. W. Jones, *Borough Politics* (London, Macmillan, 1969), Chapter 16.

11. See, for example, Alt, 'Some Social and Political Correlates', and Boaden, *Urban Policy-Making*. Also see M. Aiken and R. Depré, 'Politics and Policy in Belgian Cities', *Politics and Policy*, 4 (1976), and T. Hansen and F. Kjellberg, 'Municipal Expenditures in Norway: Autonomy and Constraints in Local Government Activity', *Policy and Politics*, 4 (1976).

12: See H. L. Wilensky, *The Welfare State and Equality* (Berkeley, University of California Press, 1975), Ch. 1, for an interesting discussion of popular misconceptions about the redistributive effects of public services, especially education.

13. There is one unusual result in Table 9.3 which has been carefully checked but which has no obvious explanation. It will be seen that education per pupil has a strong positive relationship with the percentage of Labour seats, but a weaker negative relationship with years of both Conservative and Labour control. This may be because the percentage of Labour seats is strongly associated with years of Labour control, and collinearity of this kind often produces strange results.

10. DOES POLITICS MATTER?

The Broad Trends

In this, the final chapter, we will try to draw together the main threads of the general arguments which we first set out in Chapter 1, and then the conclusions to be drawn where these arguments have been subject to verification against our data in the intervening chapters. Briefly, we claimed that whereas the advent of output analysis was to be warmly welcomed as a laudable attempt to determine in a systematic fashion whether politics, and especially parties, did in fact have an impact on public policy, output analysis had been too restricted in its application of independent variables, or had assumed a conclusive quality to its findings that was unwarranted and premature. These early conclusions were premature and unwarranted principally because they were mainly based on a model of the representative process that assumed that policy was largely the reflection of certain socio-economic characteristics of the population.

In this model the representative process was, in effect, a kind of transmission belt in which the political mechanisms as such had little independent effect on public policy since they merely performed the task of reflecting in policy terms the presumed wants derived from the socio-economic structure of the participative citizenry. Politics, therefore, did not matter, since what a government did was to all intents and purposes predetermined by factors outside its control, factors such as per capita income, age structure, or population density.

Quite how these population characteristics, as the inputs into the political system, were transformed into outputs was never adequately discussed; indeed it was very rarely considered at all. The assumption was simply that per capita income, age structure, and population density, or whatever, would somehow get transformed into a particular set of local policies. The nub of the problem here is how population characteristics can possibly be 'inputs' into the decision-making system, when they are simply inert statistical abstractions describing the given jurisdiction's population.

When the transmission model underlying some output studies failed in its explanatory task, because the relationship between demographic characteristics and outputs was found to be weak or entirely non-existent, recourse was made to the famous 'black box' which was somehow supposed to translate inputs into outputs. But since we may presume that the black box does not work by magic, we must assume some powerful mechanism which is able to transform the descriptive abstractions of the statistician into coherent policies. Only by making such an assumption could the transmission theory remain intact. Crucial as it was for the theory, the mechanism was, however, never specified.

Often a call was made for case studies instead. These, it was argued, would reveal the workings of the black box. But such a call was largely redundant since there were already many case studies of local politics which examined the component parts of the political process — the media, elections, parties, pressure groups, councillors, bureaucrats, and so forth — often in considerable detail, so it is difficult to know what more case studies could do to reveal the mysteries of the black box.

In our study we have rejected the transmission model and with it the orthodox input → black box → output view of the public policy-making process. We fully recognize, of course, that socio-economic structure has a close bearing on some outputs, and we have documented this in the preceding pages. But we also assume a largely autonomous decision-making system in which *all* outputs are viewed as being a product of the political process. Some outputs are likely to be more predetermined by the structural characteristics of the society concerned, but seldom, if ever, solely determined by them. To be logical — and resolve once and for all the long and by now somewhat gamy debate as to whether politics matters — the procedures of output studies should be transformed so that all outputs are assumed to be the product of the political process. This assumption would only be relaxed to the extent that factors that are external to the policy process itself are shown to have a significant association with the output in question. Only if an overwhelmingly strong association is revealed would it be permissible to claim that such a factor 'determined' the policy. Old and perhaps frustrated hands in output analysis will no doubt note that such a change will also have the happy effect of enabling them to 'explain' all outputs. However, rare as it is in the social sciences, the sheer success of a new solution to an old problem does not automatically rule it out.

It is the fact that all policies have first to be decisions made by those authorized to do so that makes them public policies and as such they are irredeemably political. The academic controversy over the relative importance of economic and political variables, what Castles has called the 'battle of the paradigms',[1] is therefore meaningless. Or, as Heclo has remarked, 'the match is a non-contest'.[2] To see economic, or demographic, variables as competing with political variables is rather like assuming that yeast, flour, sugar, and baking are all competing determinates of bakery. Yeast is clearly a necessary ingredient of bread, sugar of cakes. But, however necessary to all forms of baking an ingredient may be (flour, say), it is still none the less only an ingredient, and, therefore, for it to play any part in the final product it is dependent on a series of human volitions we call baking. Of all the elements that make up the final product it is only the *process* of baking that transforms them into that final product. Likewise the political factor, of which party colour is, as we have shown, usually one key element, is not an ingredient of policy — in the sense, say, that age structure unquestionably is for primary school policy — it is the whole process of policy-making.

Viewed as the whole process of policy-making, the political factor embraces not just the determination of public policy outputs, but also the selection and processing of the inputs of the political system. To return to our earlier examples, per capita income, age structure, and population density are simply inert descriptive statistics, with the same objective status as religious affiliation, eye colour, or left-handedness, until they are given policy significance by the political system. In other words, they are not inputs unless and until they are made so by a set of political values and actors. In most parts of England, for example, religious affiliation is not a politically relevant population characteristic, but in Northern Ireland it is. Similarly, the number of family units is a determinant of an important element in French welfare policy — the family allowance — yet it is of no consequence for American welfare policy since there is no family allowance. In Germany a sizeable slice of public health expenditure is devoted to combating the ravages of middle and old age via the *Kur*; six million Germans relished its watery and oozy benefits in 1981 alone. In most Western countries however, the *Kur* is not even recognized as being part of orthodox medical treatment.

The socio-economic inputs of conventional output analysis are, then, not just processed by the political system, they have first to be selected and defined and even created by the political system. The political system is to public policy what an individual's perceptual set is to his cognition: it abstracts some features of the social and economic environment and gives them political salience. We may all be able to agree as to the facts of a situation, but how we interpret and respond to such facts is always in the realm of value. There may, of course, be a very high level of consensus about the interpretation of a problem and about how governments must respond to it, but for many policy areas this situation is likely to be rare and only for a narrow range of policies can we assume such unanimity.

The conception of the political system as an intervening mechanism between inputs and outputs is preferable to that which sees it merely as a bundle of characteristics — party colour, turnout, decision-making structure — all jostling as it were with per capita income, age structure, or whatever to make their presence felt on public policy. Nevertheless, its intervening role, ensconced in the black box, although implying that the political system is something more than a population characteristic, is still inadequate.[3] For not only is the transformation process shrouded in mystery, the black box theory still denies the political process its true primordial status. Hansen, in his discussion of public policy models, makes precisely this point.

My point of departure has been the primacy of politics as policy determinants. I reject the suggestion made in earlier studies that socio-economic factors exert a direct and independent impact on the level of public expenditures for specific services. Any such relationships have to be established by the political decision-making bodies.[4]

Not only does the political system constitute the policy process; it also extends out into its own environment in order to shape, influence, and alter it. In the modern era it is never merely the passive recipient of demands from that environment. At the level of the nation state the government has ultimate power, the power of coercion. It may also have the power to change the rules in its own favour and it can certainly promote policies to strengthen its own support. It also has supremely important tasks, which we will come to in a moment, that determine the success of what is usually regarded the most decisive factor in policy-making in the advanced industrial democracies, the economy itself.

Viewed in this way it may seem puzzling that the battle of the paradigms was ever joined. Doubtless there are a number of reasons, but one is merely a semantic one. For many output studies, the only variables that are viewed as being political are those associated with the electoral process, such as party colour and turnout; they are also, of course, those for which adequate statistics are available.[5] The post-electoral process of determining the dependent policy variable is deemed to be something other than political. Peterson, in his study which is wholly devoted to what influences local and state decision-makers when formulating broad policy, provides an illuminating example of this restricted view of what is political. He claims to side-step the battle of the paradigms on the following grounds:

Until a scholarly consensus is reached on the methodological questions, the debate on the relative importance of political and environmental variables will continue on its meaningless course.

He then adds (our emphasis):

My approach is quite different. From the perspective of the unitary model, *political variables are assumed to be unimportant*. State and local units of government are presumed to be unitary systems that rationally respond to environmental conditions with policies that maximize their economic well-being. To test the model the relative importance of various environmental variables is examined: *political variables are left out of the equation altogether.*[6]

Far from assuming political variables to be unimportant, still less leaving them out altogether, his study makes a powerful and persuasive case for the primacy of the political, since it is almost wholly confined to discussing which factors decision-makers take into account in making broad policy.

We have no wish to understate the role of parties; on the contrary one of the most important findings to emerge from this study is their importance for policy variation. Nevertheless, the futile battle of the paradigms will remain unresolved, or output researchers like Peterson will assume they are side-stepping it, if the actual processes and institutions of decision-making are not regarded as being just as political as parties. Social structure, per capita income, and population density form part of the environment of decision-making; for some policies, as we have said, the most important part of that environment. Parties also seem to provide crucial elements in the decision-making process. Perhaps the best analogy to a party in this context is that of a prism; the party transforms other major elements in line with party ideology and the need to get re-elected.

Our results reveal that, contrary to the findings of a great deal of earlier research, parties do very much matter provided the appropriate measures are applied to the appropriate outputs. Not only do they matter in the sense that quite strong relationships emerged between party control and expenditure distribution, but also most of these relationships, though we freely admit not all, were in the predicted direction. In short, Left parties do tend to spend more on redistributive and ameliorative services, and Right parties do spend more on police and highways. The results also strongly suggest that parties do not usually operate in a vacuum, they affect each other, and an equally important set of results reveals the importance of the party system effect.

Although we were not able to pursue the matter in our analysis, there is also the need to take account of the interlevel party effect in a system like the British one where the parties operate at the local as well as at the central level in full partisan glory. Intergovernmental relations in such systems are automatically coloured by party, especially when the 'mid-term effect' operates; that is to say, when the honeymoon relationship between the electorate and the newly elected central government comes to an end and the electorate punishes the government by electing the national minority party to power locally. A uniform swing like this acts as a signal and a justification for resistance by the opposition-controlled localities to the centre as a prelude to the opposition party's return to power nationally.

Also, some central governments set out to transform not just the local policy framework, but the very nature of the central-local relationship, such that the local system as a whole experiences a sea change in its role. Such, in our view, was the case during the 1945-50 Labour government and the Conservative government elected in 1979.

Another reason why the battle of the paradigms was joined is the need for academics to defend their respective disciplinary deities from attack. But if this is the case, then in this instance one discipline seems to have triumphed, for there can be little doubt that nothing has been as important in sustaining the dispute as economic determinism. This has become one of the dominant influences in the social sciences, it unites many diverse and unlikely soul mates including all the various branches of neo-classical economics with Marxists and neo-Marxists, as well as public choice theorists, and some branches of modern analytic political theory.

But even where there is no explicit claim for the pre-eminence of the economy, economic factors are assumed to be more decisive than the social, and particularly, the political. Indeed the political is often denied any decisive autonomy and becomes simply an epiphenomenon of something else. Government is defined as a kind of residual of market failure. Perceived in such an intellectual climate it is hardly surprising that in policy-output analysis the economic characteristics of society are given a higher status that those of the process of policy-making itself as possible determinants of policy. That is to say, to return to our earlier analogy, that flour has been assumed to be more important than baking in making baked goods. Nor is it surprising that economic factors have been found to fulfil the large expectations placed in them and have emerged as being more decisive than the political, or rather, what has been defined as the political.

This is not the place to attempt either to explain why economic determinism has achieved its dominant position in the social sciences nor to refute it. However, it bears repeating that historically the state and its concomitant, taxation, pre-dated the emergence of money and certainly the market mechanism by a wide margin. Even more important, it must be emphasized that there is only one 'economy' or 'market' that is external to or prior to the key political jurisdiction — this being the state — and that is the world market. This market apart, it is overwhelmingly the state (and in a few cases for specified products, state groupings) which defines the market — by enforcing and maintaining the boundary — and shapes and sustains the market, and not vice versa. For there can be no market without the enforcement of contracts, and the provision of a currency and uniform weights and measures.

The other key constituent element of the environment in which local decision-makers make policy forms the second major element of our study. This is the role of the individual authority as an entity within a wider, sub-regional, regional, or national system. This is what has been termed the unitary model and our study demonstrates conclusively that it applies for certain services, either in terms of a local authority's position in the urban hierarchy, or its role as a specialized centre within the national system.

There are three further broad features of the study that must be emphasized at this point. The first is the importance of having time series data to analyse, and our data covers a sixteen-year period. The need for time series was especially important for examining the effect of party since it enables us to relate party effect to length of office, and to establish that different types of party require different lengths of time to effect their policies; Labour being able, apparently, to change its predecessor's policies more rapidly than the Conservatives.

Another general conclusion arising from our study that we wish to emphasize is the importance of disaggregating expenditures. Analysis only of total expenditure or whole service expenditures, it seems, critically affected the results obtained.

Limiting analysis to high levels of aggregation tends to mask variations that occur at what we have called the operational level; that is, at the sub-departmental or agency level. In Chapter 4, we demonstrate how important it is to take this disaggregated operational level as the unit of analysis if incremental theory is to be adequately tested. This is especially the case for local government where the tax constraint is likely to enforce an incremental approach, with service expenditure as a function of its proportionate share of total expenditure, and not, as the incrementalists claim, as a function of limited knowledge, limited cognition, or conformity to some pluralist theory of the proper limits of government. Equally, in Chapter 9, disaggregation to levels around which parties actually conflict was shown to be critical if the party effect was to be adequately assessed.

Finally, we wish to emphasize a general technical point. There is a tendency for social scientists, when presented with a body of data relevant to a general theoretical problem, to reach for their computer terminal. However, most of the theoretical headway made in this study has developed from very simple statistical techniques. In our view, there is a tendency to use complex techniques where they may not be appropriate, but also to use them as a trawling device to see what emerges rather than to harness them to a hypothesis. We found that the most complicated analytical techniques, in the shape of multiple regression analysis, cluster analysis, and hierarchical cluster analysis, initially failed to produce anything of much interest. It was only when the technique of regression analysis was linked to a well-defined theory and body of empirical propositions that it produced sensible results. Furthermore, the material in the counties chapter (Chapter 8) suggests that the most complex statistical methods employed by the government, the Rate Support Grant (RSG) regression formulae, were actually highly misleading and resulted in a maldistribution of large sums of money. This is because regression analysis gives disproportionate weight to extreme cases (statistical outliers) which in this particular case happened to be a few Welsh counties. It also assumes that there is a single, homogeneous set of counties, all of which behave in much the same way, whereas our results suggest that there is a special Welsh effect which differentiates between English and Welsh counties, and which means that the statistical relationships which obtain in one set of cases are not repeated in the other. A close look at the county data indicates that regression analysis is of limited use in an understanding of local outputs, at least in England and Wales, unless all due care and caution is exercised.

Establishing the Case for an Output Study

In this study we felt that it was necessary to precede the core analysis of the data with a clearance of the ground by means of a thorough and rigorous survey which established the case for the output approach in the context of British local government, and this we did in Chapters 2, 3, and 4. In Chapter 2 the

clearance took the form of an investigation into the capacity of the local government system to exercise sufficient autonomy to justify the assumption implicit
in our analysis that the main units of local government (counties and county
boroughs) during the period covered were sufficiently independent agents. Our
firm conclusion was that neither the growth of central grants nor the expansion
of central controls, up to and during the study period, constituted a significant
impediment to local autonomy that would undermine our assumptions. We were
also able to back this conclusion with some revealing statistical evidence of the
degree of variation in service expenditures within the local government system.

In Chapter 3 we examined the relative success of other research methods as
compared with our own for ascertaining the causes of policy variation. The first
was the Tiebout hypothesis, which on careful examination was ruled out as a
tenable explanatory method, in our view, by the inherent improbability of its
main assumptions. Secondly, we examined two conventional output approaches,
what we have called the demographic approach and factor and cluster analysis.
Both are considerably more plausible than the Tiebout hypothesis, and when
applied to our data did reveal, as they usually do, a clear capacity to show
statistical relationships between certain socio-economic characteristics of local
authorities and their outputs. However, in the case of the demographic approach,
this capacity was limited, particularly in the case of indivisible services such as
police, parks, libraries, and highways. It was more successful, though not a great
deal so, in the case of divisible services such as education, housing, and social
services. But for most services, whether divisible or indivisible, the bulk of
variance remained unexplained. If anything, a distinctly more inferior set of
results was achieved when the factor and cluster analysis was applied to our data.

In Chapter 4 we assessed the last conventional approach for explaining output
variation against our data. This approach is the theory of incremental budgeting
and, although there was evidence of incrementalism tending to operate for large
budget items in the counties, it did not apply with any precision in the county
boroughs. Nor did the incremental model apply for smaller and disaggregated
budget items in either type of authority. Again, disaggregation was seen to have
a critical relationship to political factors.

The Core Analysis

Chapter 4 concluded the first phase of our analysis which, broadly speaking, also
set the stage for the analysis in the subsequent chapters in which we applied to
our data the key explanatory concepts which seek to account for output variation.
These were the two basic types already mentioned. The first is based on the
unitary model and is derived from the conceptualization of the government of a
city as having tasks to perform that are related not to the city's internal social
characteristics, but to its role as a holistic entity in relation to the external world,

either as a service centre within the national urban hierarchy for a hinterland that extends beyond the city's political boundary, or in relation to some specialized economic role that the local community performs within a national division of labour. The unitary model is in sharp contrast to the transmission model, which has tended to dominate most output research and which, as we have noted, sees the bulk of a government's policies as being internally derived. That is to say, most policy is seen as the reflection of the needs of the population. Socio-economic statistics which describe that population, it follows, will be strongly linked with policy. Both aspects of the unitary model — service centre and specialized role — were applied to our data in Chapters 5, 6, and 7 and a fairly clear pattern emerged. First, certain service expenditures, mainly for quasi-public goods such as police, highways, parks, libraries, and sports facilities, did seem to be related to the city's position in the urban hierarchy. That is to say, they were related to the size of the population in the city's hinterland for whom it provided market services. Secondly, our results showed that a city's role within the national system also seems to affect service patterns in the expected directions. This was notably the case for seaside resorts, conurbation centres, and county towns.

In Chapter 8 we have tentatively extended the unitary model to the counties. We would not, however, wish to lay too great an emphasis on the results obtained, for the obvious reason that counties are in socio-economic terms very different animals to cities. We do, none the less, feel that the results we set out in Chapter 8 reveal that some counties, despite their relative heterogeneity, have acquired a unitary role within wider systems.

In Chapter 8 we have also applied another geographical model. This is a regional one whereby the service expenditures of the Welsh counties as a group were compared with those of the English counties, and the Welsh group emerged as consistently spending considerably more on all of their services, especially on education, than English counties. Moreover, this difference was not explainable in terms of socio-economic variables (for example population density) or the available political variables (for example uncontested seats). It follows that there is a very strong likelihood that this difference reflects a different conception of the appropriate level of public expenditure on the part of policy-makers in Welsh counties as compared with their English counterparts. That is to say, some sort of cultural-cum-ideological difference between Welsh and English decision-makers seems to have been at work. It would be interesting to see if other regional differences in expenditure patterns occur in Scotland and Northern Ireland.

The second major group of new, or non-conventional, output techniques were applied in Chapter 9. These were exclusively political and sought to improve on the existing work on the effect of party variables by first, using a better list of party variables (for example length of time in office, rather than just which party in control), and by relating these variables to a broader range of specific services, rather than using the single measure of total expenditure. Our treatment of the dependent variable is, we think, in this case more rigorous than has previously been achieved. We also introduced an equally rigorous set of measures in order to gauge the party system effect on aspects of the role of party that have been curiously neglected. Again these measures were perhaps more refined than have been applied in previous research.

Both the party effect and the party system effect were revealed as having a critical bearing on outputs, not only in the sense that different parties seemed to have different effects on expenditure patterns, as did different types of party system, but also in that these differences broadly arose in the expected direction; the Left party (Labour) tended to spend more on the ameliorative and redistributive services and the party of the Right (Conservative) tended to spend less on such services and more on the non-distributive services.

Contrary to a great deal of previous research then, politics, and parties in particular, were unquestionably seen to matter, and this emerges as one of the major findings of our study. However, a possible criticism of this conclusion must be met. We have emphasized that one characteristic of the very early research on the party effect, which influenced the general conclusion that politics did not matter, was that the parties in question were American. Their relative lack of ideological commitment, we argued, and in particular the absence of a socialist or Labour party, could account for the absence of a party effect.

By the same token, it could equally plausibly be argued that just as American parties tend to be relatively non-ideological, so British parties tend to be the reverse. It follows, so this criticism might claim, that our results reveal not so much that parties matter, but that British parties matter.

Certainly there is some prima-facie evidence that this may be the case. In terms of comparative party style there are the claims of the 'adversary' school, which makes precisely the point that British parties are unusually combative and prone to transmute most political issues into an ideologically rooted conflict, to the point where such behaviour, so the school has claimed, was actually endangering the democratic process.[7]

Although this school's concern for the future of British democracy seems to have rapidly and mysteriously subsided since the election of the Thatcher government in 1979, there are some fairly solid constitutional grounds that lend credence to the claim that British parties are likely to be hostile to each other.[8] Whether this is a threat to democracy raises questions that lie outside our study and may therefore be safely left to the students of the adversary theory — should they resume their labours.

The adversary theory is exclusively related to central government, it can be argued, but the institutional reinforcement of the adversary style in the British system is as pervasive at the local as at the national level, especially in urban areas.

Virtually all the county boroughs during our study period were run on fairly well-developed party lines for all major, and some minor, policies. Such rigidity is unusual in most Western countries and unknown in some, for, whereas in Western Europe at least elections are partisan and often mirror those at the national level, overt and full-blooded party conflict does not, as it does in Britain, always persist in the council chamber and decision-making process. The main institutional reason for this is that British local government lacks a unitary executive like the French *maire* or German *Burgermeister*, or a plural but multi-partisan executive like the Scandinavian Executive Committee. Both types of executive tend to dilute the pure milk of party doctrine. The unitary executive because it personalizes, and thus tends to neuter, policy-making. The plural executive is less ideological because, by its very nature, it excludes the possibility of major decisions being a one-party monopoly.

As prima-facie evidence that British local government ought to be more partisan, all this may be conceded, and it may very well be that the greater partisanship of British local government is one factor influencing the very clear relationship that our analysis has revealed between local expenditure patterns and party colour, and, indeed, party system. But it is very unlikely that it is the only factor; for, as we noted in Chapter 1, as more research applying more refined dependent variables has been undertaken in other Western countries besides the US and Britain, so the party effect has been revealed as having as strong a relationship with certain types of output as in Britain.

We conclude that British local government, whatever influence its peculiar institutional arrangements may have on policy formation, is not a special case in terms of party effect. Parties, we repeat, are a much more potent factor in influencing governmental outputs than much of previous output research has recognized.

As we have already argued, the primacy of the political factors as broadly understood was also revealed in the second major aspect of our analysis, the geographic. That is to say, expenditure patterns were shown to be not only a reflection of the socio-economic character of the local community, but also of its role as a unitary specialized service provider within an external system.

It is true that the geographic determinants of the unitary model that we have deployed — mainly the urban hierarchy and the city typology — are external to the political process, but that does not mean they pre-determine the policy that the local decision-makers choose in relation to their local government's role in the external system. City fathers cannot, of course, make their domain into something fundamentally different from their community's inherent character. As we have noted, seaside resorts have to be on or near the coast. Similarly, a city's service centre role is circumscribed by the degree of proximity of competing centres. But local councils can and do vary the intensity with which they reinforce and support the unitary role of their community. Moreover, no external system within which the community may have a role is immutable and it may be subject to change — in demand or technology, for example — which requires its policy makers to adjust their policies if the community is to maintain its prosperity. As Peterson has emphasized:

Local governments operate on an ever-changing environment to which they must be prepared to respond. Just as the nation state must be prepared to counteract forces in the international arena, so a local government must anticipate not only the immediate changes in surrounding towns and communities, but even the longer-term trends shaping relationships among states and regions in the country as a whole . . . Just as the nation state wishes to maximize its power in the international system, and the private firm wishes to maximize its profits, so the local community wishes to maximize its economic well-being, its social standing, and its political position relative to other local units.[9]

As Peterson also points out, local government rarely has any control over the forces making for change to the external system in which it operates, whichever option it chooses in order to maximize its opportunities is unlikely to be either predetermined or self-evident; it will be a product of political choice and judgement.

Precisely the same considerations apply to the striking results that emerge from our analysis of the Welsh county outputs. Here, almost beyond the shadow of a doubt, is a political factor at work. What its precise form is will require the techniques of another research mode — the case study — to elucidate. Here is an example of the way in which the macro output approach links up with the micro case study which we noted in Chapter 1, and one claim we wish to make is that we have provided a basis for future case studies. We do so not merely to avoid confronting tricky questions of causality arising from macro research, which, as we argued earlier, seems to be the case with some black box theorists. Rather, we do so in the hope that the case study can be designed precisely in order to elucidate further the determinates of policy variation. For by selecting cases from the types of local government we have identified, the inferences we have made from the macro data about the principal determinants of policy may be put to a searching and detailed test.

Case studies will be essential in any event if the determinants of outputs are to be fully revealed, since some of them are almost certainly not susceptible to output analysis. These are principally those political factors that play a part in policy formation, but which could not be analysed in this study. One of the most important of these omitted factors is the role of the bureaucracy.[10] Another is the role of leadership cadres among the elected representatives, especially, in our case, individual leaders in the one-party dominant and the strongly Independent-controlled authorities.

Both of these elements, leaders and bureaucrats, also contribute to what may not be susceptible even to the case study. This is what may be termed a polity's decision-making tradition. There are no decision rules to cover every eventuality, even in the most rigidly controlled organizations. Every organization has therefore to evolve some of its conventions for itself, and governments are relatively free agents in the creation of their own decision rules; nation states more so than decentralized governments, of course. Anyone who has ever studied in a systematic fashion how governments, whether they be local, intermediate, or national, make policy, becomes quickly aware that these traditions have a decisive impact not only on the process of decision-making — their ostensible function — but also on the policy outcome.

So, while we may fairly claim that by our extension of the independent variables we have reached a level of explanation of expenditure variation rarely achieved, we are only too aware that much unexplained variation remains and is probably likely to remain if only the output technique is employed.

One last point. We have consciously set out, both in our preliminary discussion in the assessment chapters and elsewhere, to treat output analysis as if it was applied to all governments and we have tended to ignore the distinctions between local, intermediate, and national government. In doing so we have no wish to pretend that local government is just national government writ small. There are fundamental differences between the two, not least those in functional range and fiscal capacity, and, above all, there is the fact that, with the exception of a confederation, sub-national government is always in some sense subordinate to national government. However, we would also like to emphasize that, despite these differences, the present compartmentalization of the cross-national and sub-national output studies is, not to put too fine a point on it, silly. Whatever the differences between the two types of polity it cannot possibly justify the almost hermetically sealed character of cross-national research. One illustration must suffice; in one of the most recent and one of the best cross-national collections, comprising six individual analyses of policy variation between nation states, over five hundred references are listed of which only three refer to sub-national output studies![11] A reader of this collection who was largely unfamiliar with the genre might be surprised to discover that the sub-national literature is far larger than the cross-national and, dare it be said, much broader in scope.

We hasten to add that in making this assertion we have no wish to endow sub-national political scientists with superior qualities *qua* political science. But there is at least one very good reason for the superiority of their work, namely the severe handicaps under which cross-national research has to labour. In endeavouring to treat output studies as a unified subject, we have no wish to denigrate cross-national research gratuitously, and indeed we readily concede that the state is prima facie a much more plausible free agent than any sub-national government. Moreover, we are equally aware that for most states there is already a very rich literature on its internal policy-making process which considerably strengthens the quality of macro analysis. No, what we have in mind is the likelihood that unified treatment will enrich both wings, but that cross-national research has two special and unresolvable handicaps which it will have to accommodate if it is to develop. Drawing freely on sub-national research, which suffers neither handicap, as part of a unified conceptual framework embracing a single unit of analysis — let us say the polity — is one way of accommodating these handicaps. The handicaps are, first, the extreme difficulty of getting commensurability of outputs cross-nationally. This difficulty is no better illustrated than by the extent to which so much of cross-national output research is limited to the somewhat meagre question: What are the main influences on certain kinds of welfare expenditures?

The second handicap that we noted in Chapter 1 is the age-old problem of all comparative research and was raised long ago by J. S. Mill, namely, the likelihood that the number of variations that will probably affect the dependent variable very considerably exceeds the number of countries that can plausibly be mustered for analysis.[12] Even the most ingenious special pleading cannot extend the group of 'advanced Western' states (the only group for which the requisite data are likely to be available in any case) much beyond twenty. In short, the time has come to link all forms of output research lest the cross-national sector expires from inanition. We hope that our study will provide a modest step in that direction.

NOTES

1. F. G. Castles, 'The Impact of Parties in Public Expenditure', in F. G. Castles (ed.), *The Impact of Parties* (London, Sage, 1982).
2. H. Heclo, *Modern Social Politics in Britain and Sweden* (New Haven, Yale University Press, 1974), p. 288.
3. See D. Ashford, 'Resources, Spending and Party Politics in British Local Government', *Administration and Society*, 7 (1975).
4. T. Hansen, 'Transforming Needs into Expenditure Decisions', in K. Newton (ed.), *Urban Political Economy* (London, Frances Pinter, 1981), p. 45.
5. An exception is Ashford, 'Resources, Spending and Party Politics'.
6. P. Peterson, 'A Unitary Model of Local Taxation and Expenditure Policies in the United States', *British Journal of Political Science*, 9 (1979), 283 and n. 7. Also see P. Peterson, 'Redistributive Policies and Patterns of Citizen Participation in Local Politics in the U.S.A.', in L. J. Sharpe (ed.), *Decentralist Trends in Western Democracies* (London, Sage, 1979). We understand that Peterson has developed these ideas further in his *City Limits* (Chicago, University of Chicago Press, 1981), but this book came to our notice too

late for us to consider it in this study.

7. See, for example, S. E. Finer's 'Introduction' to S. E. Finer (ed.), *Adversary Politics and Electoral Reform* (London, Wigram, 1975); S. E. Finer, *The Changing British Party System 1945-1979* (Washington DC, American Enterprise Institute, 1980), especially Part Two; J. Rogaly, *Parliament For The People* (London, Smith, 1976); M. Stewart, *The Jekyll and Hyde Years: Politics and Economic Policy Since 1964* (London, Dent, 1977), Ch. 7; and Lord Hailsham, *The Dilemmas of Democracy* (London, Collins, 1978).
8. G. Peters, 'Types of Democratic Systems and Types of Public Policy', in P. Lewis, D. Potter, and F. G. Castles (eds.), *The Practice of Comparative Politics* (London, Longman, 1978).
9. Peterson, 'A Unitary Model of Local Taxation and Expenditure', 283-4.
10. For an excellent example of a study that links output analysis with a case study and is thus able to explore the role of the bureaucracy, see R. Winters, 'Political Choice and Expenditure Change in New Hampshire and Vermont', *Polity*, XII (1980).
11. Castles (ed.), *The Impact of Parties*. All these sub-national references occur in Castles's own essay.
12. B. Barry, 'Methodology Versus Ideology, the Economic Approach Revisited', in Elinor Ostrom (ed.), *Strategies of Political Inquiry* (Beverly Hills, Sage, 1982). Also see Castles, 'Introduction: Politics and Public Policy', in Castles (ed.), *The Impact of Parties*.

APPENDICES

Introduction

The Appendices contain most of the technical and methodological details of the study. They have been collected together at the back of the book so that the flow of the discussion in the individual chapters is not continuously interrupted by diversions concerning statistical methods, data sources, methodological problems, and so on. Nevertheless, the Appendices contain important information for those who wish to examine the foundations of the study, and to follow up its points of finer detail. They are organized as follows.

Appendix 1 General Background to the Data File

1.1 *The Scope of the Study*

The discussion of the theory and methods of output studies in Chapter 1 points to the need for time series research covering as long a period as possible. Therefore, we searched for the longest unbroken set of comparable local financial statistics in the post-war period. This turned out to be bounded in the early years by changes in the way in which central government calculated and paid its grants to local government, and by the consequences of these changes for the ways in which local authorities present their expenditure figures. There was a major change in 1958 from specific grants to a block grant, after which more detailed and systematic figures for all major local authority service expenditures became available. Although figures for services and some sub-services were published before 1958, this is the first time in the post-war period that a complete series of figures was produced that is strictly comparable both across services and across years. The great bulk of the financial data on the file, therefore, record major service expenditures, starting with the financial year 1960/1, and then at four-yearly intervals until 1972/3.

For reasons which are discussed in the chapter on incrementalism, it is also necessary to cover as long a period as possible when tracing change in spending figures which are disaggregated into reasonably small budgetary items. Fortunately disaggregated figures of this kind are available for a limited number of services from 1956/7 onwards, and from these education, fire, and health services were selected. These three services represent a reasonable spread of large and small services, distributive and redistributive ones, and divisible and indivisible ones. The disaggregated data file thus starts in 1956/7, and like the major service expenditure file, continues at four-yearly intervals until 1972/3.

Ad hoc changes in county and county borough boundaries, such as the creation of Torbay, Teesside, and the GLC (discussed in Appendix 3.2), altered the number of top-tier local authorities, but did not affect the nature of the local government financial system as such. However, the time series is brought to an abrupt halt by the reform of local government in 1974. Major changes in both boundaries and service functions introduced in that year make it impossible to compare the old and the new systems in the exact manner required by this study. In addition there is some evidence that spending patterns in the last year of the old system were unusual because some authorities seemed to have spent all their balances before they went out of existence, rather than hand them over to their successors. However, the financial year 1972/3 did not suffer from this problem, and is the last set of figures which can reasonably be analysed. In any case, by starting at the earliest possible date of 1960/1 for major services, and 1956/7 for disaggregated figures, and by taking every fourth year thereafter, the study ends up with 1972/3.

A virtually complete set of figures is available for all the fifteen major services of the county boroughs, and all ten major services of the counties, plus, of course, an overall total for both types of authority. Such gaps as do exist in the service expenditure section of the data file are both rare and random, and offer no obstacles to proper and systematic analysis.

With the exception of London, the study examines the spending of all top-tier authorities in England and Wales — i.e. all the counties and county boroughs. London is excluded for the same reason that the study had to finish in 1972/3, namely that London was fundamentally reorganized in 1964. Scotland and Northern Ireland are also excluded because they have their own local government, financial, and accounting systems which cannot be compared directly with those of England and Wales.

1.2 Sources and Reliability of Financial Data

Local authority expenditure data for the major services of the county boroughs are taken from *Return of Rates*, which was compiled and published by the Institute of Municipal Treasurers and Accountants — now known as the Chartered Institute of Public Finance and Accountancy (IMTA and CIPFA). This publication appears about a year after local authority budgets have been set, and it gives budget figures, not final expenditure figures. For the county councils, the Society of County Treasurers (SCT) compiles and publishes *Rate Precepts and Estimated Expenditures per Head*, which also gives budget figures and not final expenditures. For the more detailed financial data on education, fire, and health, the data sources are the IMTA and SCT publications, *Education Statistics*, *Fire Service Statistics*, and *Health Service Statistics*.

A check on the reliability of budget figures as an estimate of final expenditures was carried out through a random sample of twenty county boroughs and ten counties. In more than two-thirds of the cases, the budget figure was within 2 per cent of the final expenditure, and in no case did the latter exceed the former by as much as 5 per cent.

A more serious objection to the IMTA and SCT statistics concerns the comparability of figures returned by different authorities. The use of different accounting practices, such as the classification of the same spending under different budgetary headings, would make sensible analysis of the data impossible. On the other hand, we must not exaggerate the possible extent of such accounting variation. It is highly unlikely, for example, that highways spending would be listed under the education budget. Nor can fire and libraries spending be easily confused, or sewerage and welfare, or education and police, and so on. More to the point, however, IMTA and SCT have had many decades' experience of collecting local financial statistics, and have had years, not to say generations, in which to sort out the ambiguities and complexities of local accounts in the search for standardization. In a local government service as professionalized as the municipal treasurers and accountants, it is difficult to argue that there are still large and undetected variations in something as routine as local authority accounting.

There are almost certainly some problems. The way in which general administrative costs are divided between services in one such. Debt charges are another problem in 1956/7, because they are not distributed between education sub-headings in that year, although they are in all subsequent years. However, these are precisely the sorts of problems which are recognized and discussed by IMTA and SCT in their financial publications, and eventually ironed out, more or less. Other problems are likely to be both small and, above all, random across services, authorities, and years. They can, therefore, be safely ignored.

1.3 Sources of Social and Economic Data

Unless otherwise stated below, social and economic data were culled from the 1961, 1966, and 1972 census reports. Other sources of data are as follows.

Source	Variable
Return of Rates (IMTA)	Local authority acreage
Financial and General Statistics (IMTA)	
Rate Precepts and Estimated Expenditures Per Head (SCT)	
Rates and Rateable Values (Ministry of Housing and Local Government/ Department of the Environment, and Welsh Office)	All rateable value figures
Registrar General's Decennial Supplement, Area Mortality Tables	Male standardized mortality rate (county boroughs only)
Home Office, *Supplementary Criminal Statistics*	Indictable offences.

1.4 Sources of Political Data

Election statistics are taken from the Registrar General's *Statistical Review* and figures for the number of council members from the *Municipal Year Book* for the appropriate years. Data on the party affiliation of council members are much more difficult to obtain and our figures are compiled from a variety of sources. There is no official record of the party affiliation of council members, of the party composition of councils, or of the party control of councils (if any). In county boroughs this is not generally a problem, since most of the councils operated on party lines, with a high proportion of the seats being taken by the two main parties. In counties, however, the situation is more confused by the substantial proportion of seats taken by Independents.

The majority of our data were obtained from *The Times* election reports, which, for county boroughs, give the new council, the seats won, the party in control, and any change in control from the year before. Obvious misprints and errors were checked and corrected. Gaps in these data were filled in either from the records at Conservative Central Office, or from information collected and kindly made available to us by Mr Phillip Williams, of Nuffield College, Oxford. In two of the budget years (1955 and 1967), the boroughs held aldermanic elections which led, in some cases, to changes in the proportions of the parties represented on the councils, and even occasionally to a change in control. To allow for this, the data were adjusted by using the results of the following years' elections to calculate back to the council composition after the aldermanic elections.

The Independents on the county councils proved to be a severe problem. Some of them had electoral agreements with the Conservatives, or formed alliances with them once elected to the council. So far as possible we tried to distinguish Independents with Conservative support from 'Genuine Independents', using data from Conservative Central Office. For the three years 1955, 1958, and 1964 we divided the Independents on the county councils into those with, and those without, Conservative support, but for the other three years the data are not available at Conservative Central Office, and we have not been able to do this. Consequently, Independents are treated as a single group in these years.

Determining the party in control in the counties is difficult because *The Times* does not give complete information. Also, there are many anti-socialist alliances, and other coalitions, which make it impossible to know which party or combination of parties, if any, controlled some of the councils. As far as possible we filled in the county figures from the sources available to us, bearing in mind the weakness of some of the figures. However, information for the years 1955, 1958, and 1964 is fairly complete and fairly reliable, and some confidence can be placed in them. The general rule followed in coding the data was that only Independents who were known to have agreements with the Conservatives were coded as such and, therefore, the figures tend to under-estimate Conservative strength.

Expenditure data were collected for the years 1956/7, 1960/1, 1964/5, 1968/9, and 1972/3. Political data were collected for each of the preceding years, because these were the years in which local authority budgets were set. In other words, the data relate to the political characteristics of the councils in the years in which budgets were set. In the case of the county boroughs there is little difficulty in collecting all the election and party data required. Elections were held every year during the period 1955 to 1971, and so information was collected for each of the relevant budget years, which were 1955/6, 1959/60, 1963/4, 1967/8, and 1971/2. In addition, information was collected about political control of the councils for each year between 1955 and 1972, in order to obtain a complete record of the political background of the councils over the whole period.

For county councils, where elections took place every three years, we recorded election and political statistics for all the election years between 1955 and 1973, namely, 1955, 1958, 1961, 1964, 1967, and 1970. Every effort was made to keep track of by-election and aldermanic election results which may have disturbed the political balance of a county council, but there is no sure way of knowing whether this was completely successful, and it is likely that the figures are in error in a few cases. The errors are likely to be fairly minor, however, and it is unlikely that correcting them, if this were possible, would make much difference to party-control or party-system variables as they are constructed in this research.

Appendix 2 The Contents of the Data File

Besides the expenditure data, the file included a large amount of material describing the social, economic, political, and locational characteristics of local authorities. The following is a somewhat abbreviated list, but it gives a generally fairly full idea of the range and number of variables included in the analysis. Each one is transformed into a ratio or percentage using the most appropriate base figure available.

2.1 *Social Data*

Social class. All seventeen socio-economic groups (SEGs) of economically active males provided by the census reports were recorded and then combined in various ways to give figures for manual and non-manual workers, upper and upper-middle class, lower middle class, skilled workers, small self-employed workers, and semi-skilled and unskilled workers, as percentages of economically active males, in 1961 and 1971.

Agricultural workers. SEGs 13, 14, and 15 as a percentage of economically active males, 1961, 1971.

Housing tenure. Persons living in privately owned, council rented, and privately rented accommodation as percentages of total population, 1961, 1971.

Overcrowding. Percentage of total population living at household densities of more than one and a half, and the percentage at less than half a person per room, 1961, 1971.

No hot water. Percentage of all households with no hot water supply, 1961, 1971.

Economically active women. Economically active women as a percentage of total economically active women, 1971.

Geographical size. Local authority area in acres, each year analysed.

Male standardized mortality rate from all causes. 1961, 1971.

Infant mortality rate. 1961, 1971.

Total population. In 1931, 1951, 1961, and 1971, plus the Registrar General's mid-year estimates for other years.

Old population. Population over pensionable age (men 65, women 60), 1961, 1971.

Indictable offences. Indictable offences known to the police by police districts, per thousand population, 1956, 1960, 1964, and 1968.

Total population in employment and resident in the area. 1961.

Population resident in the area but working elsewhere. As a percentage of total population in employment and resident in the area, 1961, 1971.

Population working in the area but resident elsewhere. As a percentage of total population in employment and resident in the area, 1961, 1971.

Inflows and outflows of working population. 1961, 1971 (the sum of the two preceding variables).

Population 0–4 years old. As a percentage of total population, each year analysed.

Population density. Per acre, each year analysed.

Population change. 1931 to 1951, 1951 to 1971, and 1939 to 1971. Full account is taken, wherever possible, of boundary changes.

Total primary, secondary, and nursery pupils for whom local authority is financially responsible. As a percentage of total population, each year of analysis.

2.2 Economic Data

Retail trade turnover, per capita. 1961, 1971, available for county boroughs only.

Total rateable value, per capita. Each year analysed.

Value of domestic property. Number of domestic properties with rateable values of less than £100, and number with values of more than £200, as a percentage of all hereditaments, each year analysed.

Rateable value of other property. Shops, offices, other commercial, industrial, crown property, and other, as a percentage of total rateable value, each year analysed.

Estimated standard product of a penny rate, per capita. Each year of analysis.

Estimated net product of a penny rate, per capita. Each year of analysis.

Total net rate and grant borne expenditure. Rate equivalent, per capita, each year of analysis.

General government grant. Rate equivalent, per capita, each year of analysis.

Rate deficiency grant. Rate equivalent, per capita, each year of analysis.

Other grants. Excluding housing; rate equivalent, per capita, each year of analysis.

Housing grant. Rate equivalent, per capita, each year of analysis.

Total rate. Rate equivalent, per capita, each year analysed.

Domestic element of rate support grant per head. 1968/9, 1972/3.

Rate poundage. Each year of analysis.

Note: Due allowance is made for the different financial systems and service responsibilities of counties and county boroughs.

2.3 Political Data

Election turnout. Percentage of qualified electors voting in contested seats.

Contested seats. As percentage of all seats, each election year analysed.

Party in control of council. Conservative, Labour, Independent, Conservative and Independent, Other, and no overall control.

Percentage of seats held by parties. Conservative, Labour, Liberal, Independent, and Other, each election year analysed.

Percentage of seats held by controlling party. Each election year analysed.

Number of changes in party control. 1955-9, 1955-63, 1955-67, 1955-71, 1959-63, 1963-7, and 1967-71.

Number of years controlled by party. Conservative, Labour, Independent, Independent and Conservative, Other, and no party control. 1955-9, 1955-63, 1955-67, 1955-71, and sensible permutations of these dates.

Party system. Non-party, one party, monopoly, one-party dominant, two party, and multi-party.

Note: Political data are compiled for each political year in which a budget was set in county boroughs (i.e. 1955, 1959, 1963, 1967, and 1971), and for each year in which the county councils held elections (i.e. 1955, 1958, 1961, 1964, 1967, and 1970).

2.4 Locational and Geographical Data

In addition to the conventional variables of the kind usually included in output studies, the file also contains additional information concerning the geographical or locational aspects of authorities, plus some data about the urban hierarchy and central places. This information applies only to county boroughs.

Coastal/non-coastal. A dummy variable indicating whether an authority is coastal — sub-divided according to seaside resorts and other authorities — or non-coastal.

Urban-Rural. A dummy variable which distinguishes between urban, semi-urban, semi-rural, and rural authorities, 1971.
  (1) *Urban.* Those authorities which are surrounded on at least 75 per cent of their boundary by other authorities with a population density of at least five people per acre.
  (2) *Semi-urban.* Those authorities which are mainly (75 per cent) surrounded by other authorities with a population density of more than three but less than five people per acre.
  (3) *Semi-rural.* Those which are mainly (75 per cent) surrounded by authorities with a population density of less than three but more than one person per acre.

(4) *Rural.* Authorities which are mainly (75 per cent) surrounded by other authorities with a population density of less than one person per acre.

Central place measures. Two main measures are on the file.

(1) *Smith Ranking.* The geographer R. D. P. Smith classifies seventy-four English county boroughs according to a variety of central place characteristics (R. D. P. Smith, 'The changing urban hierarchy', *Regional Studies*, 12 (1968), 1–19). He then groups the authorities into a set of eighteen ranked categories which serve as measures of the urban hierarchy. Although Smith's classification is based on a broad range of central place characteristics, the fact that he groups the authorities into only 18 categories has the effect of blunting his typology, which turns out to be less useful than that of another geographer, W. I. Carruthers.

(2) *Carruthers Ranking and Measure.* W. I. Carruthers ('Major shopping centres in England and Wales', *Regional Studies*, 1 (1967), 65–9) ranks seventy-four county boroughs in England and Wales according to three aspects of their shopping patterns in 1961. First, he considers the type and amount of trade in each authority, giving each a weighting, with a small extra amount for non-food trade. Second, he estimates the theoretical net loss or gain of trade for each authority – how much trade is gained or lost from nearby authorities. And third, he weights authorities according to their provision of specialist services which are known to bear a strong relationship to centrality; namely, shops for shoes, menswear, women's wear, furniture and furnishings, radio, electrical, cycles, jewellery, and leather and sports goods. Each of these scores was used in correlation and regression analysis, but, in general, they did not relate to service expenditures as closely as the sum of all three, which was, therefore, employed in the bulk of the analysis.

Appendix 3 Detailed Problems of the Data File

Any data file, particularly if it is time series, is likely to meet a whole series of problems about missing data, changes in the definitions of variables, inadequate data, complications about exact dates, changes of boundaries, and so on. Missing data are not much of a problem in this case since local authority and census reports almost always cover all the top-tier units of local government for all years. There were, however, a wide range of other problems which had to be solved in an *ad hoc* manner. It is not possible or necessary to discuss the small details of each of these, because some of them were trivial, referring to one service of one authority in one year, and because others were more general but still inconsequential. (These are noted or discussed in the code book for the data file.) There were some more major problems, however, which should be briefly discussed.

3.1 *Education Expenditure*

The computation of per pupil education expenditure figures is complicated by the fact that some pupils are educated in the public sector, but outside their own local authority area. In general, the boroughs are net 'importers' of pupils, while the counties tend to 'export'. In 1960/1, eleven of the eighty-three boroughs imported more than 10 per cent of their secondary pupils, the most striking being Canterbury which received 40 per cent of them from surrounding authorities. Only five of the county boroughs imported more than 5 per cent of their primary pupils, so the problem applies in the main to secondary education figures. However, imported and exported pupils tend to be more expensive than the others, probably because they are special in some way, or because of travel costs.

At the same time it is impossible to discover exactly how many school-aged children are normally resident in any given authority, partly because a small proportion of these are likely to be educated privately. Allowance is made for the small number of pupils who are financed by local authorities to attend private schools, but there are no figures for pupils who are educated and financed privately. The census reports give figures for children of different age groups, but some of these — the rising fives, and those above minimum school-leaving age — may or may not be attending schools. On the other hand, the IMTA and SCT sources give figures for the numbers of pupils on nursery, primary, and secondary school registers, but do not say what proportion of these are the financial responsibility of the authority keeping the registers, and the IMTA and SCT age group classifications do not match those of census reports. The best solution is to calculate per capita education expenditure on the basis of census data about school-aged populations, and to calculate per pupil education expenditure on the basis of school register numbers, though these do not make allowances for the extra cost of 'imports and exports'. Although it is assumed that the census and school register figures are directly comparable, this is not, in fact, the case, and it is likely that there are, therefore, some discrepancies in the calculations. They are likely to be no more than marginal in the great majority of cases, but they may be quite large in a small number of authorities, such as Canterbury.

3.2 Boundary changes

The number of counties and county boroughs changes over the period of analysis because of boundary changes caused by the creation of the GLC, the merging of some county boroughs, and the creation of others. The following were affected by major boundary changes between 1956 and 1973.

County boroughs
Croydon, existed up to 1.4.65.
East Ham, existed up to 1.4.65.
Hartlepool, existed up to 1.4.67.
Luton, existed from 1.4.64.
Middlesborough, existed up to 1.4.68.
Smethwick, existed up to 1.4.66.
Solihull, existed from 1.4.64.
Teesside, existed from 1.4.68.
Torbay, existed from 1.4.68.
Warley, existed from 1.4.65.
West Ham, existed up to 1.4.65.
West Hartlepool, existed up to 1.4.67.

Counties
Cambridgeshire, existed up to 1.4.65.
Cambridge and Isle of Ely, existed from 1.4.65.
Huntingdonshire, existed up to 1.4.65.
Middlesex, existed up to 1.4.65.
Huntingdonshire and Peterborough, existed from 1.4.65.
Isle of Ely, existed up to 1.4.65.
Soke of Peterborough, existed up to 1.4.65.

Due allowance has been made, whenever possible, for boundary changes affecting other authorities, although the changes are small and affect only a small proportion of cases.

Whenever possible, expenditure data are matched with census data for the nearest year (i.e. 1956/7 and 1960/1 expenditure data are run against 1961 census data, but 1964/5 expenditures are run with 1966 sample census data), but boundary changes sometimes make this impossible. In these cases, the next nearest census data are used. For 1964/5 expenditures, 1961 census data are used for the following:

Boroughs	*Counties*
Croydon	Essex
Dudley	Kent
Northampton	Peterborough

Boroughs	*Counties*
Smethwick	Staffordshire
Walsall	Surrey
West Bromwich	
Wolverhampton	

3.3 *Housing Tenure and Quality*

Housing tenure figures are not classified in the same way in the 1961 and 1971 census reports. In 1971, only four of the six categories used in the 1961 census were used, and those not fitting any of the four were allocated to the nearest one by the census enumerators. To achieve approximate comparability of 1961 and 1971 figures, the fourfold and sixfold classifications were collapsed into three, namely owner-occupied, local authority rented, and other, which includes tied housing in urban and rural areas, and furnished and unfurnished privately rented accommodation.

The variables dealing with household amenities do not cover all types of tenure, but only those in private housing. The correct base has been used in calculating proportions in any given authority involving two or more types of housing tenure. In addition, the treatment and definition of different kinds of housing amenities vary from one census to the next, the availability of hot water being one which changes the least, and which was selected for use in this study. The category of households with no hot water was used because the figures are given in percentage form in the census reports.

3.4 *Police and Fire Authorities*

Between 1956 and 1972 the number of police and fire authorities declined, as authorities were merged. This is particularly true of police districts, of which there were only forty-four in 1972/3. The figures for rate equivalent expenditures are given for each county and county borough throughout the period, as if there were discrete figures for each separate local authority, but it must be borne in mind that this is not so. The merging of authorities blunts the analysis quite considerably, and readers should not be misled by the analysis in this study which proceeds as if each local authority had its own separate police authority with its own spending figures.

Apart from this very general problem about police statistics, the fact that some counties fell partially within the Metropolitan Police Authority (MPA) in 1960/1 and 1965/6 also presents some difficulties. Middlesex had no police service of its own, so it has been given the appropriate MPA figure. Parts of Surrey, Kent, Essex, and Hertfordshire fell within the MPA, but they have been given spending figures for the areas outside the MPA, as in the SCT sources. The merging of fire authorities results in the same general problem as for police districts, although it is rather less acute, since there were fewer amalgamations, and consequently more fire districts. Nevertheless, readers are warned that the analysis proceeds as if each local authority had its own, separate fire service, whereas, in fact, this is not the case. To this extent, the analysis of fire and police service spending is misleading, but it is not invalidated as a method of trying to understand variations in spending on these services.

3.5 *Expenditure Statistics*

Figures were collected for the needs, resources, and domestic elements of the rate support grant, but the last element is treated as a partial derating of domestic property, as is the intention of the grant. Care was taken not to count it twice when considering both domestic rates and the domestic element of the RSG. Since counties do not levy rates they have no domestic element in their rate support grant, and hence the problem does not arise for them.

For some inexplicable reason there are no figures for parks expenditure in any of the county boroughs in 1968/9.

3.6 *Political Data*

In many of the counties, and in some of the county boroughs as well, the council was controlled by an alliance of Conservatives, Liberals, and Independents, and these have been classified under the 'Other' heading. In some cases it is likely that the Conservatives made up the bulk of the alliance, but too little is known about this group of councils to enable them to be classified under Conservative, or Conservative and Independent headings. In the counties, a distinction is drawn between Independents controlling a council without any public electoral support from the Conservatives, and those who have such support. It is likely that some Independents have private support from the Conservatives, but the strictest definition and classification has been used in this study. As a consequence some authorities may be classifed as Independent or Other, when they are really Conservative and Independent. This has the effect of reducing the number of observations in some of the tables dealing with party system and party control effects.

The party systems typology is drawn from J. Stanyer, *County Government in England and Wales* (London, Routledge and Kegan Paul, 1967), pp. 111–12. His classification is as follows:

Non-party	Independent or non-party members take 60 per cent or more of the seats
One-party monopoly	One party takes 80 per cent or more of the seats
One-party dominant	One party takes from 60 to 70 per cent of the seats
Two-party	The leading party takes less than 60 per cent, and no third party takes more than 5 per cent of the seats
Multi-party	The leading party takes less than 60 per cent, and two or more other parties each take over 5 per cent of the seats.

For the purpose of this classification, alliances between parties or between parties and groups of Independents have not been taken into account. In other words, the definitions are the strictest possible.

Appendix 4 Statistical Problems

4.1 *Problems of Skewness*

Inspection of the SPSS condescriptives showed a number of highly skewed variables, and since correlation and regression analysis is based upon assumptions about a normal distribution, all those variables with a skew of 2.0 or more were corrected by using a log transformation, or in the case of a negative skew, the square of the variable. To see if these precautions were adequate two tests were then applied.

(a) Correlations between dependent and independent variables in their transformed and untransformed states were compared, and those cases where the difference was ±0.1 were noted.

(b) An untransformed variable was also correlated with its transformed variant, and it was found that where the correlation was less than 0.9, there was most usually a correlational difference of ±0.1 between a dependent and an independent variable — as in (a) above.

Therefore, it was decided to transform variables when their skewness was 2.0 or more, and where there was a correlation of less than 0.9 between the transformed and the untransformed variable. The main (but not the only) variables used in a transformed state in this study were:

Population aged 0–4
Number of nursery pupils on school registers
Number of primary pupils on school registers
Number of secondary pupils on school registers
Total pupils on school registers
Number of pupils for whom local authorities are financially responsible
Percentage of agricultural workers in county boroughs
Percentage of economically active women
Percentage of domestic properties with low rateable value
Percentage of total rateable value made up by offices
Percentage of old people
Total population.

4.2 *The Problem of Spuriousness, or Definitional Dependency*

The problem of spuriousness, as originally defined by Galton, arises when the correlation between two rates or indices is affected by the fact that they have the same figure in their denominators. This is also known as the problem of definitional dependency and the strength of tendency depends on the relative variance of the terms of the indices. The problem is ignored or overlooked in the great majority of output studies but we examined ways of dealing with it. Two main methods have been suggested.

(1) Either, one can use raw data (i.e. not expenditures per capita, but absolute

figures) and fit a regression line to the population at risk. This regression is then assumed to represent the relationship between total spending and total population, and the residuals, which are then used for the analysis proper, are assumed to be that part of total expenditure which is not explained by population size. In this way, one avoids total population appearing on both sides of a regression equation which, for example, relates per capita spending on a service to the percentage of the total population of a given age. Or, amounting to much the same thing, a principal components analysis of the raw data can be carried out, and the first component, which is assumed to represent size, taken out, leaving second and subsequent components for analysis. These methods were rejected on three grounds. First, to assume that the first regression or component deals with size is to assume an answer to one question which the study sets out to examine in the first place, i.e. it assumes that population size is an important determinant of per capita service expenditures. Second, even if this were a reasonable assumption for this particular study, it would make it impossible to investigate the relationship between population size and spending, and, perhaps more important, it would make it extremely difficult to examine the relationships between spending and variables which might be important in their own right, but closely related to population size — for example rank in the urban hierarchy. Third, the use of principal components analysis would raise all the problems of this kind of statistical technique, particularly the problem of interpreting and labelling the components. It was thus decided to reject these methods of dealing with the problem of spuriousness.

(2) The terms in the correlation or regression equations which are likely to create problems of spuriousness can be standardized by dividing each by its own standard deviation. This method was tried on a set of ninety correlations, and the results with standardized and unstandardized variables were compared. In thirty cases the standardized results differed by 0.1 or more, but no pattern could be discerned in terms either of the size or the difference in the relationships. In sixty cases, the differences were small, and accounted for less than 1 per cent of the variance in the dependent variable.

Since the problem of spuriousness was shown to be not at all severe for our particular data set, it was decided to carry out correlation and regression analysis without using either of the methods of correction. There is no evidence to suggest that this impairs the analysis in any way; on the contrary, to have tried to counteract the small problems which do appear would have raised considerably greater problems than it would solve.

4.3 *Significance Tests*

There is some controversy surrounding the use of significance tests in studies like this one, which deal with a total universe of observations. Since significance tests are intended to set the limits around probable sample errors, and since we deal not with a sample, but with all top-tier authorities in England and Wales, it could be argued that significance testing is unnecessary. However, such tests serve another purpose, since a set of correlations between columns of random numbers is likely to contain some figures of a considerable and significant size, and it is necessary to set limits around the probability of this happening. Blalock uses an example which is particularly apposite for this study: 'Let us say we have found that Southern states spend relatively larger proportions of their budgets on highways but less on higher education. Before we can make any claims that our explanation should involve looking for causal factors producing this regional difference, we might think of the hypothetical sceptic who could pose a very simple alternative for our finding, namely "chance" processes. In effect, he might say: "You claim to have found a difference due to regional characteristics. But I could have used a table of random numbers to divide up your 50 states. Or perhaps they might have been divided up alphabetically according to the third letter of their names. If I could show that such a random or nearly random process could have a difference as great or greater than yours, then your explanation is no more plausible than mine"' (Hubert M. Blalock, *Social Statistics* (New York, McGraw Hill, 1972), p. 239). We find this argument compelling. Besides, without significance tests, every correlation and regression coefficient would be 'significant', and it is necessary to use a cut-off point of some kind of other to eliminate trivial results from the discussion. The statistical basis of significance tests make them less arbitrary than other cut-off points, so we chose to use them in all correlation and regression analysis in the work. Those who accept the logic of this position will find significance levels useful, and those who do not agree can choose to ignore them.

4.4 *Regression Analysis*

Some thirty-two social, twenty-one economic, twenty-one political, and eight locational or geographical variables were available for inclusion in regression analysis. In order to reduce these to a more manageable short list of the most powerful independent variables, each was correlated with the major service expenditures. Those which were not significantly correlated with the expenditures, or which were only weakly correlated with a few of them, were dropped from the analysis. Those remaining were then correlated with each other, and where two correlated at ±0.70 or more, the one which was least strongly associated with expenditures was also dropped. This left fourteen social and economic variables which were either strongly related to one spending measure, or significantly related to four or more of the service expenditures. The fourteen were:

(1) Household overcrowding
(2) Absence of hot water
(3) Mortality rates (which can be treated as measures of poverty and poor social conditions)
(4) Manual workers

(5) Council tenants
(6) Retail trade turnover per capita
(7) Offices as a percentage of total rateable value
(8) Industry as a percentage of total rateable value
(9) Population density
(10) Rateable value per capita
(11) Old population
(12) Inflow of population into the local authority for work
(13) School-aged population
(14) Population size.

Given that these are the variables left after a fairly drastic weeding-out process, there is every reason to believe that they represent the strongest social and economic variables available to us.

The same procedure was followed in order to produce a short list of the most powerful political variables. That is, of the twenty-one on the original list, those which were only weakly or rarely correlated with expenditures were dropped, and of those remaining which correlated strongly with each other, only those with the stronger association with spending levels were included in the final regression runs. In this way, fifteen political variables were dropped, and six retained for inclusion in the regressions, as follows:

(1) Election turnout
(2) Percentage of uncontested seats
(3) Percentage of Conservative seats
(4) Percentage of Labour seats
(5) Percentage of Conservative and Independent seats
(6) Percentage of other Independent seats.

INDEX